The Oxford Introductions to U.S. Law

Property

The Oxford Introductions to U.S. Law

Property

THOMAS W. MERRILL

AND

HENRY E. SMITH

Dennis Patterson, Series Editor
The Oxford Introductions to U.S. Law

Oxford University Press, Inc., publishes works that further Oxford University's objective of excellence in research, scholarship, and education.

Oxford New York
Auckland Cape Town Dar es Salaam Hong Kong Karachi Kuala Lumpur Madrid Melbourne
Mexico City Nairobi New Delhi Shanghai Taipei Toronto

With offices in
Argentina Austria Brazil Chile Czech Republic France Greece Guatemala Hungary Italy
Japan Poland Portugal Singapore South Korea Switzerland Thailand Turkey Ukraine
Vietnam

Published by Oxford University Press, Inc.
198 Madison Avenue, New York, New York 10016

Library of Congress Cataloging-in-Publication Data
Merrill, Thomas W.
The Oxford introductions to U.S. law. Property / Thomas W. Merrill, Henry E. Smith.
p. cm.—(The Oxford introductions to U.S. law)
Includes bibliographical references and index.
ISBN 978-0-19-531476-2 ((pbk.) : alk. paper)
1. Property—United States. I. Smith, Henry E. II. Title. III. Title: Property.
KF561.M47 2010
346.7304—dc22 2010002669

8 9

Printed in Canada on acid-free paper

Note to Readers

This publication is designed to provide accurate and authoritative information in regard to the subject matter covered. It is based upon sources believed to be accurate and reliable and is intended to be current as of the time it was written. It is sold with the understanding that the publisher is not engaged in rendering legal, accounting, or other professional services. If legal advice or other expert assistance is required, the services of a competent professional person should be sought. Also, to confirm that the information has not been affected or changed by recent developments, traditional legal research techniques should be used, including checking primary sources where appropriate.

(Based on the Declaration of Principles jointly adopted by a Committee of the American Bar Association and a Committee of Publishers and Associations.)

To our students

Acknowledgments

IN COMPLETING THIS BOOK, we have happily incurred many debts of gratitude. The substance of the book greatly benefited, as always, from comments by Bob Ellickson and Carol Rose. We also thank the anonymous reviewers at Oxford University Press for their valuable suggestions. Our students at Yale and Harvard also deserve thanks for their insights and encouragement in test runs of the book in our classes, and we especially thank our research assistants, Claire McCusker and Sarah Beth Berry.

There are many others who deserve our thanks for their contributions to this project. We would like to thank the staff of Oxford University Press, especially Lori Wood and Chris Collins. Professor Smith is also grateful to the Hoover Institution at Stanford University for its generous financial support as a member of its Task Force on Property Rights, Freedom, and Prosperity.

Finally, our deepest appreciation extends to our families whose support made this book possible.

Contents

ONE

The Institution of Property

THE COMMON LAW IS TYPICALLY DIVIDED into contracts, torts, and property. A contract, roughly speaking, is a legally enforceable promise. A tort is a civil wrong based on the violation of a duty not arising from contract. Where does property fit into the picture?

One way to think about property is that it defines the entitlements people can enter into contracts about, or can sue in tort in order to protect. Thus, contract law and tort law presuppose the existence of property. If *A* sells Blackacre (the proverbial name for a generic plot of land) to *B*, the transfer is governed by a contract. But what *A* and *B* are contracting about is the property rights in Blackacre: Before the contract, *A* owns Blackacre; after the contract, it is owned by *B*. Likewise, if *B* enters Blackacre without permission or sends foul odors wafting onto Blackacre, *A* might bring a tort action in trespass or nuisance against these interferences. These tort actions provide protection for *something*; that something is *A*'s property rights in Blackacre.

We can describe the fundamental nature of property in relation to contract and tort another way. One can imagine a world without contract or tort. It would be a highly inconvenient place to live. Without contracts, people would have to make do with what they already have rather than trading for other things. Without tort, the only recourse for those wishing to protect their possessions would be self-help (i.e., putting up fences or using guard dogs) or, in the case of more aggravated violations, criminal law. But it would be much more difficult to imagine a world without property. In the broadest sense, property delineates the rights people have to control and derive value from resources in the world. Property tells us what is mine and what is not mine. Without rules about this, the world would be a chaotic and probably quite violent place.

What exactly then is property? Some people, especially economists, tend to regard any expectation about being able to derive value from some resource as "property." In this broad sense, one's expectation of being able to stay in a friend's apartment overnight, or being able to collect mushrooms on public land, would be regarded as property. Notice that "expectation" here need not have any normative force or legal enforcement. Indeed, on this understanding one could say that someone has property rights in coconuts if he or she is the only one who knows how to climb a tree.[1]

This conception of property as pure expectation is too broad to capture the meaning of property in law. Rather, legal scholars (and more legally attuned social scientists) would require at a minimum some kind of social guarantee for an expectation to count as property. For *A* to have property in some thing, *A*'s expectation of a special claim to the thing—whatever that claim is—must have some social recognition. Some scholars argue that this recognition need not consist of legal enforcement. On this view, fishers with informal "rights" to fishing spots may have their expectations recognized by other fishers, which may be all that is needed to call the right property. Practically speaking, this may mean that other fishers will tolerate self-help on the part of fishers defending their spots, or it may mean that other fishers will come to the aid of a fisher whose spot is threatened by someone else.

For still others, the concept of property is reserved for a *legally protected* entitlement. On this view, the informal right to a fishing spot resembles property: there is an expectation of a benefit from it and that expectation is recognized and supported in a relevant

---

1. John Umbeck, *Might Makes Rights: A Theory of the Formation and Initial Distribution of Property Rights*, 19 ECON. INQUIRY, 38, 38–39 (1981).

social group. But it would not be property in the legal sense unless its holder could vindicate his or her rights in a court of law.

In this book, we will use the term "property" to refer to entitlements to resources protected by formal legal institutions. If the fisher cannot go to a court of law to vindicate a claim to a spot, that claim may be a social norm or a custom, but it would not be regarded as property. As we will note from time to time, customs are sometimes, but far from always, incorporated into law. So the boundary between custom and law is fluid, rather than fixed.

Property in the sense of legally protected entitlements comes in a variety of forms. The paradigmatic legal property right would be full title to a parcel of land or an object like a car—real property and personal property (or "chattels"), respectively. But the law also affords legally enforceable claims to nontangible resources. Intellectual property—chiefly, patents, copyrights, and trademarks—is regarded as property despite not being a right to any physical thing. Intellectual property rights are rights in intangibles. Likewise one can own a debt or an account at a bank or other financial institution. These too are property rights in intangibles.

Who is eligible to serve as an owner of property? There are many possibilities. Individual persons, small groups of persons who have some close relationship (co-owners), private entities that have a legally established governance structure (partnerships, corporations, nonprofit organizations), and governments (cities, counties, states, the federal government) all can and do own property. Some commentators argue that certain close-knit communities can be said to have property rights in resources like fisheries and common pastures, in the sense that persons who are not members of the community are excluded from participating in the resource. And some property, for example some beaches, might be said to belong to the general public—they are "inherently public" in the sense that even the government cannot bar members of the pubic from access to it. Seeking to bring some order to these possibilities, one popular classification scheme distinguishes between private property (property owned by individual persons, co-owners, or private entities), common property (resources collectively controlled by some close-knit group), and public property (property owned by governments and/or the public).

Property as an institution embraces these many forms, and different societies have various mixtures of them. The property systems in the United States and other countries with market-based economies rely heavily on private property, but with important components of common and public property. Socialist countries rely more heavily on public property, but they too typically permit private property in personal goods, like clothing and books. The relative advantages of different mixtures of private, common, and public property is an important question, over which academic and political conflict has been waged for a long time.

Exclusion and the Bundle of Rights

The great diversity in the types of things that can be property as well as in types of owners gives rise to the question whether there is any essential feature or element that distinguishes property from other types of claims or rights. One school of thought holds that there is an essential core to the nature of property: the right to exclude others from some thing. This view is captured by William Blackstone's definition of property as "that sole and despotic dominion which one man claims and exercises over the external things of the world, in total exclusion of the right of any other individual in the universe."[2] Here a designated thing—Blackacre, a car, an invention, or a bank account—forms the focus of the right. To describe someone as an owner of some thing is to say that such person has the right to exclude others' use of the thing and,

2. WILLIAM BLACKSTONE, 2 COMMENTARIES *2 (1766). Blackstone was probably engaging in some self-conscious hyperbole here; and after this definition, Blackstone went on to discuss the various exceptions and modifications to the right to exclude.

at least by implication, has the right to use the thing unless some other restriction—zoning law or criminal law, for example—prevents the owner from taking the action in question. This focus on exclusion does not mean that ownership cannot be supplemented with additional rights and privileges—for example, the owner may have an easement to use an adjacent parcel for driveway access. But on the "Blackstonian" view, the right to exclude others from some definite thing is central to what the owner owns and forms the core of the concept of property itself.[3]

Another school of thought denies the existence of any essential core to the concept of property. Rather, property is just a word denoting a bundle of rights—or more metaphorically, a bundle of sticks—in which each individual stick (whether it be a right or privilege) can be added or removed without necessarily changing the characterization of the bundle as "property." No particular stick in the bundle—including the right to exclude—is privileged, and the measure of which bundles are preferred to which others is simply a matter of social policy. Thus, if *A* owns Blackacre, but society finds that Blackacre would be an undesirable location for a factory, the government may remove the factory-building stick from the bundle of rights. Nonetheless, it is still possible to describe the remaining sticks as "property." The Legal Realist movement that started in the 1920s advanced this alternative view in order to debunk the notion of property as a natural right protected by the Constitution against fundamental reform.[4] The bundle of rights view achieved the status of conventional wisdom in academic circles in the course of the twentieth century, and despite increasing questioning from various quarters, it retains a great deal of influence today.

---

3. *See, e.g.*, J. E. PENNER, THE IDEA OF PROPERTY IN LAW (1997); Thomas W. Merrill, *Property and the Right to Exclude*, 77 NEB. L. REV. 730 (1998).

4. *See* Thomas C. Grey, *The Disintegration of Property*, *in* PROPERTY: NOMOS XXII 69 (J. Roland Pennock & John W. Chapman eds., 1980).

Many views in between these poles—traditional Blackstonian exclusion and the Legal Realist bundle of rights—are possible, and to a large extent the differences are a matter of emphasis. Thus, a variant of the traditional view is that a trinity of rights—to exclude, to use, and to transfer—defines the core of property.[5] Use and transfer are certainly important to property. But one can point to entitlements that are conventionally thought of as property without the right to transfer. For example, a doctor can own a medical license, with procedural protection in this "property," but transfer of such a license would be illegal. In other cases, transfer is allowed by gift but not by sale (organs for transplant purpose)—or permitted by sale but not gift (assets of an insolvent company on the eve of bankruptcy). Nevertheless, one can say that as the rights to use and transfer are removed, we move away from the prototypical property right.

More generally, the difference between the traditional and the bundle of rights views may be largely a matter of focus. The proponents of the traditional view must acknowledge that modern law imposes many constraints on the right to exclude. Some of these limits are conventionally thought of as belonging to the law of property itself and represent a shift from an exclusion strategy for managing resources to a governance strategy that delineates rules of proper resource use.[6] That is to say, the law shifts from giving the owner dictatorial control over who and what to exclude (or include), and instead seeks to prescribe rules about permissible and impermissible uses that constrain all relevantly situated owners. We will see many examples of exclusion shading off into governance. Perhaps the most paradigmatic is the shift from trespass, which governs large intrusions on land and has an exclusionary character,

---

5. *See, e.g.*, RICHARD A. EPSTEIN, TAKINGS: PRIVATE PROPERTY AND THE POWER OF EMINENT DOMAIN 59 (1985).

6. Henry E. Smith, *Exclusion Versus Governance: Two Strategies for Delineating Property Rights*, 31 J. LEGAL STUD. S453 (2002).

to nuisance, which governs small intrusions and often engages in interest-balancing to delineate proper use. Likewise antidiscrimination laws are among the governance-style limits on the owner's right to exclude. On the exclusion-based view, however, the right of the owner to act as the gatekeeper over some thing—deciding who and what to exclude and include—is still the starting point for understanding property.

For their part, the proponents of the bundle of rights view must account for the fact that property rights are not typically broken down into long lists of discrete rights and privileges. Instead, the rights of property owners are "lumpy." Ownership of Blackacre gives the owner an expectation of being able to use Blackacre for a wide range of uses without the need to explicitly spell out what those uses are. Drawing up a master list of uses and the rights to engage in them, holding between all pairs of members of society, would be prohibitively costly.

One advantage of starting with the right to exclude as a "baseline" conception of property is that this permits us to protect a wide range of interests in use, without requiring outsiders like officials or judges to know much about those uses. If *A* owns Blackacre and can invoke the law of trespass to keep out unwanted intrusions, then *A* can use Blackacre and invest in it secure in the knowledge that such intrusions can largely be prevented. The law itself need not provide for a right to grow crops or a right to build a house or a right to park cars; instead, by delegating the "gatekeeper" right (the right to exclude) to the owner, the owner can select among these uses without the law having to spell out all potential use-rights or interests at all.

Indeed, to a large extent, we might say that the various interests in use (crop growing, house building, car parking, etc.) are reflected in *privileges* (or liberties) rather than rights (or claims). Property allows a wide range of uses—maybe even as yet unforeseen uses—to be protected with the simple exclusion strategy. Only selected situations of major resource conflict are likely to lead to rules governing particular uses; we will encounter covenants and easements, nuisance, and zoning as examples of the law's attention to particular use conflicts. Alternatively and in a closely related fashion, when problems become serious enough, they may call for a reconfiguration of the property rights themselves; examples would be the more finegrained tradable fishing quotas to deal with overfishing or the unitization of a fragmented oil field under a single operator to prevent overdrilling. But much of the law's response to use conflict is in a sense implicit: the right to exclude is a sort of "black box" giving the owner decision-making authority over such questions. Thus, an initial approximation of the Blackstonian bundle of rights would include both the right to exclude from a thing and a host of privileges to use it—most of which shelter behind the right to exclude—supplemented by rights and duties of proper use.

The Thing's the Thing

In some legal systems, property is called the "Law of Things." The Latin expression for this is that property rights are *in rem*, which comes from the word *res* or thing, and indicates that property rights pertain directly to things, rather than people. A related use of the term in the law of civil procedure—jurisdiction in rem—refers to the power of a court over a thing, such as a ship. One of the more interesting in rem actions is the quiet title action. This allows a person to place some thing under the authority of the court, which will, after providing to all identified claimants the requisite notice and opportunity to be heard, make a definitive adjudication of who owns the thing. Such a judgment is binding on all conceivable claimants, whether or not they have participated in the proceeding. Here we see a direct acknowledgment of the centrality of the thing in the law of property.

It is instructive in this regard to return again to the relationship among contract, tort, and property, but now to draw a distinction between contract, on the one hand, and property and tort, on the other. Contract rights are created by particular agreements between particular persons, which create obligations binding on these persons with respect to each other and no one else. (Duties to third parties can arise under third-party beneficiary law, and contracts can often be assigned, but the rules in this area are somewhat special and uncharacteristic of core contract law.) A short-hand expression for this confinement of contract rights and duties to identified interacting parties is that contract rights are *in personam*: They are personal or are rights with respect to persons. Contract rights do not exist automatically as a matter of law. They are created only when persons engage in certain acts (offer and acceptance, giving consideration) that create obligations specified by the contract and binding only on the parties to the contract.

Property rights, in contrast, bind the world, not just a particular pair of parties. Property in the broadest sense is a set of claims that people have in resources that correspond to duties of respect in others generally. It is this feature of binding the world that is frequently referred to when we speak of property rights as being "in rem." Because the right attaches to the object, rather than to particular people, it is universally binding on all who encounter the object. Personal rights protected by the law of torts are similar; individual rights of bodily integrity, privacy, and reputation apply automatically to persons as persons (here persons, rather than objects, are the *res*) and bind all other persons in the world. We could say these personal rights are also in rem, in the sense of "in rem" as "good against the world."

As we've seen, the Blackstonian view places great weight on things in property law, namely the right of some person to exclude all the world from a thing. The bundle of rights picture, in contrast, relegates things to the background, and stresses that property affects the rights of persons with respect to things. One reason for the focus on things and rights to exclude is that property has a distinct audience. When we say that property rights are "good against the world" or "*in rem*" this means that the flip side of the owner's right is the duty of the other members of society to keep off, to respect the right, unless the owner has given permission to enter or use the thing in question. Property rights are thus like the hub of a wheel with innumerable spokes radiating out from the hub representing the general obligation imposed on all of the many persons standing on the rim.

But what is a thing? A complete answer to this question would take us far afield. For purposes of property law, some examples of things are already furnished by our everyday knowledge. A car is a thing, as is a painting. Identifying other things requires some legal definition, but partly relies also on our prelegal knowledge. A parcel of land like Blackacre requires the drawing of legal boundaries; still, a convention not to jump fences is very easy to communicate to the lay public and depends in part on lay knowledge. Finally, some things are almost wholly legally constructed: Patents require elaborate applications with written descriptions and detailed claims (and often diagrams) because the world does not come precarved into inventions—the things of patent law. Likewise for other intangibles.

We noted earlier that property can be real or personal, tangible or intangible. Nonetheless, not every thing can be property. One implicit limitation on the set of things that are subject to ownership is that they must be things worth managing through the exercise of exclusion rights. Thus, the stars and planets in the heavens are not objects of ownership, because there is currently no technologically feasible way of extracting anything of value from them. A related limitation requires that there be some way of demarcating the resource in question and enforcing exclusion rights in it at a cost that is reasonable in relation to the value of managing the resource. Traditionally the atmosphere and the oceans were said to be ineligible to be objects of ownership, probably because it was too difficult to delimit and enforce ownership shares in these resources, given the gains that might accrue from such an exercise. There are also important moral and cultural limitations on the types of things that can be the objects of ownership. Human beings were once commonly owned as slaves, a form of property now universally regarded as morally repugnant.

Blackstone refers to the objects of property as the "external things of the world," suggesting that the object of the property relationship must be differentiated from the person or group owning it. In ordinary discourse we do not speak of ourselves or our body parts as being property. It is true that John Locke grounded his theory of property on the proposition that people own their own bodies and hence their own labor.[7] Thus, Locke argued, when a person mixes his or her labor with resources that are unclaimed by anyone else, these resources also become his or her property. But the idea that we own ourselves or our own labor should probably be regarded as metaphorical. For most purposes some separation between owner and owned thing is assumed. Thus, we do not speak of our hair as property when it is growing on our heads, although after it is cut—that is, after is it separated from the body—a lock of that hair could well be regarded as property.

General Justifications, General Concerns

What, then, are the general justifications for a legal institution that gives exclusive rights to persons over the things they own? A wide variety of justifications for private property have been offered. We will mention five.

First, the institution of property provides an effective way of managing society's resources. We can imagine a variety of techniques for managing resources, ranging from government bureaucracies to local customs to a system of might-makes-right. The property strategy for resource management can be seen as one that delegates near-dictatorial powers over particular resources to individual owner-managers, which powers are then backed up by the authority of the state. This strategy, to a greater degree than

7. John Locke, Two Treatises of Government, 285–302 (Peter Laslett ed., Cambridge University Press 1988) (1690).

government bureaucracy, allows for decentralization in the management of resources and permits the owner-managers to specialize in developing the knowledge and skills pertinent to their particular resource. The decentralized nature of property also permits experimentation with new uses and techniques for managing resources, rendering it more dynamic than a consensus-based system of local custom. And, so long as the state provides a sufficient degree of security for ownership, the property strategy is more stable and requires fewer expenditures on defensive measures than does a might-makes-right system.

Second, the institution of property provides a powerful set of incentives for persons to make investments in and engage in effective management of the resources they control. A homey way of expressing this is that property allows the owner to "reap where he has sown."[8] Farmers who own land, for example, can decide what kind of seeds to plant, how much effort to put into cultivating them, and when and how to harvest the crops, knowing that the effort and skill they put into the process will be reflected in the yield they ultimately obtain. Other forms of resource management create much less incentive to expend these kinds of efforts to make productive use of resources, because they provide no assurance that those who put in effort to improve the resource will be able to appropriate the fruits of their efforts. This is because no one is in a position to exclude others from interfering with or seeking to capture the benefits of their efforts.

Third, the institution of property facilitates the making of contracts regarding the use and control of resources. In order to contract for the exchange of or modifications to the use of resources, it is necessary to know who controls what resources and, hence, who may make contracts with respect to those resources. Property gives us the answer to these questions. Two types of contracts regarding property are especially important. One is the exchange of property rights.

8. *See* Int'l News Serv. v. Associated Press, 248 U.S. 215, 239 (1918).

Suppose I own Blackacre but am too old and tired to make much use of it. If I can enter into a contract to sell it to someone else, then this resource may be used more effectively, making society better off. Another is a contract modifying the use of property. If my neighbor is using his or her property in a way that causes me discomfort or irritation, one solution is to enter into a contract with the neighbor in which the neighbor promises to desist from this use.

Fourth, property is an important source of individual autonomy. Property provides the material means for individuals to achieve a degree of independence from others. By giving individuals control over resources, it allows them to control the direction of their lives. Particular items of property may also be critical to personal identity or to the development of individual personality. Many people's identity is closely wrapped up with their homes. For others, particular shops or factories may be vital to how they see themselves. Most of us have books, photos, memorabilia, items of clothing, or collections of things to which we attach significance, and which we would be pained to lose.[9]

Fifth, property is important to the preservation of liberty. Morris Cohen once wrote that property is a form of sovereignty; the right to exclude others from things is a source of power over other people.[10] This is true, but it also means that if the ownership of property is distributed widely enough, then property ownership can be a source of countervailing power to the power of the government—or the power of other property owners. Checks and balances are thought to be vital to preserving liberty, and dispersed property ownership provides an important source of checks and balances. For example, private property allows individuals to organize opposition parties and distribute literature critical of the government; if the

---

9. *See* Margaret Jane Radin, *Property and Personhood*, 34 STAN. L. REV. 957 (1982).

10. *See generally* Morris R. Cohen, *Property and Sovereignty*, 13 CORNELL L.Q. 8 (1927).

government controls all the resources it is easy to squelch dissent.[11] And property allows unpopular minorities to resist threats from the government to cut off government-granted benefits or employment.[12]

Although property has been applauded for these positive functions, certain general concerns have also been raised about the institution of property.

One pervasive problem goes by the name "externalities." The private property strategy entails dividing the world up into separate parcels of land and discrete objects of personal property, each with its individual owner. But the owner-managers of these individualized units of property may use them in ways that have spillover effects for the owner-managers of other units of property. Spillover effects that have adverse consequences for others, known as negative externalities, are a particular matter of concern. *A* can use *A*'s land in a way that generates pollution damaging to his neighbor *B*. Or *C* can allow her car to deteriorate into an unsafe condition, posing a danger on the road to *D* and other drivers. In fact, the very strategy of allowing owners to appropriate the gains from their property creates an incentive to try to foist as many of the costs associated with property as possible onto someone else. Any set of legal rules governing property will thus have to come up with strategies for trying to control negative externalities.

Another concern about property is monopoly. Property, by its very nature, confers a monopoly of control on someone with respect to a particular resource. Every property right is in this sense a monopoly right. Ordinarily, this is of no concern. For example, a farmer can be said to have a monopoly over the farmer's own land. But if there are thousands of farmers producing a substantially identical commodity—say, wheat—there will be vigorous competition among the farmers in the market for wheat, and the monopoly each farmer has over some particular private production facilities

---

11. Milton Friedman, Capitalism And Freedom 7–21 (1962).

12. Charles A. Reich, *The New Property*, 73 Yale L.J. 733, 771–74 (1964).

will have no effect on the price that consumers must pay for wheat. In other circumstances, however, granting property rights can create monopolies that do have troublesome social consequences. For example, if I own the only piece of land on which it is feasible to build a bridge across a river, this may give me a monopoly on river-crossings, and with it the power to extract large tolls from the public for the privilege of using the bridge. Similarly, the award of patent rights or copyrights may in certain circumstances allow the owners of these rights to extract very large payments from the public, if there are no good substitutes for the thing they have created. This concern therefore suggests that the property strategy will become problematic insofar as the monopoly rights conferred by property coincide with a distinct market for particular goods or services. It may be necessary in these circumstances to modify property rights by applying antitrust laws or some form of regulation.[13]

Another concern about property is that it leads to commodification of values and social relations. Property conceives of the world in terms of owners dominating or controlling objects. Many people resist thinking this way about their bodies, their intimate relations, their networks of friends and colleagues, their pets, and so forth. The concern here is with the scope or domain of property rights. The more we extend the sphere of property, the more we think about the world in terms of owner-object relations. Insofar as it is important to preserve a sphere of life that is organized according to different principles, then we must exercise caution about how far the system of property rights extends.

---

13. Related to monopoly are problems that can arise when too many people have exclusion-like claims on resources. If multiple persons or institutions can veto the use or transfer of a resource, then a kind of gridlock (or "anticommons") can set in that leaves the resources of society underdeveloped. See MICHAEL HELLER, THE GRIDLOCK ECONOMY (2008). In some cases, a resource may be subject to more than one property regime (as in a "semicommons") in order to serve different goals and to benefit from operating on multiple scales—for example, otherwise private parcels subject to a public easement for transit or copyrights subject to fair use. See Henry E. Smith, *Semicommon Property Rights and Scattering in the Open Fields*, 29 J. LEGAL STUD. 131 (2000).

Finally, property has long been attacked on the ground that it promotes inequality. Property, at least if it is well managed, tends to beget more property. This is because property, by allowing the owner to exclude others, permits the owner to capture the fruits of the property, to reap what has been sown. Much of the captured "fruit" is attributable the skill and industry of the owner—but not all. Some is attributable to rising demand for resources generally, and to sheer luck. The component that can be ascribed to luck or general conditions of scarcity represents a kind of built-in multiplier whereby those who have property get more property, without regard to their individual desert. If we combine this with a general right of inheritance, then a robust system of private property can create conditions where the rich generally get richer. This is not to say that abolishing property would create greater equality. Communist systems were notorious for providing special perks for party leaders that gave them a lavish lifestyle far beyond what ordinary workers could aspire to enjoy. But it does suggest a rationale for imposing higher burdens of taxation on those with significant property to offset the dynamic tendency toward greater inequality. Whether this greater burden should be greater than proportionate with wealth or income (i.e. progressive), and if so, how much so, has been a topic of lively debate—as has the question of whether to use taxes or the rules of property itself to achieve distributive ends.

Further Reading

C. B. MACPHERSON, ED., PROPERTY: MAINSTREAM AND CRITICAL POSITIONS (1978) (includes key readings from Locke, Bentham, Marx, Mill, and others).

Thomas W. Merrill & Henry E. Smith, *What Happened to Property in Law and Economics?*, 111 YALE L.J. 357 (2001) (argues that lawyers and economists have overlooked the *in rem* feature of property rights).

TWO

Original Acquisition and the Scope of Property Claims

HOW DOES PROPERTY GET STARTED? We are familiar with the process by which someone acquires private property in some external thing by transfer (sale, gift, will, etc.) from a previous owner. But where did that owner get the property? Most likely through another such transfer. How do such chains of title begin? What is the process by which something that is unowned enters into the world of owned things?

Property theorists have long been concerned about the need to justify the origins of property. Perhaps most famously, John Locke theorized that in the beginning all resources were held in common; private property came into being when one person mixed his or her labor with some portion of these common resources, and in so doing claimed it as his or her own.[1] Locke thought that this story justified the institution of private property. Most of the value of the appropriated thing, Locke claimed, was attributable to the labor expended in appropriating it. As long as the appropriator left "enough and as good" for others and did not engage in waste, it was only just to award the thing to the person who labored to acquire it.

Locke's tale is of course a fable. No one knows exactly how the institution of property arose in human societies in prehistory. The best we can do is examine the modes of original acquisition that exist today, together with those from the past that are reasonably

1. JOHN LOCKE, TWO TREATISES OF GOVERNMENT 285–302 (Peter Laslett ed., Cambridge Univ. Press 1988) (1690).

well documented, and consider why they have been adopted for initiating claims of title to property.

First Possession

The most general mode of original acquisition is first possession. Possession, as we will see, is a ubiquitous concept in property, with different shades of meaning depending on context. Generally speaking, to possess some thing means to be in control of it. Control implies intention. One does not generally control some thing one does not know one has, or one is trying to throw away. Control also implies power. To possess some thing is to have power or dominion over it. The basic idea of first possession is that the first person to possess an otherwise unowned object becomes the owner. This means, generally speaking, that the first person who both intends to assert control over the object and who establishes a significant degree of power over the object is deemed to be the owner—provided no one else has any claim of ownership to it.

Courts that have applied the concept of first possession have sought to identify the required acts that demonstrate the appropriate intention and degree of power over the contested object. *Pierson v. Post*,[2] the most famous case in property law and a frequent starting point for the course, struggles to specify the acts that define first possession in the context of acquiring original ownership of a wild fox. Post was pursuing a fox as part of an organized hunting party on a "beach," which apparently was stipulated to be wild and unpossessed in order to remove issues of claims by the landowner. Pierson, knowing Post was in pursuit of the fox, killed the fox and took it away. Post sued and won at trial, and Pierson appealed.

The court assumed that foxes are wild animals (*ferae naturae*), and that ownership of such an animal is established by the rule of

---

2. 3 Cai. R. 175 (N.Y. Sup. Ct. 1805).

capture, which is a version of first possession. The issue that divided the parties and the justices was how close one must be to capture in order to be deemed in possession of a fox. Clearly, killing the fox and bagging it would count. But what acts short of this also would do the trick? The majority and the dissent agreed that merely spotting the fox or pursuing it would not be enough. But between mere pursuit and bagging the fox, the opinions diverge. Justice Tompkins's majority opinion requires *certain control*, which in the case of a fox means at least mortal wounding coupled with continuation of the chase. Justice Livingston's dissent would have required only a *reasonable prospect* of capture, which here would mean close pursuit.

In arguing for their respective positions, the majority and dissent stressed different authorities. Justice Tompkins relied almost exclusively on legal treatises, ranging from Justinian's Institutes of the Roman Empire, to European writers such as Pufendorf and Bijnkershoek, to old English authorities such as Bracton. The assumption seems to be that there is a universal definition of possession, true in all times and places, which can be determined as a matter of law. The dissent also cited treatises, but in addition tossed off the suggestion that the dispute should be submitted for resolution to the arbitration of sportsmen—who would presumably find for Post, the hunter. This implies that the definition of possession varies from one time and place to another, and should be regarded as a question of fact.

The justices also engaged in a debate about the policy implications of different rules. The majority stressed the need for a clear rule in order to reduce conflicts in the future, suggesting that the dissent's "reasonable prospect" rule would produce too many disputes. The dissent makes much of the need for incentives to encourage the killing of foxes and the importance of protecting investments by people like Post in the institution of fox hunting.

Pierson thus raises issues of institutional design and incentives, but the questions are more complicated than either of the justices acknowledges. It is an empirical question whether imposing clear rules is more likely to prevent conflict than following customs, and many have suspected that Justice Livingston was right that the customs of hunters favored Post. It is also an empirical question whether protecting a pursuer would lead to more or fewer dead foxes, either by encouraging hunts or by making the Posts of the world overly complacent. Analogous issues arise throughout property law, and are prominent in recent controversies over intellectual property: What level of patent protection promotes the most invention without stifling the process?

The case has about it a contrived air, and recent scholarship underlines the artificial nature of the conflict and the opinion. The fox itself was not worth much and seems to be symbolic in some way, perhaps as a flash point in the struggle between nouveaux riches like the Posts and old elites like the Piersons.[3] Also, it turns out that foxes, unlike wild animals in general, were regarded as vermin that could be killed wherever found. Fox hunting was primarily a recreational activity, so much so that in some places hunters even paid farmers to raise foxes.[4]

Even if incentives to engage in fox hunting were important, the rules for determining when possession has been established perform another important function—notice to others. Recall that property is in rem: At the end of the process of original acquisition, a right is good against all others. An important part of the process of acquisition, then, must be notice to others that such a claim is being asserted. So, for example, even if it turned out that awarding exclusive rights to the first to spot the fox would encourage fox hunting, such a rule, without more, would provide very little notice to others. The lack of notice might lead others to compete with the original hunter—not to mention the possibility that more than one

---

3. Bethany R. Berger, *It's Not About the Fox: The Untold History of* Pierson v. Post, 55 Duke L.J. 1089 (2006).

4. Andrea McDowell, *Legal Fictions in* Pierson v. Post, 105 Mich. L. Rev. 735 (2007).

hunter would claim to have spotted the fox first—thereby leading to wasted time and resources.

These two issues, of incentives and notice, are deeply entwined with the potential problems of the commons. The term "commons" is associated with ambiguity: We will distinguish between an *open-access* commons and a *limited-access* commons. The well-known problem of resource depletion dubbed the "Tragedy of the Commons" is characteristic of the open-access commons.[5] For example, fishers in an open-access fishery obtain the full benefit from each fish taken from the sea, whereas leaving fish for another day (perhaps to reproduce) redounds to the benefit of all the fishers. Only a tiny fraction of this benefit inures to the fisher making the decision to forbear. Given this set of incentives, each fisher has an incentive to overfish, and a group (especially one open to additional members) can easily exploit the resource to ruin. Many problems from road congestion to air pollution have this structure that tends toward overuse. By contrast, a limited-access commons such as the medieval grazing commons (mistakenly cited by Hardin as an open-access commons) were not tragic in this sense: The set of farmers with access was limited, and their behavior was further controlled by the group in the interest of resource preservation.[6]

In light of the tragedy of the commons, why is first possession ever the rule in property law? For one thing, the end result of first possession is private property, and to the extent that private property has advantages in terms of security of expectation, investment, planning, and so on, a process that gets us into the realm of private property gains some favor. A further advantage of the first possession rule is its simplicity: It decentralizes the process to the

---

5. Garrett Hardin, *The Tragedy of the Commons*, 162 SCIENCE 1243 (1968); *see also* Thráinn Eggertsson, *Open Access versus Common Property*, *in* TERRY L. ANDERSON & FRED S. MCCHESNEY, PROPERTY RIGHTS: COOPERATION, CONFLICT, AND LAW 73 (2003).

6. *See generally* ELINOR OSTROM, GOVERNING THE COMMONS: THE EVOLUTION OF INSTITUTIONS FOR COLLECTIVE ACTION (1990).

appropriators who decide whether to engage in the pursuit. And here is where notice comes in: first possession is much less wasteful of resources if a clear winner emerges early on in the process of appropriation. If among those pursuing the fox or staking a homestead claim, one can tell relatively early which appropriator is likely to win, the others will give up and the wasteful race will be cut short. By contrast, where many are equally well-positioned to win the race, competition can remain fierce until the end—the end being tragic overall. It is an empirical question, and often a difficult one, whether first possession is beneficial or tragic and which first possession rule—certain control, reasonable prospect, or something else—will be most cost-effective.

Might custom be a way out of this thicket of empirical issues? Some have hypothesized that close-knit groups will develop customs that are efficient, as applied to that group.[7] And in the historic example of medieval grazing commons, this seems to have been the case; the appropriators prevented the tragedy of the commons through custom. Some fisheries, too, have been maintained in part through customs among fishers. Nevertheless, if the resource is not entirely under the control of the group, the custom may work well for the group but cause externalities or a larger tragedy of the commons. Whalers may have had customs that regulated their interactions but collectively still tended to drive whales toward extinction. To return to *Pierson*, hunter customs fail to take into account the wishes of preservationists or animal rights activists—not to mention those of foxes. Some of the impact on out-group actors is informational: If expert fox hunters are the only ones likely to encounter a fox, the custom need only be known to hunters. But if nonhunters come upon a fox, the law is asking a lot by requiring the nonexpert to know the custom, at the pain of expending fruitless effort in getting the fox. Whether people should be expected to know of a custom is relevant to its suitability for incorporation into the law.

---

7. Robert C. Ellickson, Order Without Law 167–83 (1991).

Put differently, when should custom supplement or even supplant the general law that can be gleaned from treatises and cases? When should custom displace nonexpert "common sense"?

The rules of first possession are in effect the regulation of a competitive process of acquiring unowned resources. This may—but need not—focus on the benefits of pursuing a commercial activity: Those hunting for a livelihood could traditionally expect more protection against someone trying to disrupt activities such as the hunt. Particularly where competition is motivated by spite—trying to prevent a benefit to the other party rather than obtain a benefit for oneself—the law is more likely to intervene. A prime example is the shooting of guns to scare off ducks from a neighbor's commercial trap, as in the classic English case *Keeble v. Hickeringill.*[8] But to some extent, spite—and by extension benefit—is in the eye of the beholder. Animal rights activists making noise to scare off prey think they are benefiting the animal and society in general, and can at least be regarded as satisfying their own preferences (for live foxes).

Discovery and Creation

Closely related to first possession as a source of original title to property are discovery and creation. In property law "discovery" loosely refers to a collection of situations in which someone establishes ownership of an object by being the first to claim it. Being first is again of paramount importance. But here the relevant act is a *claim* of ownership, as opposed to actual possession of an object. Claiming is a form of signaling, and thus intention and notice loom especially large here. By comparison, actual control over the object, in the sense of power over it, recedes into the background.

8. 103 Eng. Rep. 1127 (Q.B. 1707).

One prominent application of discovery refers to the process, lying at the root of titles in the United States, by which colonizing powers made claims to dominion over the "New World." Under the principle of discovery, the first European power to claim an area populated by non-Europeans would have dominion or sovereignty over it, subject to rights of occupancy in the indigenous population. The native population had the right to continue to occupy the land until this right of occupancy was extinguished by the colonizing power. If and when their right of occupancy was extinguished, then European settlers could move in and occupy the land, under whatever rules of settlement the European power decided to establish. This set-up, to which most titles in the United States historically trace, has led to litigation stretching from current disputes in upstate New York back to the famous case of *Johnson v. M'Intosh*,[9] another frequent starting point for Property courses.

In *Johnson*, the U.S. Supreme Court was faced with two conflicting titles, each with its own chain extending back into the past. Plaintiff Johnson traced his title back to a group of white settlers who had purchased deeds to certain lands in Illinois from two Native American tribes, the Illinois and Piankeshaw, in 1773 and 1775. M'Intosh traced his title to a grant from the United States in 1818 (which had acquired the land by treaty with the tribes).[10] The opinion would have grave consequences for Native Americans. But they were not represented in the proceedings.

Speaking through Chief Justice Marshall, the Court framed the issue narrowly in terms of which of the contending parties had the better title. The usual starting point in such a case is the principle that no one can transfer that which one does not own. (We return to this principle, sometimes called *nemo dat*, and its exceptions

---

9. 21 U.S. 543 (1823).

10. The Court implies the two chains of title are to the same lands, but this has recently been called into question. *See* Eric Kades, *The Dark Side of Efficiency:* Johnson v. M'Intosh *and the Expropriation of American Indian Lands*, 148 U. Pa. L. Rev. 1065 (2000).

in Chapter 7.) At first blush, Johnson appeared to have better title because his predecessors had purchased the land before the tribes ceded it to the United States. But the Court invoked the principle of discovery: The United States traced its claim over the land back to Cabot's discovery of North America, thereby giving the United States the sole right to determine who would deal with the Native Americans to extinguish their right of occupancy. Because the only interest the tribes had was the right of occupancy, and only the United States had the power to extinguish that right, the Native Americans had nothing to convey to Johnson. M'Intosh's title over the land, although established at a later date than Johnson's, was therefore confirmed.

The principle of discovery operates as between the European sovereigns and only with respect to the "New World." The Court acknowledged that if the Native Americans were regarded as fully sovereign, their claims would have been accorded full property protection—at least that was the rule of international law that applied to conquered peoples in Europe. But the native use and occupancy of the land, Marshall suggested, did not count as possession in the Western sense. Viewed through the lens of Western property concepts, native land use was not intensive or exclusive enough to count as property. In fact, Native Americans *did* have property concepts, mixing private property in implements with various mixtures of private property, common property, and open access for agricultural and hunting uses.[11]

Chief Justice Marshall's opinion ostensibly expressed reservations about the morality of the operation of the principle of discovery but treated its use as inevitable. The principle of discovery was embodied in a variety of laws and decrees in force at various times, and the Court seemed to view it as a background custom incorporated into Anglo-American law. Many have also speculated that the

11. *See* WILLIAM CRONON, CHANGES IN THE LAND: INDIANS, COLONISTS, AND THE ECOLOGY OF NEW ENGLAND 58–61 (1983).

Court feared the backlash that would have attended the opposite result: Thousands of titles to land in the United States depended on the validity of acts extinguishing Indian title that would have been regarded as violations of international law as applied to conquered peoples in Europe.

In retrospect there is much to deplore in this history. But it is worth asking what the principle of discovery as applied to westward expansion can tell us about property in general. For starters, as between the European powers, the principle of discovery probably had the beneficial effect of lessening potentially deadly conflicts. For the Native Americans, discovery and the consequent exclusive right in the discovering power to determine with whom they might deal meant that they faced a monopsony (monopoly on the buyer's side) in selling their rights. This buyer's power, sometimes along with deception, coercion, outright violence, and the effects of European diseases, depressed the prices that natives could get for their land. At the same time, Chief Justice Marshall's insistence that the federal government was the only party that could directly deal with Native Americans may have to some extent displaced even harsher regimes that states and individual settlers would have put into place. The history of westward expansion is one of limited federal ability to control the activity of its own citizens, until well into the nineteenth century. Yet as federal control solidified, the federal government came to be understood to have a special trust obligation to protect Native Americans against hostile state law, and this understanding is attributable in part to the analytics of the doctrine of discovery, as explicated in *Johnson*. Finally, the principle of discovery also clarified title. It was not so clear, at least to settlers, who—if anyone—had the authority under native law to make a deal to transfer title to land. A morass of conflicting claims might well have resulted without the principle of discovery.

It is usual these days not to take the notion of European "discovery" of America too literally, but discovery is also important in mining law. To establish a claim to minerals under the Mining Act of 1872, a claimant must both locate and discover a valuable mineral deposit. Again, discovery does not imply full control in the possessory sense but being the first in the eyes of the law to identify and claim the resource is key.

Closely related to discovery are the many contexts in which people make property claims based on bringing to light new information or expressions. Sometimes this process is termed *creation*, and it forms a key basis for intellectual property. Although one can create a table from wood using tools, one's effort at creation is only part of the story: The ownership of the wood and the tools are also relevant. In the case of information, one may build on previous information (inventions, in the case of patents, or expressions, in the case of copyright), but the incremental informational discovery involved in creation is the key characteristic that underlies the recognition of many intellectual property rights.

From a property point of view, *International News Service v. Associated Press*[12] illustrates both a claim based on creation and some of the limits of this approach. The Associated Press (AP) sued the International News Service (INS) for—among other things—copying or using (after rewriting) uncopyrighted news reports from the AP's newspapers for its own newspapers. (In those days, copyright required registration, which would be impractical in the case of news stories. Today, copyright attaches as soon as an expression is fixed in a tangible medium of expression, so copyright protection for the expression—but not the facts or ideas—would be available to the AP). The majority held the AP had a quasi-property in the news it had gathered, and held that the INS had misappropriated this right. Why "quasi-property"? The majority was at great pains to limit the duty against misappropriation of hot news to competitors; presumably, a reader could quote the stories around the water cooler. The Court was uneasy declaring news to be a thing from which all others could be excluded, but it did afford protection for hot news vis-à-vis competing news organizations. By contrast,

12. 248 U.S. 215 (1918).

Justice Brandeis's dissent declared that when it comes to information, the default should be that it is "free as the air to common use."[13] Only specific property rights established by Congress, like copyright and patent, should derogate from this important baseline.

As with previous acquisition principles, the quasi-property in hot news may have had some basis in custom. News organizations generally respected each other's right to scoops.[14] In *INS v. AP* this custom broke down when the INS was denied access to news and transmission facilities by the allied authorities in World War I, who did not appreciate the coverage they were getting from the Hearst-owned newspapers of the INS. As a legal problem, the question would be whether the "hot news" custom is certain enough to apply as a legal rule. Also, does it implicate other values, reflected in the First Amendment, that came into play in the *INS* case itself?

Another way to read *INS v. AP* is as a judicial recognition of the Lockean principle that labor and desert lie at the heart of property: that one should be allowed to "reap where he has sown." Read this way, *INS v. AP* would be a powerful generator of property rights. But the reap-sow principle bumps up against other acquisition principles. For example, a stranger is not allowed to sow or to reap on someone else's privately owned land—or usually on public land for that matter. When it comes to owned land, the reap-sow principle is secondary to ownership of the land on which the growing might occur.

In the years since *INS v. AP*, the case has come instead to stand for a much narrower application of creation as a mode of acquisition. News organizations have a right to prevent their competitors from free riding on efforts to gather hot news, as long as the news remains hot. Competitors are allowed to investigate using the story

---

13. *Id.* at 250 (Brandeis, J., dissenting).

14. Richard A. Epstein, International News Service v. Associated Press: *Custom and Law as Sources of Property Rights in News*, 78 VA. L. REV. 85, 101–02 (1992).

as a lead (in effect engaging in "reverse engineering") or to publish the story after the news value has decreased sufficiently. But other more extended applications of creation have been rejected, for example in the context of dress designs. Fashion is time-sensitive (and can be "hot"), but is open to copying by competitors.[15] Some would argue that nonprotection has been beneficial in promoting the generation of new fashions.[16]

Although *INS v. AP* involves a peripheral form of intellectual property, the debate in the case about whether and how much protection is needed for investments in efforts at creation and commercialization of new information are at the heart of intellectual property policy. Likewise, Justice Brandeis's concern for the public domain looms over intellectual property debates because information has special qualities that set it apart from other resources. Not only is it difficult to exclude others from information, information is what economists call "nonrival": one customer can use the information without diminishing the enjoyment of others. Although *A* and *B* cannot both eat the same bite of an apple, both can enjoy the plot of a sitcom. From this point of view all information should be maintained in an open-access commons; additional copies of a song can be made at virtually zero extra cost and in a competitive market we expect the price to come down to this extremely low marginal price. But the costs of creation (and commercialization) need to be covered, and a competitive price does not do this. Various methods, ranging from first-mover advantages to prizes to intellectual property rights, have been advocated for allowing people to recover their fixed costs in the creation and development of information-related goods. The right mixture of these devices, and the proper boundary between the public domain and intellectual property rights, remain keenly debated questions.

---

15. *See* Cheney Bros. v. Doris Silk Corp., 35 F.2d 279 (1929) (Hand, J.).

16. *See* Kal Raustiala & Christopher Sprigman, *The Piracy Paradox: Innovation and Intellectual Property in Fashion Design*, 92 VA. L. REV. 1687 (2006).

Accession

The acquisition principles we've seen thus far all involve someone performing some action, whether taking possession of something previously unowned, discovering it, or creating it. With the principle of accession, the emphasis is on status rather than action. Accession assigns unowned or contested objects to the owner of property that has the most prominent connection to the contested object. In other words, accession uses ownership of one thing to establish ownership over yet another thing.

A number of legal doctrines incorporate the principle of accession. One folksy example is the rule of *increase*. Baby animals are owned by the owners of the baby's mother. A number of factors support this rule: the mother-offspring bond, the need for care of young animals by their mothers, and the ease of identifying the mother. The rule is recognized in all legal systems we know of, and admits of few exceptions. Even if the father is a prize-winning bull, absent a contract, the owner of the mother nevertheless gets the calf.

Another example of the principle of accession is a doctrine that is called, somewhat confusingly in American law, "accession." (The Romans called this the doctrine of *specificatio*, and it might be advisable to revive this term in the interest of reducing confusion.) Under this doctrine, if one mixes one's labor with some thing owned by someone else, one gets to keep the improved thing—not always, as this would be the worst sort of invitation to thieves and intermeddlers. For this doctrine of accession to apply, several tests or factors come into play. The degree of transformation of the object is important. The more difficult it is to identify the original object in the final product, the more likely it is that courts will award the final product to the laborer. The classic example is pressing grapes into wine. The comparison of relative values also matters. The more value added by the labor, the greater the chances the laborer will be given the final product. Thus, if one makes barrel hoops from trees one does not own, and the value of the hoops is 28 times the value of the standing trees when they were cut down, the improver can keep the hoops.[17] Finally, to reflect the worry about destabilizing the system of ownership, only those who in good faith mistakenly mix their labor with an owned thing can invoke the doctrine of accession. Courts take a dim view of bad faith improvers, generally making bad faith a flat bar to accession. If under these tests the improver wins, the improver must compensate the owner of the original object in the amount of the value of unimproved thing or furnish the equivalent in kind. If the owner of the original object wins, however, the laborer can at most hope to make a (difficult) claim for restitution for the value of the labor.

Wild animal cases also feature a version of the principle of accession, which is variously called the doctrine of *ratione loci* (by reason of place) or *ratione soli* (by reason of the ground). When this doctrine applies, wild animals that are captured are awarded to the owner of the land on which the capture occurs, not the first possessor. Ownership of one thing, the land, gives ownership of another thing, the animal—another example of the broader principle of accession. The court in *Pierson v. Post* neatly dodged this doctrine by assuming that the place where the fox was captured was a wild and unpossessed beach.

There is an even more sweeping version of this instance of the principle of accession: the *ad coelum* doctrine. Under the *ad coelum* doctrine, ownership of the surface brings along with it ownership of the air space and the subsurface in a column or carrot of space running upward and downward from the surface boundaries. "*Ad coelum*" is short for "*Cujus est solum, ejus est ad coelum et ad inferos*," which means "one who owns the soil owns also to the sky and to the depths." The law of trespass crucially relies on the bright line furnished by the *ad coelum* doctrine in order to define an invasion. This doctrine allows buildings to include both foundations and basements and to rise to more than minimal height. Absent special agreements, the *ad coelum* doctrine also determines the ownership

17. Wetherbee v. Green, 22 Mich. 311 (1871).

of minerals (even of caves), and at one time landowners argued that it potentially applied to airplane overflights.

A moment's thought reveals the pointless chaos that would ensue from allowing land owners to block all airplane (not to mention spaceship) flights in the column of space defined by a literal application of the *ad coelum* rule. Instead, the law makes an exception to the *ad coelum* rule for airplane overflights where the owner is not actually using the space through which the airplane flies. This exception to the *ad coelum* doctrine can be rationalized in a variety of ways, most usually by recognizing public rights in a navigation (or in this case "avigation") servitude.[18] We return to public rights in the next chapter. Low-flying airplanes might be nuisances, but as we will see, nuisance—unlike the simple *ad coelum*-based law of trespass—requires proof of injury and is not nearly as strict.

Other examples of the principle of accession include accretion (under which land is augmented by alluvial deposits left by the ocean or a river), the principle that interest earned on a fund of money belongs to the owner of the principal, and the law of *fixtures.* Fixtures arise in a wide variety of situations. When *A* sells premises to *B*, or *C* leases from *D*, or *E* mortgages land when borrowing from *F*, there is a question as to whether certain items, such as appliances, mirrors, drapes, and so forth, go with the premises or are personal property that the seller, lessee, or mortgagor can take away. Absent a special agreement, the law of fixtures determines whether the item should stay or go. Intent matters, but not a hidden subjective intent. Custom can be a guide: Is this item something people expect to take with them or not? This can change: Bathtubs at various times have been considered separate or built in. Being physically attached ("bolted") makes something more likely to be a fixture. If a mirror is affixed to a wall, especially if damage would be caused by its removal, it is a fixture. Likewise, if something is specially suited or custom-built to the premises, it is likely to stay.

18. *See* United States v. Causby, 328 U.S. 256 (1946).

Courts also look to the identity of the party who provided the improvement for the improver's likely intentions as manifested by objective acts. Thus, owners are more likely to be presumed to wish to "enrich the freehold," as they say, than are tenants. So, if an owner builds custom book shelves that are not bolted but fit into a special niche, the owner might be considered to have made a fixture; but if a tenant built the shelves the tenant might be allowed to remove them at the end of the lease.

Accession, then, is a very general part of the law. Based on considerations of salience (e.g., smaller and less valuable goes with bigger and more valuable), accession allows the rich to get richer as it were. In this sense accession, like first possession, creation, and discovery, is a principle of acquisition.[19] But by solving the question of what-goes-with-what, accession can also be regarded as a principle of asset definition. If property is a right to a thing, then the principle of accession goes a long way toward telling us what a thing is. Even with other principles of acquisition, like first possession, when someone acquires a thing we need to know what it is. Why can't I acquire rights to the ocean by pouring a can of tomato juice in it (as Robert Nozick famously asked)?[20] Because tomato juice neither forms the majority of the value of the ocean-tomato juice mixture nor transforms the ocean. Accession does not apply. So even when one acquires an unowned thing by a Lockean process of mixing labor, we need something like accession to tell us what (and how much) one has thereby acquired. Much of the time we can implicitly identify a thing, but in cases of doubt the principle of accession—often through one of the specific doctrines such as increase, and so forth—is there to help us decide what is the "thing."

---

19. Thomas W. Merrill, *Accession and Original Ownership*, 1 J. LEGAL ANALYSIS 459 (2009).

20. ROBERT NOZICK, ANARCHY, STATE AND UTOPIA 175 (1974).

Adverse Possession

First possession, discovery, creation, and accession do not require anyone's consent in order for acquisition to happen. This is why these doctrines operate as a source of original title. None of these modes of acquisition, however, cuts off some other person's established right of ownership. Once ownership is established, we usually think that subsequent ownership of an object must be determined by transfer (sale, gift, will, or inheritance). Nevertheless, nonconsensual acquisitions can occur and, perhaps surprisingly, are sometimes allowed by the law. Adverse possession is a method by which someone, without the owner's permission, acquires a new root of title to property already owned. The adverse possessor acquires title in this fashion by possessing the property until the statute of limitations for the relevant action by the title owner to recover possession has run—ordinarily ejectment in the case of land, and replevin in the case of chattels.

For an adverse possessor to prevail over an owner, the relevant possession must meet a number of requirements. Most importantly, the adverse possessor must enter and remain in possession (that key concept again!) for the requisite period of time established by the statute of limitations. Thus, if *A* enters *O*'s land and acts as an owner would for the right number of years (usually somewhere between ten and twenty), *A* may become the new owner. This goes beyond the normal result from the running of the statute of limitations. Suppose the statute of limitations is twenty years. Ordinarily, this would mean that *O* cannot sue for any wrong committed more than twenty years ago. *O* would still be allowed to sue for the wrongful possession by *A* within the last twenty years. Under the law of adverse possession, however, once the twenty years is past, *O* cannot sue *A* at all—the entire course of wrongful conduct is treated as having occurred at the moment of entry—and *A*, in effect, becomes the new owner. Moreover, *A*'s new title "relates back" to the point of original entry, so that *A* is entitled to keep any rents and profits earned in the last twenty years (but also must pay any taxes owed for the last twenty years).

To gain title the adverse possessor must meet a number of additional requirements beyond the running of the statute of limitations. These can be said to constitute a specialized definition of what "possession" means in this context. The occupancy must be exclusive, open and notorious, actual, continuous, and adverse under a claim of right. The central point uniting these requirements is that the adverse possessor must act as an ordinary owner would, in terms of restricting others' access (or giving them permission), using the land, and so on, and must not have interrupted this activity. Many cases involve seasonal homes, and the issue is whether the adverse possessor's use is as continuous as a ordinary owner's would be. The requirement of continuity does not require the same adverse possessor to engage in adverse possession for the statutory period, but allows various adverse possessors to "tack" their periods of adverse possession, as long as the transfer from one adverse possessor to the next is consensual. But if one adverse possessor ousts another, the clock starts over.

Crucially, the adverse possessor's use must be without permission ("adverse"). If *O* has given permission for *A* to enter the land, there is no adverse possession until the permission is exceeded (or withdrawn). Courts differ as to whether the adverse possessor must be in bad faith (knowing of the rights violation), good faith (not knowing) or whether the adverse possessor's state of mind matters at all. Interestingly, regardless of the law on the books, courts tend to look unkindly on bad faith adverse possessors.[21] Squatters and thieves have trouble convincing courts to award them title by adverse possession, even if a long period of time has elapsed since the original dispossession.

---

21. R. H. Helmholz, *Adverse Possession and Subjective Intent*, 61 WASH. U. L.Q. 331 (1983).

The statute of limitations can be suspended if the owner is laboring under one of a small class of disabilities, such as being under age or insane. Disabilities, however, cannot be "tacked": if the true owner at the time of the adverse possessor's entry is a child, who later becomes insane, the statute is only suspended until the true owner becomes 18 years old. It is a little hard to see why one insane person should be expected to sue when another is not. Perhaps the rule is meant more to prevent adverse possessors from choosing to enter the land of owners under disabilities; once entry has occurred, a different or later disability is less likely to enter into the adverse possessor's decision to stay. Thus, the disabilities rules can be seen as another reflection of distaste for bad faith adverse possessors.

Personal property can be acquired by adverse possession as well. Here the relevant statute of limitations is the action for replevin (or conversion in states that allow recovery of possession through this action). Adverse possession is particularly important for valuable and long-lasting chattels such as art work and jewelry. Unlike in the case of land where the owner can easily find out whether an adverse possessor is possessing the land, personal property is harder to keep track of. (This is one reason we do not have well developed title records for personal property.) So when should the statute of limitations start ticking in the case of personal property? For thieves and converters, the statute is held to start running from the moment of the theft or conversion. From that moment, the true owner has a cause of action against the wrongdoer. Things are a little more complicated in the case of a good faith purchaser, such as a person who buys artwork from a dealer without realizing it was originally stolen. Some jurisdictions, such as New York, have adopted a demand rule: The clock does not start ticking until the true owner demands the return of the chattel and is refused.[22] Other jurisdictions, including New Jersey, hold that the clock starts ticking when the owner either knows or reasonably should have known through the exercise of

22. Solomon R. Guggenheim Found. v. Lubell, 569 N.E.2d 426 (N.Y. 1991).

reasonable diligence the identity of the person who has the object.[23]

These are highly fact-intensive inquiries, and whether they make sense depends on which rationale for adverse possession (if any) one subscribes too. Longer, more difficult applications of the statute of limitations protect true owners at the expense of adverse possessors. One oddity is that the clock typically starts ticking earlier when the chattel is in the hands of a thief than when it has come into the possession of a good faith purchaser. It is hard to see why thieves are more deserving of protection, and as we will see, as between owners and good faith purchasers, U.S. law generally tends to be more protective of owners (and less protective of good faith purchasers) than other, especially civil-law, systems.

Why have adverse possession at all, especially considering its close relationship, in bad faith cases, with theft? Justifications for adverse possession fall into three broad classes. Consistent with adverse possession's origins in the statute of limitations, one rationale emphasizes the slothfulness of the true owner. One can argue the owner is a less worthy gatekeeper than the adverse possessor, or losing the property will hurt the owner less, as evidenced by the owner's indifference in not suing within the limitations period. A second class of theories focuses on the adverse possessor and sees adverse possession as rewarding a diligent possessor who has built up a connection to the property that would be painful to break. (Sometimes this is reinforced with references to the endowment effect in psychology, which seeks to explain the apparent gap in some settings between the higher price people require to give up something they already have than the price they would pay to acquire it.) A third class of rationales are those that emphasize system-wide effects: land records and other questions of title are simpler when old history becomes less relevant. This too is reminiscent of the general reasons for having statutes of limitations, related to the difficulty of proving—and defending against—"stale" claims.

23. O'Keeffe v. Snyder, 416 A.2d 862, 868–70 (N.J. 1980).

Adverse possession wipes away old claims on a rolling basis. As we will see, the effect of adverse possession on land records is not just simplifying but complicating as well: purchasers of property must investigate the "facts on the ground" to see if there are potential adverse possession claims not revealed by the records. Sometimes these three theories point in opposite directions but sometimes they coincide; they coincide in cases where, if not for the owner's tardiness, the adverse possessor's reliance would not build up and evidence would not get stale.

Adverse possession illustrates how seriously the law takes possession in yet another way. When an adverse possessor takes possession, the adverse possessor has rights good against everyone but the true owner. Possession is a close proxy for ownership—but not identical. An owner can give possession to another without losing ownership, as in bailments (see Chapter 4) and leases (see Chapter 6). Such voluntary surrenders of possession do not lead to adverse possession. Likewise, an adverse possessor in possession can maintain trespass actions against all others except the true owner, who in turn is expected to sue or kick off the adverse possessor before the statute of limitations has run. This is an example of the relativity of title: The adverse possessor does not have full ownership, but is like an owner with respect to people other than the true owner. What if one adverse possessor (AP_1) is ousted by another (AP_2)? Here AP_1 has better rights than AP_2, illustrating the relativity of title. So it is not just that adverse possessors have better title than all but owners; an adverse possessor has better rights than all but the owner and anyone with better (here, prior, involuntarily surrendered) possessory rights: $O > AP_1 > AP_2$.

Sequential Possession, Finders, and the Relativity of Title

Relativity of title finds even more dramatic expression when we come to the law of sequential possession, including the law of finders.

The most famous illustration and formulation of the law of finders is the case of *Armory v. Delamirie.*[24] A chimney sweeper's boy found a ring and took it to a goldsmith's shop. The apprentice took the stones out and showed it to the master, who offered to buy them for a trivial sum. The boy refused, whereupon the apprentice returned the ring with the socket empty. Somehow the boy managed to bring an action in trover (damages for conversion of personal property) and won. The court chose to measure damages by the finest jewel able to fit in the socket unless the defendant could prove otherwise. The court stated that a finder has title good against all but the true owner. This demonstrates again the relativity of title, but goes further than necessary for the case. The court could have simply said that finders beat converters, as the boy was a finder, and the goldsmith effectively stole the stones from him.

More difficult cases involve earlier finders against later finders or earlier converters against later converters. Most courts (in the few relevant cases) have found that the first finder or converter beats the second finder or converter. Recall too that in the case of adverse possession the first adverse possessor wins over a later adverse possessor. Generally, courts have sought to protect the stability of possession by awarding the property to the party earlier in the chain of possession. No court that we know of has had to decide earlier converter versus later finder.

Finally, in a move reminiscent of accession, some courts and statutes make a distinction between *lost* property and *mislaid* property, the latter being property placed deliberately by the owner and then forgotten. If such a distinction is made, mislaid property is kept by the owner of the locus where the property is found, pending a claim from the true owner. This has been explained by hypothesizing that the true owner is more likely to recover the object if it is kept by the owner of the *locus in quo*, because the true owner is

---

24. 1 Strange 505 (K.B. 1722).

likely to retrace his or her steps to inquire of all places previously visited in an effort to find the property.

The Mosaic of Acquisition Principles

The conflict between a finder and a locus owner highlights the problem that the acquisition principles we've discussed can sometimes come into conflict. What if the fox in *Pierson v. Post* had been on private land? The law has varied on this question, but in the case of wild animals U.S. law has tended to favor hunters by making it harder to claim trespass in hunting situations (see Chapter 4). Outside the wild animal context, an intriguing set of cases comes from the law of meteorites, which as they enter the atmosphere have no known owners. Here locus owners almost invariably win over finders, and even over tenants in possession.

Reconciling the various acquisition principles can seem like a hopeless morass of analogies. Coming up with a clear answer is key, and courts prefer not to reward people who violate entitlements. Thus, trespassers tend to lose to locus owners, absent some widely accepted custom in favor of the finder. In some cases, custom may supply an answer as to how to treat finders versus locus owners (as when someone finds bees and follows them onto someone's land). Sometimes the law of employment can furnish some guidance. Cleaning staff at hotels are usually held to be acting as agents for their employers. But in the end, tough cases remain.

Further Reading

Richard A. Epstein, *Possession as the Root of Title*, 13 GA. L. REV. 1221 (1979) (justifying first possession as moving resources into private ownership with minimal government intervention).

Dean Lueck, *The Rule of First Possession and the Design of the Law*, 38 J.L. & ECON. 393 (1995) (analyzing the circumstances under which first possession is efficient).

Thomas W. Merrill, *Property Rules, Liability Rules, and Adverse Possession*, 79 Nw. U.L. Rev. 1122 (1985) (summarizing theories of adverse possession).

Carol M. Rose, *Possession as the Origin of Property*, 52 U. Chi. L. Rev. 73, 78, 85 (1985) (emphasizing the role of notice in first possession).

Henry E. Smith, *The Language of Property: Form, Context, and Audience*, 55 Stan. L. Rev. 1105, 1115–25 (2003) (examining the communicative function of rules of original acquisition).

THREE

The Domain of Property

IN THIS CHAPTER WE CONSIDER the domain of property. What sorts of things or interests in things can be held as property? Does the domain of property change over time, and if so how do we account for such changes? What principles determine the limits on the range of interests that can be regarded as property?

The Demsetz Theory

We start with a famous theory offered by Harold Demsetz to explain changes in the domain of property over time.[1] According to Demsetz, property is an institution for internalizing externalities associated with the use of scarce resources. An externality is some benefit or cost generated by one person's activity that is involuntarily borne by some other person.

Suppose you own land abutting a small lake. One of your neighbors dumps waste material into the lake, with the result that large numbers of fish in the lake die. The pollution of the lake is a *negative externality* associated with the neighbor's dumping activity that is borne (in part) by you, the landowner. After this episode, suppose another neighbor builds a fish hatchery in an attempt to restock

1. Harold Demsetz, *Toward a Theory of Property Rights*, 57 AM. ECON. REV. PAPERS & PROC. 347 (1967).

the lake. To the extent the neighbor succeeds, the restocking will be a *positive externality* experienced (in part) by you, the landowner.[2]

Starting with a famous article about externalities written by Ronald Coase in 1960,[3] economists have long been aware that one way to internalize positive and negative externalities is through contracts. Suppose the landowner in the previous example identifies the would-be dumper before the pollution takes place. Such an identification might lead to a contract between the owner and the dumper, in which the dumper would agree, in return for some consideration, not to dispose of the waste material in the lake. The offer of such a contract would internalize to the would-be dumper the negative externalities that otherwise would be borne by the landowner, because now the dumper would have to take those costs into account—as represented by the price the landowner is willing to pay to secure the agreement of the dumper not to pollute. Similarly, the neighbor thinking of starting a fish hatchery might decide to condition his or her willingness to do so on the other landowners on the lake agreeing to contribute to the hatchery. The offer of such a contract would internalize the positive externalities associated with the hatchery, because now the neighbor would take into account more of the benefit when incurring the cost of providing it.

The Demsetz theory posits that another way of internalizing externalities associated with the use of resources is by establishing property rights in the resource. Property rights, as Demsetz understood them, are rights to exclude others from specific things

2. It is commonly thought that negative externalities result in excessive activity levels, and positive externalities lead to underprovision of the good in question. Although this is true in many situations, it is not always the case. A flower garden is nonrival, in the sense that additional people can enjoy it at no extra cost. Nevertheless, you may enjoy planting it so much that you will do so regardless of whether additional passers-by enjoy it or not. In such a case the spillover benefit is called an "irrelevant" externality.

3. R. H. Coase, *The Problem of Social Cost*, 3 J.L. & ECON. 1 (1960). We will return to Coase at greater length in Chapter 8.

or resources. By creating such exclusion rights and conferring them on an identified owner, many of the benefits and costs associated with the use of the resource—which otherwise would be experienced as externalities by others—will instead be borne by the owner. By giving the owner exclusive control over the resource, decisions that affect the value of the resource in a positive or negative direction will be captured by the owner. The owner thus has a powerful incentive to take these benefits and costs into account in deciding how to use the resource, just as one would if one could enter into contracts with other affected persons about these benefits and costs.

As Demsetz further observed, this incentive extends to costs and benefits that will be realized after the owner's death. As he put it, "an owner of a private right to use land acts as a broker whose wealth depends on how well he takes into account the competing demands of the present and the future."[4] When resources are held in an open-access state, in contrast, there is no such broker to represent the interests of the future, because there is no owner who can internalize the claims of future generations. The result is likely to be that "the claims of the present generation are given an uneconomically large weight in determining the intensity with which the land is worked."[5]

Consider again, by way of illustration of these points, the small lake in our previous example. Suppose, first, that no one owns the lake; it is an open-access resource (see Chapter 2). Under this arrangement, if one person pollutes the lake, this imposes a cost in the form of reduced opportunities to catch fish in the future. This cost will be borne by all persons who might want to fish in the lake. Consequently, most of the cost is experienced as an externality by persons other than the one who pollutes. Similarly, if one person were to stock the lake, this would create a benefit in the form of

4. *Id.* at 355.

5. *Id.*

increased opportunities to catch fish in the future. But again, most of the benefit would be experienced as an externality by persons other than the one doing the stocking. The predictable result of this open-access arrangement would be too much polluting—overconsumption of the resource—and too little stocking—underinvestment in the resource.

Now, change the arrangement so that one person is the owner of the lake and hence can exclude all other persons from the lake. If the owner of the lake pollutes, the cost this imposes, in terms of reduced opportunities to catch fish in the future, will be borne entirely by the owner. Likewise, if the owner decides to stock the lake, the benefits this creates, in terms of increased opportunities to fish in the future, will be captured entirely by the owner. Even if the owner is too old to look forward to catching these fish during the owner's own lifetime, the stocking will increase the value of the lake, and the owner can capture this higher value by selling or donating the lake to others who can look forward to catching them. Because the owner internalizes the full costs of pollution and the full benefits of stocking, the owner has an incentive to weigh these costs against the advantages of polluting activities, and to weigh the risks and potential return from stocking. The problems of overconsumption and underinvestment associated with the open-access regime are significantly reduced.[6]

If property has these desirable cost-internalization features, why aren't all resources owned? Here Demsetz offered an important insight: Just as Coase pointed out that making and enforcing contracts to control externalities is costly, so Demsetz observed that

---

6. If property rights are limited in scope, as they always are, then externalities will never be completely eliminated by creating property rights in resources. There will always be spillovers from one unit of property that affect other units or actors. For example, if the owner of the lake destroys a marshy portion of the lake that serves as a habitat for migratory birds, this could impose costs on persons who like to go bird watching or bird hunting in areas outside the lake. The destruction of the marsh imposes an external cost on bird watchers and hunters in other areas where the birds migrate.

establishing and enforcing property rights is costly. It is necessary to define the resources subject to ownership, specify how owners are identified, set up an institution to resolve disputes over ownership, and devise mechanisms for enforcing ownership rights. These activities consume resources that could be devoted to doing something else. Putting together the advantages of property, in terms of internalizing the costs and benefits of resource use, and the costs of property, in terms of the resources needed to establish and enforce property rights, we get the complete Demsetz theory. Stated affirmatively, this says that property rights in resources will be established when the internalization benefits associated with property rights exceed the costs associated with establishing and enforcing property rights. Stated negatively, if the costs of establishing and enforcing property rights exceed the benefits of internalization from establishing and enforcing property rights, resources will remain in an unowned (open-access) state.

The Demsetz theory has several important implications for the types of things that will be owned as property. First, for something to be governed by a property regime, there must be enough demand for the resource relative to its supply that internalization of externalities associated with use of the resource will produce significant benefits. Some things are so *plenteous* that, even if they are very important to sustaining human life, there will be no perception of scarcity and hence no point in internalizing externalities. The atmosphere and the oceans have historically been regarded as the "common right" of all mankind, in part because they have been regarded as so plentiful that no one would bother to try to assert exclusive rights over them. This can change of course. In recent decades, one important resource associated with oceans—fisheries—have become increasingly distressed, and stocks of fish have declined, sometimes precipitously. In response, we have seen movement toward establishing exclusive economic zones in ocean fisheries, regulatory limits on total catch in certain ocean fisheries, and even the creation of systems of individual permits to fish that are bought and sold, called individual tradeable quotas (ITQs).

Evidence suggests that ITQs where implemented have generally halted and sometimes reversed the trend toward collapse of fisheries.[7] This broad movement toward exclusion rights in response to scarcity is consistent with what the Demsetz theory would predict.

Second, if something is regarded as having no value, or negative value, it is also unlikely that the thing will be treated as property. Animal droppings, for example, are generally regarded as a nuisance—a *negative value product*—and ordinarily no one claims property rights in animal waste. Tellingly, however, if such waste does have value, disputes over ownership can arise. This is suggested by a famous case about horse manure gathered in piles at the side of a public roadway.[8] The manure had no value to the travelers whose animals dropped it. But once collected it had positive value as fertilizer, and this gave rise to a dispute over who owned it (the gatherer as it happened).

Third, property in a given class of resources is unlikely to exist if there are *high costs of establishing and enforcing* such rights. A famous example is provided by rangeland in the American west.[9] Rangeland was regarded as an open-access resource for most of the nineteenth century. Any one could graze animals on the open range. This led to overgrazing, which quite arguably reduced total output from raising livestock. In theory, division of the land into separately owned tracts would have offered a solution, but this was far from costless. One problem was that traditional fencing materials, such as wooden rails, were scarce on the plains, which made it expensive to demarcate individual grazing tracts by fencing. With the invention of barbed wire, it became much cheaper to divide rangeland

---

7. Christopher Costello et al., *Can Catch Shares Prevent Fisheries Collapse?*, 321 SCIENCE 1678 (2008).

8. Haslem v. Lockwood, 37 Conn. 500 (1871).

9. See Terry L. Anderson & Peter J. Hill, *The Evolution of Property Rights: A Study of the American West*, 18 J.L. & ECON. 163 (1975).

into separately owned parcels. Consistent with the Demsetz theory, widespread enclosure of the land soon followed. Cheaper fencing material lowered the costs of defining and enforcing private property in land, and this changed the cost-benefit equation.

In general, rights in some assets are easier to delineate and enforce as property than other assets. Rights in land and tangible personal property such as clothing and automobiles are relatively easy to delineate and enforce as property. Rights in other resources, such as wild birds, water in underground aquifers, or abstract ideas are much more difficult to delineate and enforce. This can be because the resource moves around (birds), or is difficult to observe (underground water), or is inherently difficult to specify (abstract ideas). Not surprisingly, we find that objects that fall into one or more of these categories tend to resist treatment as property.

Notice that the Demsetz theory identifies some general conditions in which property, especially in the sense of exclusion rights, are likely to emerge, but has nothing to say about whether the response will be to create traditional private property, communal property, public property, or some type of public regulation such as a permitting scheme. Demsetz suggested that the particular history and cultural conventions of the society will be important in determining the "type" of property that evolves. This is undoubtedly true, but does not provide much guidance in predicting the path of future institutional development.

Notice too that the Demsetz theory fails to specify a causal mechanism by which property rights get created. Resources are held in an open-access state at time T_1, under one combination of benefits and costs, and then move to a property regime at time T_2, under a different combination of benefits and costs. But we are not told exactly how the change from T_1 to T_2 comes about. Commentators have debated whether the causal mechanism is more likely to be bottom-up, with property evolving from informal social norms, or top-down, with "property entrepreneurs" lobbying the government to pass laws that authorize new forms of property.

The top-down theory has a certain plausibility if creating a new type of property entails a large upfront investment. Assume a lake subject to open access yields $1000 worth of fish to ten different fishers. Assume further that creating a system of exclusion rights, such as a program of ITQs, would raise the value of the yield to $2000, by eliminating the take of young fish before they spawn. Finally, assume that the costs of lobbying the government to create the ITQs would be $400. If the existing ten fishers have relatively equal-sized operations, such that they would most likely divide the ITQs equally, it will be difficult to raise $400 for the lobbying campaign. Each fisher would gain only about $100 from adopting this scheme, so unless there is some way to compel each fisher to help underwrite the lobbying costs, the change may not happen. Suppose, in contrast, that one fisher has a disproportionately large operation, equal to 50 percent of the take, and that this operator would likely command 50 percent of the ITQs. Such an operator would stand to gain $500, which is enough to create an incentive for this one operator alone to incur the $400 lobbying costs needed to make the change. This example suggests that property rights may be most likely to emerge in markets with heterogeneous producers, some of whom would benefit disproportionately from the creation of property.[10]

The principal point established by the Demsetz theory is that there are practical constraints on the domain of property. Plenteous resources, negative or low-valued resources, and resources that are hard to pin down or observe are unlikely candidates for inclusion in the domain of property. Conditions that make enforcement of property rights difficult, such as a scarcity of fencing materials or the absence of a functioning court system, will also make it difficult for property to thrive.

---

10. *See* Katrina Miriam Wyman, *From Fur to Fish: Reconsidering the Evolution of Private Property*, 80 N.Y.U. L. Rev. 117 (2005). Conversely, to get multiple parties to contribute, homogeneity of interests is likely to facilitate bargaining. *See* Gary D. Libecap, Contracting for Property Rights 22–23 (1989).

Personhood

Another strand of theorizing justifies property in terms of personhood. Human actors act on the world and exercise dominion over external things, and in so doing they constitute themselves as individuals. This is an idea tracing back at least to Hegel,[11] and is the springboard for the theory of property developed in the early work of Margaret Jane Radin.[12] According to Radin, property that contributes to personhood is deserving of more protection than "fungible" property. Thus, a wedding ring on the hand of a loving spouse is personhood property, whereas a ring in the inventory of a storeowner is fungible property. The loss is far more of a personal wound in the former than the latter case. Of course operating a store can be the expression of individual personhood, and Radin would not necessarily disagree. But Radin sees danger in "fetishizing" things, and takes a dim view of the personhood and property claims of capitalists in particular. Although certain features of law such as the homestead exemption in bankruptcy can be regarded as reflecting a version of personhood concerns, in U.S. law personhood issues come to the fore primarily in placing constraints on what can be treated as property.

The personhood perspective suggests that even if conditions identified by the Demsetz theory are fully satisfied, there are reasons of social policy for refusing to regard certain kinds of resources as property. We can distinguish two types of social policy constraints grounded in personhood concerns. Strong personhood constraints counsel against treating persons themselves as property. Weak personhood constraints counsel against treating certain things closely identified with persons as property for some purposes such as permitting commercial sales.

---

11. G. W. F. HEGEL, ELEMENTS OF THE PHILOSOPHY OF RIGHT (Allen W. Wood, ed.; H.B. Nisbet, transl. 1991) (1821).

12. Margaret Jane Radin, *Property and Personhood*, 34 STAN. L. REV. 957 (1982).

Human slavery provides the clearest example of the strong personhood constraint. Throughout much of human history, ownership of one person as property by another was permitted. Today this is universally regarded as a violation of basic human rights. The ban on slavery reflects the principle that all human beings, without regard to race or nationality, should be regarded as autonomous moral agents rather than objects controlled by other persons. The principle is so strong we forbid individuals to contract into a state of slavery or servitude. Various explanations have been given for this, including paternalism (we do not trust people to make an informed choice about this), external costs (others may be anguished by seeing slaves), and the immorality of slavery in all its forms however it arises. Whatever the explanation, it represents a baseline principle about property rights: People can be owners of things but cannot be objects of ownership.

The strong personhood constraint is also reflected in modern conceptions about relations among members of families. At one time, and still today in some places, parent-child and spousal relations were conceived of in a property-like fashion. Parents had absolute control over the children, as husbands did over their wives. Today, parent-child and husband-wife relations are governed by legal norms of family law different from those that apply to property ownership. Like the rule against slavery, these norms are designed to protect the basic understanding that all persons are autonomous moral agents, not simply objects owned by others.

When we move beyond the core case of one person owning another, we are much more likely to encounter weak personhood constraints.[13] Consider in this regard the many vexing questions about the legal status of human body parts, bodily fluids, and

---

13. Weak personhood constraints are often expressed in terms of the danger of "commodification" of personhood interests. For discussion and applications in a variety of contexts, including trade in sex, children, and body parts, see MARGARET JANE RADIN, CONTESTED COMMODITIES (1996); RETHINKING COMMODIFICATION (Martha M. Ertman & Joan C. Williams eds., 2005).

genetic material. The most widely discussed case here is *Moore v. Regents of California*,[14] which is often cited for the proposition that human body parts are not property. Moore was being treated for leukemia at UCLA Medical Center. Physicians removed cells from his spleen and, without informing him, used these cells to develop a new cell line for which the medical center obtained a patent. The new cell line was thought to have potentially valuable commercial applications. Moore sued the physicians and UCLA, seeking damages for conversion of his spleen cells. The California Supreme Court held that Moore's complaint stated a cause of action for breaching a fiduciary duty and failing to obtain his informed consent for the medical treatment (by concealing the plans for commercial use of the spleen cells). But the court found he had no action for conversion, because he did not have any "property" interest in his spleen cells.

There are many puzzling aspects of the *Moore* case, including the court's apparent assumption that although Moore had no property rights in his spleen cells, UCLA did have such rights in the cells after they were removed. In general, the court seemed worried about imposing unexpected liability on downstream medical researchers who had previously used body tissue or cells for research without inquiring whether they had the right to do so. The court also noted that commercial sales of organs and bodily fluids for purposes of treatment and transplantation are prohibited by the Uniform Anatomical Gifts Act. The court thought it best to await legislative action before treating body cells as the property of the person from whom they are drawn.

Another puzzle is whether the court in fact succeeded in denying Moore a property right in his spleen cells. If property crucially involves the right to exclude, then in a sense the California Supreme Court *did* give Moore the right to exclude, because once the doctors provided him with complete information about the possible

---

14. 793 P.2d 479 (Cal. 1990).

commercial use of the cells, he could always refuse to consent to the surgery. The right to give informed consent assumes the right to say no, which is functionally the right to exclude the doctors from getting their hands on the cells. Of course, this right to exclude would apply only to Moore's treating physicians; it would not impose any duty on downstream researchers or persons using any medical products developed with Moore's spleen cells. The right recognized by the court was in personam, not in rem. So maybe the court did succeed in denying Moore a full-fledged property right after all.

A narrower characterization of the court's holding would be that Moore could not sell his spleen cells in a commercial transaction, and hence could not recover damages based on the market value of the cells. So construed, the decision reflects a concern about permitting commercial transactions in human body parts. This concern can usually be vindicated by eliminating one of the incidents of property—the right to sell. It is not necessary to deny other incidents of property, such as the right to exclude, to use, or to gift. Indeed, nothing in the court's decision suggests that Moore could not make a gift of his spleen cells for medical research, or could not refuse to permit them to be used for any purpose after they were removed. On this reading as well, then, the court was overstating things in saying that Moore had no property in his spleen cells.

More recent decisions tend to confirm a narrow reading of *Moore.* In one case, the Ninth Circuit held that the next of kin have a sufficient property right in the body of a deceased relative to demand a due process hearing before body parts are removed by the coroner for transplantation.[15] Another California case held that frozen sperm cells are the property of the estate of a deceased person, subject to disposition by a probate court.[16] The general pattern seems to suggest that the person from whom body parts or fluids are removed has the right to direct or veto how these resources

15. Newman v. Sathyavaglswaran, 287 F.3d 786 (9th Cir. 2002).

16. Hecht v. Superior Court, 20 Cal. Rptr. 2d 275 (Cal. Ct. App. 1993).

are used after removal. In this sense, persons do have property rights in their body parts and fluids. But there is continued uneasiness about permitting individuals to contract to sell body parts or fluids, at least without affirmative legislative authorization, perhaps out of concern that this would lead to body harvesting or other types of degradation that violate the principle that humans are moral agents and not objects of ownership.

Certain types of cultural objects have also been placed off limits from being treated like ordinary property. The Native American Graves Protection and Repatriation Act (NAGPRA),[17] for example, has been interpreted as prohibiting commercial transactions in certain Native American artifacts that cannot be sold under native customary laws. Again, the concern is with commodification of objects that are regarded as being integral to native cultural practices. There is no suggestion that cultural patrimony is not property for other purposes, such as protection against theft or destruction.

In sum, there are both strong and weak personhood constraints on the domain of property. The strong constraint is represented by the rule that no person can own another person as property. The weak constraint, which is reflected in the cases involving body parts and cultural patrimony, is more accurately characterized as a concern about commodification, and prohibits buying and selling certain kinds of resources. But the weak constraint does not deny the status of the resource as property for other purposes, such as the right to exclude, use, or gift.

Inherently Public Property

A different and opposite limit on the domain of private property involves resources that must be maintained in an inherently public or open-access state. Here, the core case is provided by navigable

---

17. 25 U.S.C. §§ 3001–3013.

waterways, which have been understood since Roman times to be a resource that must remain open to access by all persons.[18] In the modern era, navigable airspace has also been described as a resource that is regarded as inherently public.[19] Many would also include highways and streets on this list of things that should remain open to all, although private toll roads are not unknown, and some European cities including London and Oslo now impose user fees on vehicles in congested areas. Public squares, parks, certain public buildings such as courthouses, and beaches are also often regarded as assets that should be accessible by all, and not subject to exclusion rights.

The legal doctrines that serve to protect the open-access status of inherently public resources are various. In the United States, the Commerce Clause of the Federal Constitution has been construed as incorporating a self-executing "navigation servitude" that trumps the application of restrictions on access to navigable waterways and airspace grounded in state law or private property rights. The public trust doctrine, which has roots in Roman law and English common law, has also been widely invoked to block efforts to transfer inherently public property into private property status. Assets covered by the doctrine are owned by the state but are subject to a "public trust," which inheres in the title. In the strong version of the doctrine, even the legislature lacks power to transfer these assets into private hands or otherwise violate the trust, because the state never had such a power to begin with.[20] If such a transfer occurs, the state can revoke the transaction without violating the Takings Clause or other constitutional protections for private property. Doctrines of customary rights, public dedication, and public

---

18. *See* Daniel J. Hulsebosch, *Writs to Rights: Navigability and the Transformation of the Common Law in the Nineteenth Century*, 23 CARDOZO L. REV. 1049 (2002).

19. United States v. Causby, 328 U.S. 256 (1946).

20. *See* Illinois Central R. Co. v. Illinois, 146 U.S. 387 (1892).

prescription have also been relied on to protect inherently public property.[21]

The federal landholdings known as the federal public domain represent an interesting and important variant on the idea of inherently public property. The public domain was originally composed of lands west of the Appalachian Mountains that were ceded to the federal government to pay off the Revolutionary War debts. The public domain was later augmented by the Louisiana Purchase, vast tracts of land acquired by treaties with Spain, Mexico, and England, and the purchase of Alaska. The original idea was that this land would be held by the federal government as trustee until it could be disposed of by purchase or otherwise claimed as private property.[22] But not all of these vast holdings were disposed of in this fashion, and today about 30 percent of the landmass of the United States consists of federal public domain land. These lands are used for a variety of purposes: grazing, timber harvesting, recreation, and mining, among others. The permissible uses are heavily regulated by the federal government. Whatever the use, however, the general rule is that these lands may be entered by any person who agrees to follow the rules. In designated Wilderness Areas, for example, all motorized vehicles and permanent structures are prohibited.[23] But access nevertheless is open to anyone with a sturdy pair of shoes and a backpack.

Why are certain resources regarded as inherently public? One theory would be that these resources are used by large numbers of people, often on a temporary or transient basis, with the result that carving up the resource into many individual exclusion zones would create very *high transaction costs*. As we noted in Chapter 2,

---

21. *See, e.g.*, State of Oregon *ex rel.* Thornton v. Hay, 462 P.2d 671 (Or. 1969) (ruling that the general public enjoys a customary right of access to dry sand beaches).

22. Pollard v. Hagan, 44 U.S. (3 How.) 212 (1845).

23. 16 U.S.C. § 1133(c).

navigable airspace provides a vivid example. If we applied the *ad coleum* rule literally and allowed the owners of surface rights to exclude airplane overflights, the costs of assembling flight easements above all the affected parcels would be enormous. At the same time, the owner of the surface typically has no good reason to exclude overflights, assuming they occur at a sufficiently high altitude that they do not interfere with construction of buildings or other activities on the surface. Similar arguments can be made about the high transaction costs that would result from carving up navigable rivers, town squares, beaches, or wilderness areas and subjecting them to private property rights.

Another theory would point to a phenomenon known as *network effects* to explain the intuition that certain resources should remain in an open-access state. A colloquial expression for network effects is "the more the merrier."[24] The idea is that certain resources become more valuable as more people use them. The telephone system and the Internet are examples. The more people have phones or e-mail accounts, the more valuable it is for others to sign up to join the system, because they have more people with whom to interact. Similarly, it might be argued that the more people use navigable rivers or airspace, the more trade and commerce flourish, and hence the more goods and information disseminate through human interaction. Leaving the rivers or the skies in an open-access state, that is, pricing access at zero, encourages this dissemination. The same is plausibly true of highways and town squares. Perhaps parks, beaches, and street fairs share this quality as well—at least up to a point. With physical assets like rivers, beaches, and street fairs, congestion may eventually set in, requiring that some kind of rationing mechanism be established. In the electronic world of telephones and the Internet, congestion is less likely to be a problem.

---

24. Carol Rose, *The Comedy of the Commons: Custom, Commerce, and Inherently Public Property*, 53 U. Chi. L. Rev. 711, 768 (1986).

A third theory is that certain resources should remain open to all in order to promote *sociability*.[25] The model here might be the agora of ancient Greece, where citizens gathered every day to trade, gossip, hear the latest news, and see and be seen. The agora provided the social glue that kept the society together. Similarly, keeping parks, beaches, and even navigable rivers open to all encourages random meetings and encounters, and allows for spontaneous gatherings of citizens. This unplanned mixing of people can help develop tolerance for persons of different backgrounds and ideas, and can perhaps build bonds of community among individuals who otherwise have few occasions to interact.

Hybrid Resources

There are also some important resources that are hybrids, in the sense that they share attributes of both ordinary goods subject to exclusion rights and public goods that remain in an open-access state. Water is a prime and interesting example. Water can be captured in a tank or bottle, in which case it is much like other commodities that are generally treated as private property and are subject to exclusion rights. But in its unconfined state—in a river or stream or pond or an underground aquifer—water has unique features that make it difficult to assimilate to the world of ordinary commodities. Water is subject to the hydrological cycle, in that it evaporates, falls as rain, and evaporates again. It also flows downhill and seeps into the ground if not kept in an impermeable container. There is thus a public-rights aspect to water, in the sense that certain uses or misuses of water by one person will affect the interests of others who might benefit from the water after it evaporates or flows away from the first user.

25. *See id.* at 775–81.

Given the unique attributes of water, the law has responded by creating regimes of rights that are unique to water. One general principle here is that water rights are usually linked to the ownership of land. In areas where water is relatively plentiful—generally speaking, in England and the eastern states of the United States—rights attach to the land where water is found. Ownership of land that abuts a body of water, called riparian land, confers rights to the water, which go with the ownership of the land. Under the *natural flow* theory that prevailed in the early common law, a riparian owner could block any diversion that significantly modified the natural flow of a river or stream or level of a lake or pond. Under the *reasonable use* theory that is more commonly used today, courts will balance the interests of different riparian owners to determine whether diversions or other uses are permissible.

In dry areas where water is scarce—generally speaking. the western states in the United States—rights to water attach to the ownership of land where the water is *used*, which may or may not be the land on which it is initially found. In its original form, this system established rights to water in accordance with temporal priority in appropriation of the water for a beneficial use. The first appropriator had the first claim, the second appropriator the next claim, and so forth. Hence this system is often called the *prior appropriation* system. Unlike riparian rights, water rights in a prior appropriation system can be sold separately from the land they are currently being used on, but the new use must not harm return flows that have been appropriated by downstream users. Over time, the pure system of temporal priorities has been extensively modified by an overlay of regulation that limits what constitutes a beneficial use and protects other users who may be harmed by diversions. Some states, notably California, have developed systems that combine features of riparian rights and the prior appropriation system.

A common feature of all water rights is the attachment of the rights to land, either the land where the water is found or where it is used (recall the discussion of accession Chapter 2). An explanation might be that this allows for water rights to be uniquely assigned to particular persons. The owners of these rights can therefore deploy the resource to maximum advantage, and internalize externalities. Yet another common feature of water rights, at least in the modern era, is extensive public regulation of uses, so as to protect the interests of other persons interested in drawing on the resource.[26] For example, consumptive uses may be restricted to amounts deemed reasonable, in light of the needs of other competing users. Similarly, transfers of water rights, especially diversions outside the watershed, typically require regulatory approval to assure that third parties are not harmed. Thus, water law simultaneously has both an exclusionary aspect, and strong public rights aspect. Which aspect dominates is driven in part by the nature of prevailing uses: Water law in the eastern United States has historically been less intense and more oriented around nonconsumptive uses such as water-powered mills, whereas Western uses such as irrigation and mining tend to be intense and make the water used unavailable to other local users.[27]

Intellectual property is another prominent resource that has a hybrid private-public quality. Here, the mixing does not mainly occur simultaneously, as with water rights, but rather by carving out "islands" of exclusion within a general sea of open access. The background rule for information goods—ideas, expressions, images, symbols—is one of open access. Anyone and everyone can use, copy, or elaborate on information goods without obtaining the permission of anyone else. The justifications for this background rule are similar to those previously mentioned for inherently public property: Exclusion rights would create high transactions costs; information goods often have network effects (certainly this is true

26. See Henry E. Smith, *Governing Water: The Semicommons of Fluid Property Rights*, 50 ARIZ. L. REV. 445 (2008).

27. Terry L. Anderson & P. J. Hill, *The Evolution of Property Rights: A Study of the American West*, 18 J.L. & ECON. 163, 176–78 (1975); Carol M. Rose, *Energy and Efficiency in the Realignment of Common-Law Water Rights*, 19 J. LEGAL STUD. 261, 290–94 (1990).

in the case of language systems and many computer programs); and making information goods freely available may enhance social interaction. In addition, once an information good is produced, it can be used or copied over and over at little or no additional cost. It costs no more for a thousand people to think a thought or recite a poem than for one to do so. Economists say that information goods are "nonrivalrous," with the implication that the correct price for such goods is zero.

This is not the whole of the story, however. As mentioned in Chapter 2 in connection with hot news, if all information goods were subject to open access and consequently priced at zero, there might be insufficient incentives for creative individuals to devote themselves to producing and commercializing new information goods. Inventors, novelists, and songwriters—some of them at any rate—might decide that there is little point in laboring to create new information goods if they have no way to appropriate the value these goods provide for others. In addition, industrial firms, publishing houses, and recording studios might decide that there is little point in improving, marketing, and distributing information goods (or things produced with information goods) if they have no way of assuring a return on their investments in these activities.

For these reasons, the U.S. Constitution authorizes Congress to create "exclusive rights" in certain information goods for "limited times"[28]—what are known as patents and copyrights. (Other intellectual property rights, such as trademarks and publicity rights, have also been created, under the federal Commerce Clause and state law, respectively.) These intellectual property rights, which give owners the exclusive right to use certain delineated information goods, are limited in scope. They apply only to a subset of information goods that meet certain prescribed criteria, such as novelty and usefulness (in the case of patents) and originality (in the case of copyrights). And they typically last for a limited time, such as the

---

28. U.S. CONST. art I, § 8, cl. 8.

period of 20 years minus the duration of the application, under the current Patent Act.

Intellectual property rights represent a different sort of compromise between private and public property. Whereas water rights combine interwoven private and public facets, the various aspects of intellectual goods tend to be either private or public, and if they are private, they are private for only a temporary period of time. Given the sharply dichotomous, either/or structure of various uses of intellectual goods, it is perhaps not surprising that there is fierce dispute over whether the islands of intellectual property are too large or too small relative to the sea of open access in which they reside. Congress's willingness to adopt repeated extensions of the term of copyrights—and to apply these extensions to existing copyrights—has been a particular source of contention.[29] The legislative willingness to expand has given rise to a backlash, which increasingly calls into question the need for exclusion rights given alternative models of cooperative production and distribution.[30] Which mix of intellectual property rights, other methods of appropriation, and open access, are appropriate in different industries raises important and unresolved empirical issues.

Further Reading

Harold Demsetz, *Toward a Theory of Property Rights*, 57 AM. ECON. REV. PAPERS & PROC. 347 (1967) (offering an economic theory of the evolution of property rights).

Margaret Jane Radin, *Property and Personhood*, 34 STAN. L. REV. 957 (1982) (stressing the role of property in sustaining individual personhood).

29. *See* Eldred v. Ashcroft, 537 U.S. 186 (2003) (upholding retroactive extension of copyright term to life plus 70 years).

30. *See, e.g.*, YOCHAI BENKLER, THE WEALTH OF NETWORKS: HOW SOCIAL PRODUCTION TRANSFORMS MARKETS AND FREEDOM (2006); LAWRENCE LESSIG, THE FUTURE OF IDEAS: THE FATE OF THE COMMONS IN A CONNECTED WORLD (2002).

Carol Rose, *The Comedy of the Commons: Custom, Commerce, and Inherently Public Property*, 53 U. CHI. L. REV. 711 (1986) (examining the importance of and exploring different rationales for inherently public property).

Symposium: *The Evolution of Property Rights*, 31 J. LEGAL STUD. S331 et seq. (2002) (papers exploring, extending, and critiquing the Demsetzian perspective on the evolution of property rights).

FOUR

Owners as Gatekeepers

ONCE AN OWNER HAS ACQUIRED PROPERTY, either by original acquisition or by transfer from a previous owner, the question becomes what exactly does such an owner have? We can frame the question in terms of the competing visions of property we touched on in Chapter 1. The everyday notion of property, reflected especially in the law of trespass, starts with the right to exclude. This suggests we should think of the owner as a kind of gatekeeper of the thing over which the owner has property. The owner, as gatekeeper, has broad discretion to decide who has access to the property and on what terms, how it will be used, and whether to deputize someone else as a gatekeeper on either a temporary or permanent basis. In this chapter we examine the extent to which the law in fact conforms to this model of owner as gatekeeper.

We find that the law does provide impressive support for the right to exclude, not only through the action for trespass, but also through various criminal and civil laws and the privilege of self-help. As we will see, this right to exclude is subject to many exceptions, such as for necessity, custom, public accommodations law, and antidiscrimination law. In addition, owners are subject to governance rules of proper use, to which we return in Chapter 8. Owners also enjoy a variety of powers ancillary to their basic right to exclude, including the power to include (licenses), to transfer temporary custody of property for limited purposes (bailments), to get rid of property (abandonment and destruction), and to transfer property in a variety of ways (sales, gifts, inheritance). Owners get not only to keep people out, but also to determine the use or nonuse of resources in a variety of ways.

After considering all these various rights or powers and their many exceptions, one might ask whether there is a theme to this pudding. The bundle of rights metaphor—another basic vision of the nature of property—has been deployed to call into question whether there really is any core content to property. Do we have a single rule or principle with exceptions, or just a collection of disparate and shifting rights and privileges? This is a very basic question with respect to all of law, indeed with respect to all sorts of rule-governed phenomena. This may sound like a purely theoretical question, with one characterization of the issue or another largely a matter of taste. But the answer we choose has real consequences. With respect to property, the critical question is what presumptive force the core right to exclude should be given when there is some rationale for relaxing or overriding it. When in doubt do we balance considerations of social policy to forge an ad hoc solution, or do we defer to the owner-gatekeeper?

Laws for Owner Protection

Both real and personal property are protected under both civil and criminal law. This gives us four combinations: criminal laws protecting real property, personal property theft offenses, civil law protections for real property, and the civil law of personal property. Although all four modes of protection backstop the owner's right to exclude, the specific degree of protection and its rationale differ within each area.

One might think that because land has traditionally been treated as important and special, the criminal law protection of real property would be robust. The law has always had very strong criminal prohibitions of burglary and arson, but these offenses are more about protection of persons than of property. More purely a matter of property is criminal trespass, but, as it turns out, criminal trespass statutes were introduced only in the nineteenth century and generally carry only modest penalties. Prior to that, it was expected that landowners would avail themselves of self-help, including the use of deadly force, to vindicate their right to exclude. We return to self-help and its limits below. Although many of the uses of criminal trespass are uncontroversial, there has always been some tension between the use of the criminal law to protect real property and other areas of law such as labor law or civil rights law.

The conflict between owner sovereignty and other values in the law of criminal trespass is well illustrated by *State v. Shack*.[1] A farmer invoked the law of criminal trespass to exclude two aid workers who wanted to consult unsupervised with migrant farm workers temporarily living on the farmer's land. The New Jersey Supreme Court, noting that property serves human values, held that the owner's right to exclude did not go this far—an owner could not use the law of trespass to isolate the workers. The court came down for balancing the right to exclude against the interests of migrant workers in maintaining contact with the outside world. The court also declined to resolve the dispute in terms of existing legal categories. Presumably, the court, if it had so chosen, could have held that the workers were tenants in a landlord-tenant relationship with the farmer and as such had a (perhaps nonwaivable) right to receive guests. Or the court could have read a strong implied term into the employment contract, prohibiting this type of isolation. In other words, *State v. Shack* raises two issues. One, are the values and interests of others enough to override the basic right to exclude of the owner? And, two, if so, how should this overriding be accomplished? The New Jersey Supreme Court is something of an outlier in this and other cases in that it is inclined to override the right to exclude using a balancing test, and a fairly case-by-case one at that. Most courts tend to stick with traditional categories to a greater degree,

1. 277 A.2d 369 (N.J. 1971).

for example by looking to landlord-tenant first before tinkering with the basic machinery of criminal trespass.

The criminal law has long protected personal property. Broadly speaking, the offense of larceny originally emphasized the wrongful taking of goods from the owner's possession (*asportation*). This was plausibly regarded as reflecting a concern with preventing violence—taking personal property directly from the owner's possession is very provoking and has a high potential for triggering resistance. As time went on, the offense was gradually expanded to include situations where an owner has been intentionally deprived of property without the owner's consent, but it is difficult to identify any wrenching-from-possession, as for example when an employee embezzles employer funds. Gradually, asportation has been deemphasized in favor of a focus on intent to convert the good to the wrongdoer's use.[2] In effect, the criminal law of theft offenses has shifted at least partly from an emphasis on preventing violence to protecting the owner's more general interest in the security of property rights.

The center of attention in a property course is on the civil side. For real property, the most robust protection is afforded by the law of trespass, under which intentional gross invasions (by objects large enough to displace possession) are subject to strict liability. No injury need be shown, and harm is presumed. In another case that sometimes begins the property course, *Jacque v. Steenberg Homes, Inc.*,[3] a company delivered a mobile home to the plaintiffs' neighbor across the plaintiffs' snowy field, over their explicit and vociferous objection, instead of using a private road with a dangerous snow-clogged hairpin turn. The trespass could not have been more deliberate, and there was evidence of scoffing at the Jacques on the part of the company foreman. The jury found one dollar in

---

2. *See* George P. Fletcher, *The Metamorphosis of Larceny*, 89 HARV. L. REV. 469 (1976).

3. 563 N.W.2d 154 (Wis. 1997).

nominal damages and $100,000 in punitive damages. This is a dramatic result, and the court (like the trial jury presumably) was outraged by the company's lack of respect for the Jacques' rights, and believed that the $30 fine for criminal trespass would not deter the defendant from engaging in similar conduct in the future. Like an injunction but more so, the punitive damages send a message to get the attention of the defendant (and those in a similar position). The court saw the right to exclude, backed up by trespass, as important and worthy of protection—enough so that it held that the usual rule that nominal damages will not support an award of punitive damages does not apply to trespass to land.

But why? The Jacques may have been a little eccentric and, evidently smarting from being on the losing end of adverse possession in the past, were very insistent on their rights. But as we saw in Chapter 2, adverse possession (or, as we will see in Chapter 8, prescription) would require nonpermissive use over a twenty-year period (in Wisconsin). Simple permission from the owner would defeat any such claim. But most observers feel there is more to the story than the stated objections of the Jacques. Certainly their autonomy was violated. But would it have been if they had known beforehand that their bundle of rights did not include the right to prohibit dragging a mobile home across the snowy field? (Query: Where would such specific determinations come from—courts or legislatures?) Or maybe the problem is that the whole point of private property is to delegate to the owner, here the Jacques, decision-making authority (the gatekeeper right) without the need to justify their decisions, and Steenberg Homes had simply offered no good reason to revisit that determination, instead bypassing the system altogether in bad faith. Whether $100,000 is the right amount of punitive damages is another question, upon which the U.S. Supreme Court has made periodic pronouncements,[4] but the availability of a

4. *See, e.g.*, Exxon Shipping Co. v. Baker, 128 S. Ct. 2605 (2008); State Farm Mut. Auto. Ins. Co. v. Campbell, 538 U.S. 408, 429 (2003); BMW of N. Am., Inc. v. Gore, 517 U.S. 559, 575 (1996).

deterrent even where a plaintiff cannot prove harm protects the basic delegation of gatekeeping authority to the owners.

Injunctions traditionally were not available in trespass actions, but the exceptions to this rule, for repeated and threatened trespass for example, eventually wound up almost swallowing the rule. Otherwise damages are the remedy in trespass. Other actions for the protection of real property tend to trace back historically to the trespass family. Ejectment is the action to remove another who is in wrongful possession; as we saw in Chapter 2, the statute of limitations for ejectment is generally the measure of adverse possession. Nuisance, to which we return in Chapter 8, protects against more ethereal invasions.

Owners of personal property who have lost possession can sue in replevin to get the thing back or can sue in conversion (sometimes called *trover*) to get damages. In the latter situation the owner is in effect forcing a sale on the converter. There is also an action in trespass—trespass to chattels—that protects personal property against damage. Unlike trespass to real property, harm must be proven, and this requirement (for jurisdictions in which it is a requirement) has given rise to controversies in the context of computer systems. The most high-profile case to date enforced a harm requirement in the context of an invasion of an intranet system by unwanted e-mails.[5] Although spammers and senders of unwanted e-mails may be liable for trespass to chattels if the volume of e-mail harms or slows down the plaintiff's system, the California Supreme Court held that other harms such as disruption to the workplace do not give rise to trespass liability. Cyberscholars generally applaud this result because in their view it promotes the openness of the Internet, whereas some others have advocated a more robust right to exclude along the lines of trespass to land. One interesting twist is that courts and most commentators seem to agree that owners of computer systems can engage in self-help: Intruders cannot complain if the owner takes defensive measures such as installing

---

5. Intel Corp. v. Hamidi, 71 P.3d 296 (Cal. 2003).

filters to keep the e-mails out. This means that the owner has a legally recognized right to exclude but no legal remedy to enforce that right. This is anomalous, given the usual assumption that every legal right has some legal remedy. Perhaps in the case of ordinary chattels such as bowling balls the law should not waste its time with providing legal redress for unwanted touchings. But whether self-help is always more efficacious than legal intervention with respect to unwanted invasions of electrons remains to be seen.

Self-Help

Self-help is not just a feature of the Internet; it is everywhere. Locking your apartment or car is self-help, as is putting a fence around your yard. Many of these measures are uncontroversial.

Some types of self-help are normally covered in criminal law. People have a limited right to defend themselves and their dwellings. The force used must be reasonable. Methods once used to protect property such a spring guns are generally not allowed any more. Again, the criminal law is a blend of protection of persons and property, and life and limb take priority over defense of property. The right in some jurisdictions to shoot intruders in an occupied dwelling does not extend to the right to use deadly force to protect unoccupied buildings (hence no spring guns even in those jurisdictions).

Property law focuses on less dramatic self-help measures that owners can take to enforce their property rights. Owners can use reasonable force (not deadly force) to eject trespassers. Closer cases involve landlord-tenant relations. In the 1970s a trend developed in which courts disallowed landlords from physically evicting tenants or locking them out. Under this approach the rule is mandatory in the sense that landlords and tenants cannot contract into a regime under which landlords would have a right to do a self-help eviction. As we will see later (see Chapter 6), the move away from self-help here can be seen as part of the wave of tenant-friendly decisions and legislation in the 1960s. Whether such mandatory rules protect tenants who are at an informational or economic disadvantage, or whether such rules hurt tenants in the long run by raising rents and making landlords choosier about tenants is a complex question, which turns in part on how competitive rental housing markets are.

In part, courts justified the move away from self-help as being compensated, in that landlords have been given expedited actions—often termed a "forcible entry and detainer" (FED)—to regain the premises. In practice, these procedures have typically not been as quick or efficient as originally envisioned. (Partly, this has been caused by the recognition of new tenant defenses to eviction, based on the condition of the premises.) Perhaps for that reason the trend toward disallowing any self-help in residential landlord-tenant law has run out of steam, leaving a mixed landscape.

Similar issues arise with personal property. Under the criminal law, one is not allowed to use deadly force to protect personal property (but one would under certain circumstances be allowed to use deadly force to prevent a physical attack on one's person, which might also involve property). A person is allowed to use reasonable force to protect personal property, so it is all right to snatch a purse back from a purse snatcher. As with real property, self-help in the law of personal property tends to come up in specialized contexts.

One such area is repossession of personal property subject to security interests. In contrast to mortgages of real estate, which have elaborate procedures for foreclosure, the holder of a security interest in personal property can use self-help to take possession of the property in question if the debt is in default. This is most familiar (in life as in the movies) in the context of auto repossession, because cars, unlike other consumer goods, are often left out in the open. Jurisdictions differ on how much self-help can be used, but where it is allowed, the "repo man" (even if thriving on confrontation[6]) must not do anything that tends to a breach of

6. REPO MAN (Universal Pictures 1984).

the peace. This usually means that if the owner objects strenuously enough, the repossession must stop. As in the case of landlord-tenant, the question involves balancing the possibility of overbearing behavior against the lower interest rates made possible by quick and cheap repossession. Nevertheless the current state of the law abounds in ironies. For one thing, in those jurisdictions where self-help repos are all right unless the owner firmly objects, people who are less physically threatening to the repo man are at a disadvantage.[7] Moreover, the process for gaining possession from a wrongful possessor in contexts other than security interests is much more elaborate and, being state action, subject to due-process constraints.[8] (Likewise, because of the high stakes, and in the case of homes because of their often personal nature, foreclosing on a mortgage on real property is a long and difficult road for the mortgage holder.)

At the beginning of this section we mentioned the uncontroversial nature of using locks as a measure of self-help. Other measures generate more controversy. Fences and walls have aesthetic implications, and in the case of gated communities, some find them troubling because they look too exclusionary. In the context of intellectual property (IP) and digital files, open access advocates often decry the exclusion of others through digital rights management (DRM). Some such situations shade off into contracts, but the question then becomes what one should think about an effort to contract for limited access with all possible users. Related to this is the fact that we do not usually hold owners responsible for failing to take cost-effective self-help measures to protect their property–there is no defense of contributory negligence analogous to what we find in the law of tort with respect to personal injuries. If you leave your front door or your car unlocked, you can still sue a

7. *See, e.g.*, Williams v. Ford Motor Credit Co., 674 F.2d 717 (8th Cir. 1982).

8. *See, e.g.*, Fuentes v. Shevin, 407 U.S. 67 (1972) (common-law action for replevin subject to due-process hearing).

trespasser or thief. Part of the delegation to the owner is not second-guessing the adequacy of the owner's self-protective measures. An exception to this is trade secret law, which partakes more of torts than other property; the owner of a trade secret must show reasonable efforts to maintain the secret in order to hold another liable. This sometimes involves lock and key, but these efforts are often contractual, in the form of confidentiality agreements.

Finally, self-help can be used in an even more limited way to enforce other rights of the owner. Notably, an owner can use self-help to abate a nuisance. So, for example, an owner can go onto the land of another to remove fire hazards such as a stack of hay next to a sparking piece of machinery. But for self-help to be available, the victim of the nuisance should give a reasonable opportunity to the other owner to abate (this usually involves some notification and request for action), and self-help may be used only where there is some urgency. Over the last one hundred years the tendency is to expect owners to resort to the legal process more and engage in self-help less. (In the old days, self-help actions to destroy a dam on a common stream were not uncommon.) In this, the self-help privilege is a little like the doctrine of necessity, our next topic.

Exceptions to the Right to Exclude

Trespass law may be very stringent, but the owner's right to exclude is neither absolute nor unchanging. On the bundle of rights theory, it is unsurprising that the bundle might take any number of forms and that these might change. On an approach that takes the right to exclude as central, the question is how easy it should be to make exceptions and modifications to the basic exclusion regime. Only by considering the range of situations in which owners' exclusion rights give way can we begin to get a sense of the overall shape of property. Here our focus is on the limits to private ownership. Some of the limits, such as necessity and custom, may officially or unofficially apply to public property as well; others, such as public accommodations and antidiscrimination, limit private owners' sovereignty in the name of public values.

Necessity

In some situations the right to exclude gives way to one facing necessity. The classic example is a person lost on a snowy mountain who breaks into an unoccupied cabin to eat the food inside. In such emergency situations, we do not expect people to respect boundaries, although the law still holds people using property out of necessity responsible for the harm they cause. Another situation would be a ship in peril that has the right to dock against the dock-owner's will but the ship owner must pay damages for harm caused to the dock.[9] One way to view this compromise is that the remedy for the property rights violation is reduced from property rule protection (injunction, punitive damages) to liability rule protection (compensatory damages). (See Chapter 8.) As a legal doctrine, necessity is, as in criminal law, very narrow: Someone who is hungry cannot break into a supermarket and eat the food. Although contestable, the idea is that a hungry person in an urban area has more alternatives, and a generalized defense of necessity would lead to too much bypassing of consensual transactions.

Another issue with necessity is whether the range of situations it covers hangs together. Necessity applies to natural disasters and fleeing from assailants, but it also covers less dire situations such as the minor damage that wandering animals may do by munching some grass along their path, or a person might cause in rescuing property that has found its way onto someone else's land. Thus, retrieving Fluffy from the neighbor's yard is necessity too. What all

---

9. Vincent v. Lake Erie Transp. Co., 124 N.W. 221 (Minn. 1910) (holding that ship owner may use dock in storm but must pay for damage done to dock); Ploof v. Putnam, 71 A. 188 (Vt. 1908) (holding that ship owner whose ship was cast off from dock by an agent of the dock owner could sue dock owner).

these situations have in common is that explicit consensual negotiations do not seem to be worthwhile. In the high-stakes examples, the emergency precludes such a transaction. In the low-stakes situations, the idea is that there is not much to be gained by requiring consent—such mundane invasions are widespread—and generally people benefit, up to a point, from a live-and-let-live approach. We hope for common sense and cooperation and try to reserve the law for situations where these don't suffice.

Custom

Custom can limit an owner's property rights. (In other situations custom might add to an owner's rights, as where the law allows an owner to claim wild animals *ratione loci*, see Chapter 2.) Much current scholarship has explored how social norms can operate outside—or even in contradiction to the law. To take but one of myriad examples, in some cities, notably Chicago, there is a norm that people have a right to keep a parking place they have shoveled out after a snow storm for a certain time (varying by neighborhood). This custom is robust but also illegal. Similarly, groups of lobstermen have demarcated and enforced—sometimes violently in "lobster wars"—exclusive territories, which seem until recently to have prevented some overexploitation.[10] Historically some areas of law have emerged wholesale out of customary regimes, as in mining and whaling. As we saw in our tour of first possession, customs such as those governing acquisition of whales may maximize value to insiders (net of the cost of enforcement) but may pose externalities on outsiders.

Here we are concerned with the way in which custom is incorporated into property law. Custom clearly featured more heavily in earlier law, and there was a time when all of the common law was

---

10. *See* JAMES M. ACHESON, THE LOBSTER GANGS OF MAINE (1988).

considered general custom. The traditional theory was that custom is legally binding of its own force even without recognition by a court, as long as the custom is of the right sort. Courts' long experience with custom was captured by William Blackstone in an oft-cited set of requirements for enforceable customary rights: antiquity, continuity, peaceable use, certainty, reasonableness, compulsoriness (not by license), and consistency.[11] In England, the antiquity requirement for custom outside of mercantile law—sometimes called "time out of mind" or "so long that the memory of man runneth not to the contrary"—often was identified with the beginning of the reign of Richard I in 1189. For custom to have much force in the United States this requirement has been reinterpreted to mean longstanding use, without great clarity on how long is long enough. Especially the requirement of reasonableness gives judges discretion to determine the substantive merits of a custom if they so choose. By requiring certainty, judges can prevent customs that require a lot of expertise from binding those outside the community of origin. For example, some customs such as the duty to report a beached, marked fin-back whale would bind outsiders, but other customs would not.[12]

Custom can be mandatory or default. In reaction against landowner power in England, early American courts were inclined to enforce a custom of access for hunters over unenclosed land. Some early versions of this custom were not avoidable by notifying a hunter that he was unwelcome (orally or by a sign).[13] Later in parts of the country where this custom is important it tends to be a default, which can be overcome by posting the land.[14] The custom now is governed by statute in many places.

---

11. 1 William Blackstone, Commentaries *76–78 (1765).

12. *See* Ghen v. Rich, 8 F. 159 (D. Mass. 1881).

13. *See* McConico v. Singleton, 9 S.C.L. (2 Mill) 244 (1818).

14. McKee v. Gratz, 260 U.S. 127, 136 (1922) (Holmes, J.).

Perhaps the most high-profile use of custom in property law these days centers on the question of beach access. Beaches are generally divided into three zones: from the low-water mark to the high-water mark (the wet sand or foreshore), from the high-water mark to the vegetation line (the dry sand), and inland from the vegetation line. States vary, but private owners of land verging on major bodies of water usually own at least to the vegetation line. The submerged land and the wet sand area is generally public, and often subject to the public trust (see Chapter 3). Owners often want to exclude the public from the dry sand area in between the high-water mark and the vegetation line as well, and much litigation has ensued. Most states allow private ownership of the dry sand areas, but some have held that the public has a right to use the dry sand area in conjunction with recreation on the wet sand area. Some courts have held that this follows from their version of the public trust doctrine.[15] Others see an implied dedication if the public has been using a particular stretch of beach. (Adverse possession is related, but often it is hard for the general public to count as an adverse possessor, in part because it is hard to sue "the public" as a defendant.) Other courts, such as those in Florida, Hawaii, Oregon, and Texas, have held that the public has rights in dry sand areas of beaches by reason of custom.[16] Courts have been ambivalent on how individualized determinations of public access to beaches should be. In the variety of assets and the owners it affects, custom is a broad brush limit on the right to exclude.

15. *See* Matthews v. Bay Head Improvement Assn., 471 A.2d 355 (N.J. 1984) (holding that under the public trust doctrine the public has a right of access over dry sand area owned by a private homeowners' association in order to reach wet sand area).

16. *See* State of Oregon *ex rel.* Thornton v. Hay, 462 P.2d 671 (Or. 1969).

Public Accommodation Laws

Related in some ways to custom is the law of public accommodations, which crystallized in the common law into a set of defined duties to the general public. At common law, common carriers such as ferries, coaches, and later railroads, and common callings such as inns, had special duties that accompanied their holding themselves out to the public as being in those businesses: They had a duty of nondiscrimination (first come, first served, unless there was good cause to exclude a potential patron) and reasonable charge (which could vary by customer as long as it was in the range of reasonableness). Later these duties were codified, and you often see a reflection of them on the back of hotel room doors (another duty was to stick to announced maximum rates). Originally the duties of public accommodations sprang from the local monopoly an inn or ferry might enjoy, which threatened travelers in unfamiliar areas with unfair surprise given their vulnerability. The concept of public accommodations was eventually broadened to include other facilities such as grist mills and grain elevators, on the grounds the owner had either received a public subsidy (e.g., eminent domain power) or the business was "affected with a public interest."[17]

The enactment of civil rights statutes has recently led to a further expansion of the notion of public accommodation. The historical connection between public accommodations and race discrimination is a contested topic: Some see the common-law definition of public accommodation as having narrowed during the era of Jim Crow, in order to give business owners more of an opportunity to exclude African Americans, whereas others see the scope of public accommodation remaining unchanged and fixed on

17. *See* Munn v. Illinois, 94 U.S. 113, 126 (1877) (holding that state has power to regulate the rates charged by grain elevators).

travel-related businesses.[18] Title II of the Civil Rights Act of 1964 contains a very broad definition of "public accommodation." Included are (1) inns, hotels, and motels, unless there are five or fewer rooms and the owner lives on the premises; (2) any restaurant, cafeteria, or lunch counter; (3) "any motion picture house, theater, concert hall, sports arena, stadium or other place of exhibition or entertainment."[19] Private clubs or other establishments "not open to the public" are excluded.[20] The provision regarding entertainment venues in particular goes beyond the common-law definition. It appears that the expansive definition of public accommodation in the 1964 Act has had some gravitational effect on the common-law definition, with the New Jersey Supreme Court finding, for example, that casinos, a heavily regulated business, had lost their common-law right to exclude for any or no reason, in this case card counters.[21] Other courts have stuck with the narrower common-law approach: As long as the facility is not discriminating based on a protected status (like race), it can revoke a license to enter a facility such as a casino or racetrack for any or no reason at all as these are not public accommodations.

We will return to the issue of takings in Chapter 9, but might the owner claim that a governmental expansion of duties not to exclude constitutes a taking? Civil rights statutes are not vulnerable on this ground, because the harm-prevention rationale is clear. But what about the inability to exclude card counters? Or what if a state prohibits a shopping mall from excluding political pamphleteers? This was the question in *PruneYard Shopping Center v. Robins.*[22]

---

18. *Compare* Joseph William Singer, *No Right to Exclude: Public Accommodations and Private Property*, 90 Nw. U. L. Rev. 1283 (1996), *with* A. K. Sandoval-Strausz, *Travelers, Strangers, and Jim Crow: Law, Public Accommodations, and Civil Rights in America*, 23 Law & Hist. Rev. 53 (2005).

19. 42 U.S.C. § 2000a(b).

20. *Id.* § 2000a(e).

21. Uston v. Resorts Int'l Hotel, Inc., 445 A.2d 370 (N.J. 1982).

22. 447 U.S. 74 (1980).

The U.S. Supreme Court held that because the owners had already invited the public in generally, they did not lose much when prohibited from excluding political pamphleteers. At the state level, the New Jersey Supreme Court, again the outlier, held that Princeton University's custom of openness prevented it from excluding a person peacefully distributing political literature.[23] What all these statutes and opinions have in common is a partial withdrawal of the delegation of gatekeeping authority to owners. In the interest of openness and free speech (and card counting?), the owner's freedom to control the business atmosphere is sacrificed. In the case of race discrimination, our next topic, society has given a clear answer. In some of these other contexts the question is far closer, especially where the original antimonopoly rationale for public accommodations does not hold. Some might see a shopping mall as a local monopolistic substitute for the town square (others might not), but it is harder to see casinos in this light.

Antidiscrimination Laws

As just noted, antidiscrimination laws have expanded public accommodation law and forbidden discrimination on the grounds of protected classes like race, sex, religion, and national origin. But antidiscrimination law has far-reaching impacts on owners' exclusion rights outside the context of public accommodations as well.

Some antidiscrimination law flows directly from the U.S. Constitution, and the Fourteenth Amendment in particular. In the famous case of *Shelley v. Kraemer*,[24] African Americans were sold property, but neighboring landowners sued to enforce a covenant attached to the property prohibiting the property from being occupied by "any person not of the Caucasian race." Overruling the

23. *See* State v. Schmid, 423 A.2d 615 (N.J. 1980).

24. 334 U.S. 1 (1948).

Missouri Supreme Court, the U.S. Supreme Court held that judicial enforcement of the covenant was state action and would violate the Fourteenth Amendment.

What gave courts and commentators difficulty (and still does) is delineating when public enforcement of private property rights is state action (and when it is not) for purposes of the Fourteenth Amendment. Generally it is assumed that owners can invoke the law of trespass to exclude unwanted guests even if the owner is discriminating on a basis that would be unconstitutional if it were accompanied by state action. Thus, mere court involvement is not the test. The enforcement of racially discriminatory wills is a closer question. In *Shelley*, one of the factors, hearkening back to public accommodations law, was that the interlocking covenants attempted in some sense to monopolize a whole area. They were the functional equivalent of zoning, which would clearly be state action. To this one might add that covenants are contracts, and one might expect that racially discriminatory covenants would be unenforceable on grounds of public policy. Perhaps the state courts' withholding of a public policy exception, in an area where such exceptions are routinely made, itself constitutes state action.

Among the statutes that cover antidiscrimination are some that focus specifically on housing. In the federal Fair Housing Act (FHA) of 1968,[25] Congress prohibited discrimination on the basis of race, color, religion, sex, familial status, or national origin, and more recently disability, with respect to availability of housing (section 3604(a)), terms and conditions (section 3604(b)), advertising (section 3604(c)), lying about availability (section 3604(d)), and blockbusting (section 3604(d)). There are very narrow exceptions, for buildings with four or fewer apartments one of which the owner occupies (the so-called "Mrs. Murphy" exception, the name itself an example of stereotyping) and for sporadic nonprofessional sales of houses. Religious institutions and senior communities receive

25. 42 U.S.C. §§ 3601–19, 3631

limited exceptions as well. The vision behind the FHA was an integrationist one, but the rights conferred are individual.

As in the rest of antidiscrimination law, the harm is in part economic, in part individual dignitary injury, and in part a matter of suppressing messages of subordination. In this regard it is important that neither the Mrs. Murphy exception nor the small-time seller exception applies to advertising. Thus the small live-in landlord cannot be sued for refusing to rent to a member of a protected class, which is a concession to the associational interests of what is thought to be a close-knit living arrangement. But an advertisement for "whites only" or even "persons speaking Polish, German, or Swedish" would give rise to liability.[26] As this last example shows, proof issues are important in this area, with courts using the familiar mechanism of a prima facie case to shift the burden to the defendant to demonstrate a proper justification once disparate treatment or effect is shown. Despite its origins in an integrationist vision, the FHA has been held to ban discrimination in order to maintain integration (for example, where a complex is oversubscribed by minorities and undersubscribed by whites in comparison to their proportions of the population).[27]

It is also worth remembering that other antidiscrimination laws can come to bear on a problem and they are cumulative. The Civil Rights Act of 1866 provides that "[a]ll citizens of the United States shall have the same right, in every State and Territory, as is enjoyed by white citizens thereof to inherit, purchase, lease, sell, hold, and convey real and personal property."[28] This statute has been held to incorporate an expansive nineteenth-century notion of "race" so that ethnic and national groups, such as Arabs, Chinese, Jews,

---

26. *See* Holmgren v. Little Village Community Reporter, 342 F. Supp. 512 (N.D. Ill. 1971).

27. United States v. Starrett City Assoc., 840 F.2d 1096 (2d Cir. 1988).

28. 42 U.S.C. § 1982.

Germans, and even Anglo-Saxons are covered.[29] Other relevant federal statutes include the Americans with Disabilities Act,[30] which mandates various accommodations for persons with disabilities. In the landlord-tenant context this Act has generated a stream of litigation over whether pets must be allowed despite a no-pets policy on the ground that they are service animals and so protected under the reasonable accommodation mandate of the statute. State and local law can also go beyond federal law. This is particularly important in areas, such as sexual orientation, in which federal law has not yet afforded protection. State courts have struggled with the issue of whether landlords with religious objections, for example, have a state constitutional right to refuse to rent to cohabiting couples who claim protection under state laws against discrimination on the basis of martial status.[31] Often state legislatures have not spoken with one voice over time about their policy toward cohabitation. States and localities are free to experiment with protecting additional classes, but at the risk of encouraging separatism of various groups. Again, there is a tradeoff between integrationism and other rationales for protection.

Owner Powers

Owners have more than the right to invoke trespass law subject to the qualifications just discussed. They also have a number of ancillary powers that fit into the "gatekeeper" family. These include the ability to grant and revoke licenses, confer temporary possession on a baliee, abandon or destroy property, and transfer property by gift, sale or to a successor upon death.

---

29. *See, e.g.*, Shaare Tefila Congregation v. Cobb, 481 U.S. 615, 617 (1987); Saint Francis College v. Al-Khazraji, 481 U.S. 604, 612 (1987).

30. 42 U.S.C. §§ 12101–12213.

31. *See, e.g.*, Attorney General v. Desilets, 636 N.E.2d 233 (Ma. 1994).

Licenses

The power to license is basically the ability of the owner to waive the owner's right to exclude. A licensee is not a trespasser, but someone who exceeds the scope of the license does trespass. A dinner guest who rifles through the host's bedroom would be an example.

License law is very confused in part because older law required that robust property rights be in writing (under the Statute of Frauds), and licenses are generally oral. Nevertheless some owners desired to make licenses irrevocable. A license coupled with a grant was presumed to be irrevocable; if a person had a right to take timber from another's land (sometimes called a "profit"), the license needed by the right-holder in order to exercise that right could not be revoked. Also, the equitable device of estoppel would apply where a licensee invested reasonably in the license (e.g., by paving a road), and it would be unjust for the landowner to revoke the license. In such situations we can even speak of an easement by estoppel. Irrevocable licenses are much like easements (rights to use), which we take up in Chapter 8, except that an easement is enforceable against third parties (in rem), and it is not clear that a license that has become irrevocable by estoppel is in rem. In any event, most disputes are between the licensee and the licensing landowner.

Although licenses are ubiquitous in everyday life, there has not been a lot of litigation over them, leaving the law in a somewhat uncertain state. What cases there are tend to be from entertainment venues such as theaters and racetracks attempting to exclude patrons. Entertainment venues are generally not considered to be public accommodations (see above), so the question arises whether a paying customer may be ejected and what remedy if any the licensee customer should have. The analysis here is clouded by uncertainty about the relationship between a license and a contract. Not all licenses are contracts: a gratuitous license, for example, would not be supported by consideration and hence would not qualify as a contract. But suppose one pays for a ticket to see a show or attend a sporting event and is then refused admission. Does one have a contract *for* a license, a contract *and* a license, or just a license that should be treated *like* a contract? Surprisingly, the answers to these questions are not clear. Some courts assume that licenses are always revocable, and the only remedy for the purchaser of a ticket is an action for breach of contract, which would ordinarily be damages.[32] Other courts have suggested that the ticket creates a license coupled with a grant to see the spectacle, which is not revocable absent good cause. Still others seem to think that the contract remedy matters here—that the theoretical availability of specific performance makes the license irrevocable.[33] Finally, there is the question of whether the owner commits an assault if he or she tries to remove a patron unwilling to leave. Does a contract right (or a right to specific performance) turn the effort to eject a patron into an assault?

The case law on these questions is in an unsatisfactory state, but the tendency is increasingly to treat a license given for consideration like a contract and to determine and enforce the terms of the contract in resolving the dispute. Because the issues here mostly affect the contracting parties, businesses that want to retain the right to exclude can make their licenses more clearly revocable. The contractual approach may also do best in meeting people's expectations. Most of the time, market pressures and concerns of reputation constrain the owners of businesses such as theaters not to eject patrons arbitrarily. This is probably the main reason these questions come up so infrequently in litigation. Nonetheless thinking about these issues is relevant for figuring out the nature of an owner's property rights, and their extent.

---

32. *See* Marrone v. Washington Jockey Club of the District of Columbia, 227 U.S. 633 (1913) (Holmes, J.).

33. *See* Hurst v. Picture Theatres, Ltd., [1915] 1 K.B. 1 (Ct. App. (U.K.) 1914).

In intellectual property, licensing is commercially important, and an IP license works differently from the traditional real property license. Like traditional licenses, an IP license is a waiver of exclusion rights. But unlike licenses generally, IP licenses are presumed to be irrevocable. In a sense IP licenses work more like easements. Restrictions in the nature of easements and covenants (servitudes) have always been regarded with suspicion when they attach to personal property and are intended to follow the property into remote hands. Similarly, under the doctrines of first sale in copyright and patent exhaustion in patent law, the owner of an IP right is not allowed to condition the sale or licensing of embodiments of the right (a book, a computer chip) upon further restrictions in the hands of remote parties. Much of the wisdom of these rules turns on whether such restrictions make the world more complicated (creating an informational externality). If so, some of the restrictions on freedom of contract from the first sale and exhaustion doctrines would be warranted.

Bailments

Owners sometimes want to give custody temporarily to another while retaining ownership. In such a relationship we call the owner giving up custody the bailor and the person who takes custody for the time being the bailee. Entrusting one's clothes to a dry cleaner, one's coat to a coat-check clerk, one's car to a valet parker, or one's lawn mower to a neighbor all are bailments. Unlike in a lease, the owner-bailor is free to resume possession at any time, and the bailment tends to give the bailee more limited rights to use than a lessee has under a lease. Because bailments serve a wide variety of purposes, the rules for finding them and the duties they imply vary by context. Many bailment cases have resulted from cars stolen from parking garages. Valet parking is clearly a bailment, but parking garages are borderline cases. The degree of control of the garage owner, expectations of security to be provided by the garage, whether the garage is enclosed, whether the owner keeps the car key, and potentially other factors relevant to whether there has been a transfer of possession and party expectations can come into play.[34] Giving a ticket or a receipt can be important in finding there is a bailment. If the bailor gets a ticket when surrendering custody, and the ticket is supposed to be matched to the item at retrieval time, this both points to there being a bailment and also absolves the bailee of misdelivery if the bailee delivers the item to someone presenting the ticket. What does not seem to do much work is the printing on the back of a ticket disclaiming a bailment. This is interesting because bailments are in personam relationships, as between the bailor and bailee, and often arise by contract.

Traditionally when it comes to liability for lost, stolen, or destroyed property, bailees have been held to a standard of care varying according to who benefits from the bailment. If the bailment is for the benefit of the bailee, the bailee is held to a strict standard of care; an example would be the neighbor borrowing the lawn mower. If the bailment is for the benefit of the bailor, the bailee is held to a standard of slight care; an example would be leaving a laptop with a friend while going to the bathroom. If the bailment is for the benefit of both parties, reasonable care is called for; many commercial bailments, such as watch repair, would be of this type. Other sources simply replace this three-tiered system with a general standard of reasonableness that will vary in part according to who benefits from the bailment.

Duties also vary by context. As noted, the reasonable care standard applies to the injury to the chattel, its loss, and its theft by a third party. However, misdelivery falls under strict liability. This could be for historical reasons based on the cause of action (conversion rather than negligence), or perhaps collusion is a particular danger in the case of apparent misdelivery.

---

34. *See, e.g.*, Allen v. Hyatt Regency–Nashville Hotel, 668 S.W.2d 286 (Tenn. 1984).

As for third parties, another set of problems in bailments concerns their in rem aspect: From the point of view of the outside world, the bailee may appear to be the owner because the bailee is in possession and possession is often (but not always) associated with ownership.[35] If the bailee is of a mind to be deceptive, then innocent third parties might mistakenly purchase the item from the bailee. In general, U.S. law is less protective of good faith purchasers from bailees than many other legal systems, but if the owner has entrusted the good to a merchant who deals in that type of good, a good faith purchaser for value will have better title than the bailor.[36] The idea is that at least in these situations the bailor has more control over creating the appearance of ownership. In other situations some kind of estoppel might apply if the bailor has done something out of the ordinary to clothe a nonmerchant bailee with the trappings of apparent ownership.

Abandonment and Destruction

Owners might want to dispose of an asset but not to anyone in particular—just eliminate their own ownership. In the case of personal property this is usually unproblematic. People throw away personal property all the time, subject to laws against littering and polluting. To count as abandonment, a person needs to have an intent to disclaim possession (and ownership) with no intent of resuming it, and perform some act manifesting that intent.

For interests that are less than full ownership of land, the rules for abandonment are similar to those in personal property. Many cases involving disused railroad rights of way raise this question.

---

35. Thomas W. Merrill & Henry E. Smith, *The Property/Contract Interface*, 101 COLUM. L. REV. 773, 811–20 (2001) (detailing the blend of contract and property elements in the law of bailments).

36. U.C.C. § 2-403(2).

Something more than discontinuing train service is usually required. Taking up the tracks would be one act that would indicate an intent to abandon.[37] For full ownership of land, abandonment is usually not an option.[38] The law seeks to prevent land in private ownership from failing to have an owner. Otherwise all sorts of nasty environmental problems and other nuisances might be left for society to clean up. (These are more likely to be covered by statute these days, but the concern retains some validity.) It is true that an owner may lose the land if taxes are not paid, but the government need not accept ownership of the land. No one is ever forced to accept ownership of any asset.

The right to destroy mainly comes up in the case of personal property but can also apply to structures attached to land. (Land itself is harder to destroy.) Generally unless a person can be found incompetent and a guardian appointed, a person is free to destroy his or her own property. You can destroy your own watch, even if it is a Rolex. Courts occasionally intervene to prevent destruction directed in a will,[39] but even here one can question the wisdom of strong constraints on owners' freedom. Although it might appear that a dead person does not experience the harm or the satisfaction from the destruction, people generally might experience happiness knowing that their instructions will be carried out after their deaths. Also, in many situations a person making the decision to direct destruction in a will could sell or devise the object (or a future interest in the object to take effect on their death; see Chapter 5), implying that the owner does take into account the opportunity cost of the destruction. (Recall Demsetz's theory that an owner acts as a broker between the future and the present; see Chapter 3.) Nevertheless, the apparent waste of an asset that has positive value

37. *See, e.g.*, Presault v. United States, 100 F.3d 1525 (Fed. Cir. 1996).

38. Pocono Springs Civic Ass'n, Inc. v. MacKenzie, 667 A.2d 233 (Pa. 1995).

39. For a dramatic example, see, e.g., Eyerman v. Mercantile Trust Co., 524 S.W.2d 210 (Mo. Ct. App. 1975).

to society is painful to observe, and in certain high-profile contexts, laws prevent destruction directly. Notably, Italy has strong laws preventing destruction of works of cultural significance, in an example of private rights being subject to overriding rights in the public, here against destruction. Historic preservation laws in the United States similarly remove an owner's right to destroy buildings that have been determined to have architectural or historic significance.

Transfer by Sale, Gift, and Inheritance

Much of the time an owner wishes to eliminate his or her ownership while creating ownership rights in another—to designate a new gatekeeper. This can be done for consideration (sale), gratuitously (gift), or by succession on death (will or intestacy).

Sales of goods are usually covered in contracts and commercial law courses. Property issues arise where the question is whether the seller really has the rights to transfer. We return to this issue, for both personal and real property, in Chapter 7. For real property, sales are quite complex and take place over an extended period of time. After the sale, the contract "merges" with the deed so that the buyer may only sue on the deed, which often includes warranties (such as of title).

Except for assets that are inalienable (which they might be for personhood reasons, for example), the policy of the law is to promote alienability. Courts distinguish between total and partial restraints on alienation. Total restraints on alienation, such as a gift of a painting to a friend on the condition that it may never be sold, are always struck down as violating this policy. Partial restraints are subject to a more nuanced treatment. Generally speaking, partial restraints are invalid only if they are unreasonable. For example, condominium units in a retirement community may be subject to a restriction that they may only be sold to someone over a certain age. This is likely to be regarded as reasonable, given that it does not unduly circumscribe the universe of potential buyers and furthers a reasonable purpose in maintaining the identity of the community. In some cases a partial restraint on alienation may even promote alienation: The original owner would not be comfortable alienating the asset without the restraint. The retirement condominium might be an example of both beneficial effects of such restraints. Nevertheless, much in this area (as in so many others) rests on empirical guesswork. If owners face the future benefits and costs of the restraints they place on their property (through the price it fetches today—recall the discussion of Demsetz in Chapter 3 and of the right to destroy in this chapter), then we might ask why a doctrine is needed to invalidate any restraints (other than ones that violate some independent public policy such as antidiscrimination). Perhaps some restraints make the alienation process in general too cumbersome by giving buyers more to be on the look out for. Or perhaps the law is a little paternalistic in this regard.

Alienation need not mean sale. Assets can be given away. Gifts are often embedded in a social context where reciprocity is expected, and there are traditional societies in which gift-giving is a major component of the economy. Neverthless, American law treats gifts as distinct from contracts and sales. For a valid gift there must be a donative intent, delivery, and acceptance. The delivery requirement can sometimes be fairly formalistic—as where *A* wants to give something to *B* but remain as bailee for *B*. To do this *A* may have to hand the thing over to *B* and then take it back.

Some gifts are conditional on an event happening. Defeasible fees, which we consider in Chapter 5, are commonly used to make conditional gifts. Another important and special type is a gift *causa mortis.* Here the owner designates someone else to receive the object on the condition that the owner dies; otherwise the owner will keep it. Think of a car owner planning to climb Mount Everest, who tells a friend that the friend is to have the car if the owner doesn't make it back.

Gifts *causa mortis* are a substitute for wills. Wills and intestate succession are the subject of a special course, Trusts and Estates, and we offer only the briefest sketch here. Basically, the ability to transfer on death is an important and well-recognized power of ownership under American law. Compared to the typical civil-law system, testators under American law have much freedom to designate who takes. One of the few exceptions is the spousal elective forced share, which allows spouses cut out of a will (or otherwise unhappy with a decedent's disposition) to take a legislatively prescribed portion of the estate, often one-third. Otherwise testators are free to designate the objects of their bounty.

Wills are subject to a variety of formalities such as attestation by two witnesses. Will formalities have been somewhat relaxed of late. But they are hard to eliminate altogether, because when a will becomes relevant the testator is no longer around to ask what he or she meant. And once the testator is dead, interested parties are only too willing to offer self-serving versions of the decedent's intent (not to mention the possibility of coercion or undue influence to write a will in the run up to the death). The reason gifts *causa mortis* and other will substitutes are sometimes regarded with suspicion is that they can wind up allowing an end run around these formalities.

If a person dies without a will (as most do), or a will is found totally or partially invalid, intestacy statutes will kick in to designate the decedent's heirs, usually the decedent's spouse and any children, and then relatives. If there are no heirs and no will, the property escheats to the state. Even in intestacy an owner can be thought of as exercising a power, in that intestacy is like a default will, and there is an attempt to mimic what the average decedent would put in a simple will if there were one. People have a natural desire to help their children and immediate relatives, but as the debates over inheritance taxes attest, there is disagreement about how much weight to give this desire as against other things society might do with resources that owners leave at death. Intestacy and even wills involve the probate process, and to avoid this, well-advised people often use trusts, a highly flexible device to which we return in Chapter 6.

Further Reading

ROBERT C. ELLICKSON, ORDER WITHOUT LAW: HOW NEIGHBORS SETTLE DISPUTES (1991) (exploring how social norms can deviate from formal law in determining the rights of a property owner).

Robert C. Ellickson, *Property in Land*, 102 YALE L.J. 1315 (1993) (comparative study of different modes of organizing rights to land).

George P. Fletcher, *The Metamorphosis of Larceny*, 89 HARV. L. REV. 469 (1976) (detailing the historical evolution of larceny toward greater emphasis on intent).

Henry E. Smith, *Self-Help and the Nature of Property*, 1 J.L. ECON. & POL'Y 69 (2005) (examining the importance of self-help in securing property in different contexts).

Lior Jacob Strahilevitz, *The Right to Destroy*, 114 YALE L.J. 781 (2005) (providing examples of legal rules and social norms governing destruction of property).

FIVE

Dividing Property Rights

SOMETIMES AN ASSET IS BEST OWNED by more than one person. This chapter deals with some basic ways for owners to divide or share ownership—over time and simultaneously, including between spouses.

Estates and Future Interests

The common law developed a very elaborate classification system for temporal divisions of property and rules for implementing that system. The study of estates and future interests was once the core of the traditional property course, but it is increasingly doubtful that this emphasis makes sense. To be sure, the vocabulary developed by the common law is still used to describe interests in family trusts (see Chapter 6). The Rule Against Perpetuities (RAP), which places limits on the control a current owner can exercise over future uses of the owner's asset, still casts its shadow over trusts and certain kinds of option contracts. And lawyers who work with charitable gifts need to know something about defeasible fees. But these areas of practice describe a relatively small portion of contemporary property law.

The common law system of temporal classification is nevertheless of considerable ongoing significance for anyone interested in exploring the nature of law. The system of estates and future interests is the nearest thing in the common law to a regime of rules, as opposed to general principles or standards. Generally speaking, a rule is a directive that prescribes an unambiguous response to a defined set of circumstances. "Maximum speed 65 mph" is an example. Rules are designed to be applied without any need for the exercise of discretionary judgment. Thus, rules are said to have the capacity to control behavior ex ante, before the behavior governed by the rule takes place. By contrast, a standard is a directive that describes a goal or purpose in a particular set of circumstances. "Drive at a reasonable speed given road conditions" is a standard. Application of a standard requires the exercise of discretionary judgment. Hence it is often said that whether one has conformed one's behavior to a standard can only be determined ex post, typically by some higher authority, after the behavior governed by the standard takes place.

The common law system for dividing property over time was developed by legislatures, judges, and lawyers to allow persons to prescribe what would happen to their property after their death. The aspiration was that people with significant property could, in consultation with a competent lawyer, create a temporal division of the property by will, deed, or trust that would precisely match their intentions about who would take what and when in the future. Because of the rule-like nature of the system, those having an interest in the property after the death of the owner, again with the help of lawyers, could faithfully carry out these intentions without recourse to litigation.

The resulting system tells us a great deal about what it is like to be governed by rules. On the one hand, the categories are sufficiently numerous and the operating principles sufficiently flexible that they can accommodate virtually any set of intentions. Consequently, the system promotes individual autonomy in determining how property will be distributed after death. It also appears that the rules have been generally successful in avoiding litigation (although not entirely of course). On the other hand, the system is complex and difficult to master. Only a lawyer can maneuver through the somewhat arcane rules with confidence. And the rules have an increasingly musty feel as time marches on. Updating and simplification would be highly desirable, but legislatures tend to have much more pressing things to attend to. The legal profession, which has invested so much in mastering the rules, has little incentive to work for streamlining that would allow accountants, Internet-based providers, or paraprofessionals to take over the task of estate planning.

The common law system of temporal classifications of interests assumed its most highly articulated form with respect to interests in land, often called "estates" in land. During the period of the development of the common law in England, land was the most important source of wealth and status. Land is also an extremely durable asset, so divisions of interests over time were both feasible and potentially problematic, insofar as they could tie up the ownership and use of an important asset for long stretches of time. Today it is often assumed that this complex system of estates also applies to personal property. Yet one rarely sees the categories of the estate system applied to personal property, except in the context of trusts composed of personal property in stocks and bonds, and (very occasionally) to works of fine art. The primary reason for this is probably that personal property is less durable than land. We take up trusts in Chapter 6.

If one were designing a system of estates in land and future interests from scratch, one might start with something called *full ownership*. Next we would want to divide property temporally between an owner who has a present possessory interest less than full ownership, and one or more owners of future rights. Conceivably, we could have a system composed of just full ownership, one type of *present interest*, and one type of *future interest*, and allow some tweaking of present interest and future interest in terms of how long they last, and in the case of the future interest, when it becomes possessory. This would make property law much simpler, and little if anything of social value would be lost. England has moved in this direction through legislative reforms. American law reformers have regularly proposed a similar simplification of American law, so far with little to show for their efforts.

For the time being, therefore, the student of American law must learn a more elaborate vocabulary of full ownership, present possessory interests, and future interests, bequeathed to us from the common law. This system traces back to the feudalism that grew up especially after the Norman Conquest in 1066. Under the feudal system, the king would grant limited rights or tenures to lords in return for services; these lords in turn would grant lesser interests or tenures in return for services; and the process would continue all the way on down to peasants who actually worked the land, again in return for services. Feudalism was abolished during and after the English Civil War of the seventeenth century, and for our purposes, the feudal legacy is mostly important in terms of the terminology used to describe the various types of present and future interests (still sometimes called "tenancies"). Perhaps the best way to think of the interests we are about to describe is as variations on our ideal of full ownership, present interest, and future interest, with the additional complication that many of the interests have distinguishing features so tightly built into them that they affect the name of the interest. For historical reasons these interests are also said to be "freehold interests," as opposed to nonfreehold (leasehold) interests (see Chapter 6, on leasing), which were subject to fewer formalities upon transfer. The freehold-nonfreehold distinction is today of limited relevance.

The chart on the next page summarizes the principal categories of full ownership, present possessory interests, and future interests that characterize the system of estates in land derived from the common law.

In considering how this system operates, it helps to think of each of the interests (other than full ownership) as part of a pair of interests—the present possessory estate and the corresponding future interest or interests. Each paired set of interests sums to the equivalent of full ownership. Or to put it another way, when full ownership is divided over time, the parts that are created include a present interest paired with one or more future interests that exhaustively distribute all of what the full owner had before the division took place.

Present Possessory Interest	*Corresponding Future Interest(s)*	
Fee Simple Absolute	[None]	
Life Estate	Reversion	
	Remainder	Vested
		Contingent
Fee Simple Determinable	Possibility of Reverter	
Fee Simple Subject to a Condition Subsequent	Right of Entry	
Fee Simple Subject to an Executory Limitation	Executory Interest	
Fee Tail	Reversion	

Under the common law system, the interest that corresponds to full ownership is called the *fee simple absolute* (or *fee simple* or *fee* for short) in the case of land and *full* or *absolute ownership* in the case of personal property. One creates a fee simple in *A* by granting "to *A* and his/her heirs," "to *A* in fee simple," or (these days) simply "to *A*." If the traditional "and his/her heirs" language is used, it is important to recognize that this is just a phrase. *A* does not have heirs until *A* dies, and so we say the word "heirs" here is part of the "words of limitation" (words that describe the interest). Only "words of purchase" tell us who gets the interest, and in all three formulations that part is "to *A*."

The fee simple not only gives the full package of rights, duties, and powers we saw in Chapter 4, it is also indefinite along the temporal dimension—it comes to no natural end. When the owner dies, a successor by will or intestacy simply steps into the fee owner's shoes. The fee simple is a present possessory interest, but, because it is of indefinite length, it leaves no room for a future interest. So in this one case there is no paired future interest that corresponds to the present interest. The present interest is everything.

The most common form of present interest—that is, a present possessory interest less than a fee simple—is the *life estate.* A life estate, as in "to *A* for life" grants full rights of possession to life tenant *A* ("tenant" is sometimes used to refer to the holder of an interest, in an echo of feudalism) during *A*'s natural life, but only for the duration of *A*'s natural life. The interest abruptly comes to an end upon the death of the holder of the life estate. The holder of a life estate can transfer the interest to someone else, but that person will hold only until the death of the original life tenant. The transferee in these circumstances is said to have a life estate *per autre vie*—a life estate for the life of another.

Because a life estate is of more limited duration than a fee simple, there is always something left over at the end of the life estate, and so a life estate is always paired with one or more future interests. Here, the most basic division is between a future interest retained by the grantor and a future interest in some person other than the grantor. If the future interest holder is the grantor him or herself, the future interest is called a *reversion.* This can be explicit as where *O* grants "to *A* for life, and then to *O*." Or it can be implicit, as where *O* grants simply "to *A* for life." Because there is something left over after the grant to *A*, the system of estates in land implies a reversion in the grantor. If the grantor holds a reversion and is dead when *A* dies, the land reverts to the grantor's successors, because the reversion passes under the grantor's will, or if the grantor has no will, by intestate succession to the grantor's legal heirs.

If the person who gets the land after the life tenant is someone other than the original grantor, the future interest is called a *remainder.* So if *O* grants "to *A* for life, then to *B*," *B* has a remainder. Remainders are further subdivided into vested remainders and contingent remainders. Some remainders have a built-in uncertainty about them. Thus, some remainders are contingent, as where *O* grants "to *A* for life and then to *B* if she has passed the bar." Here the remainder is contingent on the event of *B*'s passing the bar. Once *B* has passed the bar, the remainder becomes a vested remainder (vested in interest, but not yet vested in possession—that will occur only when *A* dies). Another type of uncertainty can revolve around who exactly will have the remainder. So for example, if *O* grants "to *A*, then to the children of *B*," we don't know until *B* has died who the set of *B*'s children might be. (If *B* already has children such a gift is said to be "vested subject to open" or "vested subject to partial divestment.")

These various distinctions among future interests that follow a life estate are relevant primarily because of the Rule Against Perpetuities (or RAP, considered more fully below). Reversions in the grantor, whether express or implied, are regarded as vested from the moment they are created, and are not subject to the RAP. Likewise, vested remainders are immune from invalidation under the RAP. Contingent remainders, however, can be invalidated if it they might vest after the period defined by the RAP. This applies to remainders that are contingent because of some condition that must be satisfied before the vesting (such as passing the bar) as well as to remainders that are contingent because the identity of the remainder-persons has not yet been established (as in a gift to "children").

The only other significant category of estates consists of a variation on one theme—the defeasible fee. A defeasible fee is like the fee simple absolute except that it can end upon the happening of some event—so it too is less than a fee simple absolute. Defeasible fees are largely encountered today in connection with charitable gifts. For example, a grantor will give Blackacre "to the school district, so long as it is used for school purposes." The objective is to limit the future use of the property to the particular charitable purpose that the grantor seeks to promote, here, its use as the site for a school. If the donee, the school district, ceases to use the property for school purposes, it suffers a forfeiture of the charitable gift—which is a powerful incentive to abide by the donor's wishes.

Defeasible fees can be classified along two dimensions: according to whether the condition that can lead to forfeiture of the defeasible fee operates automatically or not, and according to whether the corresponding future interest belongs to the grantor or to some person other than the grantor. Because there are two choice points here—automatic versus nonautomatic and future interest in grantor versus third party—one would think that there would be four types of defeasible fees; but one would be wrong. Instead there are just three.

Consider the situation in which the future interest is in the grantor, that is, defeasible fee plus grantor future interest. Here the terminology of the present possessory interest—the defeasible fee—varies according to whether the future interest kicks in automatically or not. If it is automatic, we have a *fee simple determinable.* The corresponding future interest is called a *possibility of reverter.* So if *O* grants Blackacre "to *A* so long as drugs are not consumed on the premises," this is a fee simple determinable. Use of drugs is called the "limitation event" that causes the defeasible fee to forfeit automatically, and the property automatically vests in the grantor (or the grantor's successors) through the possibility of reverter. Durational language such as "as long as," "so long as," while," or "during" is characteristic of the fee simple determinable and its automatic ending feature.

What if the defeasible fee followed by a future interest in the grantor is not automatic? Here the defeasible fee is called a *fee simple subject to a condition subsequent.* The corresponding future interest is a *right of entry* (also sometimes called a *power of termination*). The future interest holder (the grantor or the grantor's successor) must take some action to cause the defeasible fee to forfeit. If the holder of the right of entry takes no action, then the fee simple subject to a condition subsequent goes along as before. So if *O* grants Blackacre "to *A*, but if drugs are consumed on the premises then *O* has the right of entry," *A* has a defeasible fee called a fee simple subject to a condition subsequent. The language "but if," "on condition that," "provided that," "provided however," and "if" are all ways of expressing the condition. If the condition is fulfilled, here if drugs are consumed, then *O*, pursuant to the right of entry, must use self-help or a lawsuit to get *A* out in order to secure the forfeiture.

Now consider the situation where the grantor sets up a defeasible fee but follows it with an interest in someone other than the grantor, that is, some third party. Here there is one complex of interests, the *fee simple subject to an executory limitation.* The corresponding future interest is an *executory interest.* So if *O* grants Blackacre "to *A* as long as drugs are not consumed, then to *B*," *A* has a fee simple subject to an executory limitation and *B* has an executory interest. This future interest is taken to be automatic; although there is a dearth of authority on the matter, there does not seem to be a future interest in a third party that is nonautomatic (along the lines of the fee simple subject to a condition subsequent). This may seem like an odd gap, but mostly it does not matter, especially because the same result could be accomplished by creating a fee simple subject to a condition subsequent and a right of entry in the grantor and transferring the right of entry to a third party—the labels and rules do not change.

The only other set of paired interests you may encounter (if only in works of historical fiction) is the *fee tail.* This was created by statute in the thirteenth century as a way of keeping land within a particular family for as long as the family dynasty lasted. It was created by granting land "to *A* and the heirs of his (or her) body." The present interest, called a *fee tail* or an *estate in tail,* was similar to a life estate in that it lasted for the life of the first generation of offspring of the grantor (typically the eldest male). This was followed automatically by a life estate in the (eldest male in the) next generation, and then by a life estate in the third generation, and so on, until the family line fizzled out, at which point there was a reversion to the grantor (and the grantor's successors). The fee tail was problematic because it tied up land for a very long period of time, making transfers of property and mortgaging property difficult. It was abolished long ago in England and in virtually every state in the United States. Different states follow different rules about what happens if some poorly advised person tries to convey land "to *A* and the heirs of his (or her) body."

One last detail remains. Sometimes a grantor will want to create a future interest that cuts off a preceding interest before its natural end. The future interest in such situations is called an *executory interest* (we have already seen an example of this in the paired future interest to a fee simple subject to an executory limitation). An example would be where *O* grants "to *A* for life, but if *A* remarries, then to *B* in fee simple." As long as such a scheme is designed for the support of *A* before remarriage and not as a penalty for remarriage, the executory interest in *B* cuts off *A*'s life estate upon *A*'s remarriage, before the natural ending of the life estate, which would otherwise occur on *A*'s death. Executory interests, like contingent remainders, are subject to the RAP. That is, they must vest in interest within the period prescribed by the Rule or they are invalid. Again, the proliferation of terminology is less important now than it used to be when remainders and executory interests behaved more differently than they now do. Both are transferable, devisable, and inheritable, and holders of both can sue for waste.

What distinguishes future interests such as reversions, remainders, or executory interests from a future sale or gift from *A* to *B* is that the holder of a future interest is regarded as having a property right *now*, namely a right to the asset in the future. So with every future interest you need to know several things. First, when will it become possessory—after the end of the present holder's life or after some other defined event? Second, when it becomes possessory (when it "vests in possession"), what kind of right is it—full ownership or some lesser present possessory interest (like a life interest)? Third, is there some uncertainty about who the holder will be or whether the event will occur that makes the interest come into force? This problem of "vesting in interest" is primarily important because of the RAP.

How the System Works

So far the system of estates and future interests might look like an arbitrary jumble of labels. Although the system does have a certain amount of unnecessary detail, one might wonder why we don't need even more types of interests, considering all the ways property rights might be usefully carved up along the temporal dimension. Further, the features that are reflected in the labels for the various interests do not seem to exhaust those needed to make the system work. Instead, a number of architectural aspects and maintenance doctrines help the system function.

First, it is useful to realize that the combinations of interests we just explored have a generative quality that simply memorizing them does not capture. The key point is that the different interests can be combined and repeated in different ways, just as phrases connected by connectors such as "and," "or," "that," or "then" can be combined to make complex sentences. For example, what if the grantor wanted to give Blackacre to *A* for life and then to *A*'s child *B* for life and then to *C*? *O* could grant "to *A* for life, then to *B* for life, and then to *C*." *A* has a life estate and *C* has a remainder, in fee simple—when it becomes possessory it will be a fee simple. What does *B* have? Because it follows a life estate and the interest is not in *O* (the grantor), *B* has a remainder. But it is not a remainder in fee simple as in our previous examples. Instead, if and when the remainder vests in possession it will be a life estate in *B*, so *B* currently has a *remainder in life estate*, followed in turn by a remainder in *C* in fee simple.

Other constructional principles help to eliminate uncertainties about the list of temporal divisions that has been created. One particularly interesting principle is the *conservation of estates*: All the estates granted plus those retained must add up to the fee simple, which, recall, has indefinite duration. So if *O* transfers *O*'s entire interest, then the total of the interests transferred from *O* must add up to a fee simple, just as the total of the interests received by the grantees must add up to a fee simple. Nothing is created out of thin air or goes up in smoke. Thus, in all the examples the final future interest must be in fee simple in order for all the pieces to add up to a fee simple. Otherwise, we might get to a situation in which an interest ended (say a final life estate) with no one to take, which is not supposed to happen. What if *O* grants "to *A* for life, then to *B* for life?" Is this a problem? No. As we noted above, in such a case there is an implied reversion in *O*, and now we can see why. The interests that *O* grants and retains must add up to what *O* had to begin with, which was a fee simple. In order for this to be true *O* must have retained a reversion in fee simple, despite not having said so. It simply follows from the way the system works, here through the conservation of estates.

When a fee simple is broken into smaller durational parts, there is a "conservation" problem in a different sense of the word. The holder of a present interest is less likely to want to conserve the resource than the future interest holder(s). The present holder, aware of not being entitled to the property forever, will favor more consumption and less preservation; the future interest holder will favor less consumption and more preservation. Neither will reflect the preferences of a fee simple owner, who would take into account all the benefits and costs of consumption versus preservation. Mainly the problem is constraining the excessive consumption and lack of investment of the present possessor because the present possessor is the one with control over the property now. Indeed the future interest holders may not even be fully determined yet (the vesting in interest problem again) making monitoring and negotiating on their part prohibitive.

This conflict between the present and the future interest holders gives rise to the action for *waste* and its associated doctrine. Under the law of waste, the present possessory interest holder may not unreasonably use the resource and must turn it over in substantially the same condition as he or she received it. Interestingly, this is a standard, tucked in the middle of a system that is largely built on rules. The problems that can arise between present possessory and future interest holders are just too multifarious to reduce to rules. Not paying taxes (and risking forfeiture) is a clear case of waste (called "permissive" waste). Excessive mining or cutting of trees would also be waste ("affirmative waste"). Rules of thumb have developed to evaluate such behavior based in part on custom and in part on rough and conservative guesses. For example, under the "open mines doctrine," a present interest holder has the right to mine only from mines open at the beginning of the interest but not otherwise. Tearing down a usable building and replacing it with another more valuable and cost-effective building can also be waste ("ameliorative waste"),[1] although most jurisdictions today would probably not impose liability for changes that enhance the economic value of property.

In theory, a good benchmark for evaluating the behavior of the present possessor would be to ask what the holder of a fee simple owner would do under the circumstances. In practice, such a standard would be quite unworkable for a court. Hence the use of rules of thumb and the bias toward conservation. Of course, an owner can leave instructions that would override the law of waste, for example, if the owner wanted the life tenant to have the right to mine land not currently being mined.

How dire the conflict between the present and future interest holders is depends in part on how long the present interest holder's interest is likely to last. (Another factor would be how much the present interest holder cares about the future interest holder, e.g., as a younger relative or a friend.) If the present holder's interest is set to last for a long time or, in the case of a defeasible fee, is not likely to come to an end, then the present holder's incentives will not be all that different from a full owner's and the doctrine of waste is less likely to be invoked. (It may also be that courts, realizing this, give more leeway to present interest holders whose interests are "larger" in this sense.) Related to this, the value of an interest depends not only on its length, but it also on how weighted it is to the present. A dollar now is worth more than a dollar a year from now because one would need to have less than a dollar now in order to have a dollar a year from now. (To figure out how much a future dollar is worth in present value terms one needs to use the appropriate discount rate, which is the product of the rate of expected

1. Brokaw v. Fairchild, 135 Misc. 70, 237 N.Y.S. 6 (S. Ct. N.Y. Cty. 1929).

inflation and the real interest rate.) Thus if you hold the remainder, it matters a lot whether the life tenant is 30 or 90 years old.

Another principle central to the estate system is the *numerus clausus.* This term, originally from civil law, refers to standardization in property law: Applied to the estate system, the *numerus clausus* mandates a fixed and closed set of forms of ownership, and owners and transactors are not allowed to add to this list. For example, stringent versions of the *numerus clausus* disallow new forms of inheritance (such as variants on the old fee tail to keep property in the family over generations) and novel types of leases such as a lease for the duration of the war or a lease for life.[2] (On the allowed forms of leases, see Chapter 6.) One cannot create a time-share in a watch, for example, Wednesday rights in a watch that would give all the rights of an owner on Wednesdays. (One can rent out a watch but this gives the lessee less than full ownership.) This standardization of property in the *numerus clausus* stands in contrast to contract law where, subject to doctrines such as consideration and the criteria for contract formation, facilitating individual customization is the name of the game.

What is the harm in allowing parties to customize their property rights? One effect of limiting the ways of dividing property may be to discourage division and thereby prevent excessive fragmentation. But as we have seen, the system of estates is characterized by its generativity (as illustrated by the repeated application of the life estate plus remainder split). What the *numerus clausus* does is prevent the proliferation of new *types* of property rights. Transactors and even courts are supposed to let the legislature take the lead in making major modifications to the list of approved forms of ownership. By reducing the number of types of property rights, the *numerus clausus* gives third parties, including courts, less to be on the lookout for.

---

2. *See, e.g.*, Johnson v. Whiton, 34 N.E. 542 (Mass. 1893) (Holmes, J.) (disallowing new form of inheritance); Nat'l Bellas Hess v. Kalis, 191 F.2d 739 (8th Cir. 1951) (disallowing a lease for the duration of the war). For a lenient approach to the lease for life, see Garner v. Gerrish, 473 N.E.2d 223 (N.Y. 1984).

This is a pervasive problem and stems from the in rem nature of property. Thus, if you create a property right in Wednesday-watches or a property right with a different remedy for trespass (150 percent damages on even numbered days and 50 percent damages on odd-numbered days), this increases the information costs for your contracting partners and successors. Such an idiosyncratic right will be less valuable to them, and they will pay less for such rights, so to this extent the costs of your preferences are internalized to you through the price you receive (compare Demsetz, Chapter 3). But your idiosyncratic tastes also raise the information costs for anyone considering whether to buy watches or land in general, as well as for those seeking to avoid violating property rights or to enforce them. These third parties now have more possibilities to investigate. Such third party costs are an externality created by your idiosyncrasy. By limiting your ability to create these kinds of oddball rights, these external costs of information gathering and processing are reduced. Other methods of reducing the third-party information costs involve trusts (see Chapter 6) and rules for registering interests, especially in land (see Chapter 7). Which combination of these information-cost-lowering devices is best is an empirical question. But recall that because the estate system itself is so flexible (from its generativity), limiting the forms of ownership has a minimal impact on the goals that can be served using the system.

Third-party information costs may also supply a reason for the law's suspicion of restraints on alienation, which we encountered in Chapter 4. One might ask why putting even an extreme restraint on alienation is a problem. If one can refuse to alienate, why can't one alienate with strings attached? And if (and it is an if) the cost of the restraint is reflected in the price one can charge for the asset, then there is no externality. But when we cast a wider glance at who might be affected, there is more cause for concern. Restraints on alienation can in effect create new ways of owning in a fashion reminiscent of what the *numerus clausus* prevents. Restraints on alienation can make the nature of property rights in general harder to investigate and make the property system as a whole operate less smoothly in the realm of transfer. Without these systemic effects, the rule against unreasonable restraints on alienation has to be justified by parties' myopia or other irrationality, or courts' superior knowledge of what is reasonable ex post.

Because property interests can last a long time, any form other than the fee simple can lead to restrictions that persist far into the future. One concern is that remote future interests will either prevent alienation altogether (because the identity of future interest holders cannot be determined until certain contingencies are resolved), or will practically impair alienation (because of the difficulty of obtaining unanimous consent from all interest holders). Another concern involves "dead hand control"—tying up the use of property for long periods of time based on the preferences and assumptions of someone who has long since departed from the scene. Here too there is a widely shared intuition that an owner should not be allowed to project his or her control "too far" into the future. Worries about such control center on the proper relation between the present and the future, implying that the increasingly small benefits and costs, in present value terms, of the restrictions in more and more remote future times should be of less concern to current owners.

One device traditionally used to limit dead hand control is the (in)famous Rule Against Perpetuities (RAP). Originally the common law provided a loose set of doctrines that would invalidate restrictions placed by owners that operate too far into the future ("perpetuities"). The common law rule crystallized into its modern form (before more recent reforms and trends to abolish it) in part through the famous formulation by John Chipman Gray: "No interest is good unless it must vest, if at all, not later than twenty-one years after some life in being at the creation of the interest."[3] Gray envisioned a rule that would have limited but highly determinate—and

---

3. John Chipman Gray, Rule Against Perpetuities § 201 (Roland Gray ed., 4th ed. 1942).

"remorseless"—effect. Violation of the rule would result in mechanical invalidation of the interest in question. Like the system of estates and future interests more generally, the rule could be applied ex ante, by a trained lawyer, so as to determine whether any interest is valid or invalid at the moment of its creation.

When does an interest violate the rule? The first thing to notice about the rule is what it is not. It is not a rule against interests lasting too long (the fee simple lasts indefinitely long) nor a requirement that the interest must become possessory at some specific time. Instead the rule requires that uncertainties surrounding interests that have not yet vested must be resolved, one way or another, within a period of time defined by the rule. The type of vesting that must occur, if at all, within the perpetuities period is vesting in *interest*, which, in the case of executory interests and options amounts to needing to know when they will vest in possession. Thus if the interest is conditioned on someone's passing the bar or being born as the child of a certain person, these events have to occur within the "perpetuities period."

Consider an example. If *O* grants "to *A* for life, then to the first child of *A* who passes the bar," there is uncertainty as to who that will be. For the remainder to vest in interest, *A* must have a child who passes the bar. The issue under the RAP is whether that uncertainty will be dispelled within 21 years after some life in being at the creation of the interest. This means that we should be able to find one or more persons, who are living at the time the interest is created, such that the interest will vest (in interest) during that life or within 21 years after that person dies. If we can find no such "measuring life," the interest is invalid under the RAP. In the example just given, *A* is the best candidate measuring life. Does *A* work? *A* is alive at the creation of the interest; but *A* could die, and *A*'s child (if any) might pass the bar more than 21 years after that. So the RAP invalidates the interest. By contrast, if *O* had granted "to *A* for life, and then to *A*'s first child who shall graduate from high school by age 21," the interest would be good. We will know the identity of all of *A*'s children by the time *A* dies, and we will know within 21 years thereafter whether any child has graduated from high school by age 21. (If the child were in utero at *A*'s death, the remaining term of the pregnancy is added in to the perpetuities period as long as the child is born alive. Statutes govern the effects of more recent innovations having to do with in vitro fertilization technology.)

Well-advised clients should have no problems with the RAP.[4] Besides being predictable to those in the know, one can also use a perpetuities savings clause to contain any problems. Such a clause in a will would state that if any interest in the will is challenged as violating the RAP, a corporate donee is designated to appoint a grantee that would most closely approximate the wishes expressed in the will. Some legislatures and courts have adopted a lenient approach to the RAP under which the courts are directed to clean up interests to make them conform to the RAP (for example, by changing 25 years to 21 years in an interest such as the high school graduation example above).[5]

Other states have pursued more far-reaching reforms. Some have adopted wait-and-see statutes, which do not invalidate an interest ex ante (as would the common-law RAP), but only if it turns out ex post that the interest does not vest within the perpetuities period. This eliminates some cases of unfairness (caused by bad lawyering?), but at the expense of creating considerable uncertainty while the waiting goes on. Sometimes wait-and-see reform statutes use a period of 90 years, or 90 years or the common law perpetuities period whichever comes earlier.[6] Recently, in an effort to attract

---

4. *But cf.* Lucas v. Hamm, 364 P.2d 685, 690–91 (Cal. 1961) (ruling that the RAP is so difficult that a lawyer drafting a trust interest that was invalid under RAP was not liable in negligence or breach of contract). For fictional examples of RAP problems (and the like) run wild, see, e.g., Louis Auchincloss, *The Power of Appointment, in* POWERS OF ATTORNEY 172 (1963); BODY HEAT (Warner Bros. 1981).

5. *See, e.g.*, In re Estate of Anderson, 541 So.2d 423 (Miss. 1989).

6. *See* UNIFORM STATUTORY RULE AGAINST PERPETUITIES, 8B U.L.A. 223 (2001), now included in the Uniform Probate Code, UNIFORM. PROBATE CODE §§ 2–901 to –906, 8 U.L.A. 61–62 (Supp. 2006).

trust business, some states have moved to abolish the RAP altogether, especially for interests created in trust.[7] Interestingly, advertisements in those states sometimes market the services of trust specialists on the ground that owners can now control the disposition of their property hundreds of years into the future. This puts the issue of dead hand control back in the spotlight.

RAP issues may seem to be of primary relevance to family wealth transmission and estate planning. But RAP issues can also arise in business settings. In some jurisdictions, notably New York and Pennsylvania, option contracts are subject to the RAP.[8] Thus if one company grants another an option to purchase Blackacre (under which it has the right but not the obligation to purchase the property at a stated price) and any of the possible exercise times could occur more than 21 years later, there is trouble. Corporations cannot be measuring lives (their lives are indefinitely long), and so the RAP, in such jurisdictions, applies a 21-year time limit on options granted to corporations. Although options reduce the market price that the underlying property could fetch, options serve legitimate purposes of risk allocation and planning. Many have criticized the rationale for subjecting such options to the RAP at all, much less a 21-year one.

Co-Ownership

Property rights can be split not only over time but can be shared at a given time. Co-ownership is used in a wide variety of situations where it is advantageous for multiple parties not just to share possession but to share the other incidents of ownership such as the

---

7. Max Schanzenbach & Robert Sitkoff, *Jurisdictional Competition for Trust Funds: An Empirical Analysis of Perpetuities and Taxes*, 115 YALE L.J. 356 (2005).

8. *See, e.g.*, Symphony Space, Inc. v. Pergola Properties, Inc., 669 N.E.2d 799 (N.Y. 1996); Central Delaware County Auth. v. Greyhound Corp., 588 A.2d 485 (Pa. 1991).

financial flows associated with full ownership. Sometimes multiple uses and risk-spreading are the reasons to share ownership. These factors can be especially important in a long-term relationship such as marriage. Shared ownership can also be accomplished using various business entities such as partnerships and corporations. Co-ownership is simply the most basic method of sharing ownership, without resorting to the law of business organizations.

The notion of shared ownership is filtered through the common law "unities." The most fundamental unity is the unity of possession. All the forms of co-ownership involve this unity, under which the co-owners each have an equal right to possess the whole. This does not mean that each co-owner must possess the whole to maintain ownership. The unity of possession only requires that each co-owner have a *right* to possess the whole. In other words, each co-owner is a gatekeeper over the resource with respect to all nonowners. The common law form of co-ownership that relies only on the unity of possession is the *tenancy in common.* Of course in most physical resources, more than one person cannot possess the whole (or even significant parts) at the very same time, so the co-owners will need to work out among themselves who will have actual possession of what. If they cannot agree, and one co-owner prevents the other from taking possession, there is an ouster.

Generally, co-tenants are not liable to each other for their use of the property. By the unity of possession each has a right to possess the whole. Only when one co-tenant ousts another does the co-tenant in possession become liable to the other for rent ("mesne profits"). An *ouster* in most jurisdictions requires more than an expression of intent to possess by the nonpossessing co-tenant and a refusal by the possessing co-tenant; usually some attempt to go into possession that is foiled by the co-tenant in possession is required. Co-tenants are liable to each other for rents received from third parties, and one co-tenant can sue another for contribution for proportionate expenses for upkeep and taxes. Otherwise courts are reluctant to enforce monetary obligations between tenants, such as for improvements, but will do so in the course of a partition.

Also, even though a co-tenant may not be liable (absent ouster) for the co-tenant's own use, the value of the use may be taken into account (as a set-off) when the tenant in possession sues a nonpossessing co-tenant for contribution to expenses, such as taxes and mortgage payments. In general, courts prefer not to measure values during the relationship but will take a more comprehensive view if the co-ownership relationship is ending, or the matter is in court on other grounds.

Another form of co-ownership is the *joint tenancy*, which is like the tenancy in common with the added feature of the right of survivorship. Like the gift *causa mortis*, mentioned in Chapter 4, the joint tenancy functions as a will substitute. Thus if *A* and *B* own in a joint tenancy, and one of them dies, the survivor winds up with sole ownership. It is important to realize that the theory is that the interest of the decedent simply disappears, leaving the survivor with the sole interest; nothing passes, in contrast to the situation in which one tenant in common dies with a will naming the other tenant as devisee (a devisee is the recipient of real property under a will). So if *O* grants "to *A* and *B* as joint tenants with right of survivorship and not as tenants in common," *A* and *B* would be joint tenants. To create a joint tenancy, additional unities—besides the unity of possession—are required. First is the unity of time, which means that the interests of both joint tenants must begin at the same time. Second is the unity of title, under which both the joint tenants must have received their interests by the same instrument (or act of adverse possession), not by intestacy or other operation of law. Third is the unity of interest, according to which the joint tenants must have identical interests in terms of duration and the basic package of rights. It does not require their shares to be equal: A tenancy in common or a joint tenancy can be set up in which one co-owner can be entitled to more than an equal fractional share of proceeds from the asset (e.g., two co-tenants sharing sixty-forty).

The only difference between the joint tenancy and the tenancy in common is the right of survivorship. Only co-owners with a very close relationship, usually married couples, those in a long-term relationship, or close relatives would consider entering a joint tenancy. For married couples, joint tenancy for the family home is quite common, and in some jurisdictions is the default option. (For nonmarried co-owners, the default is the tenancy in common.) With respect to any other issue, the tenancy in common and the joint tenancy are exactly the same. So in either co-tenancy each co-owner has most of the rights of ownership: Each can exclude or admit strangers to the property, each can use property for enjoyment or profit, and each can sell his or her interest to a stranger.

The right of survivorship can be eliminated by "severing" the joint tenancy, leaving the joint tenants as tenants in common. To sever a joint tenancy one of the unities of special relevance to the joint tenancy—time, title, or interest—must be destroyed. If one joint tenant conveys to a third party, this destroys the unities of time and title and severs the joint tenancy. So if *A* and *B* are joint tenants, and *A* conveys to *C*, then *B* and *C* wind up being tenants in common. One common maneuver was for *A* to convey to *C*, and *C* to convey right back to *A*, where *C* would be considered a "strawman" or "straw." These days many courts will consider the joint tenancy severed if one conveys to oneself as tenant in common.[9] Courts are more divided over whether other actions, such as leasing, sever the joint tenancy.[10] Of particular interest are the questions of whether a mortgage by one of the joint tenants severs the joint tenancy, and what effect the death of either one of the joint tenants has on the mortgage.[11] Under the older "title theory" of mortgages, the mortgage took the form of a deed, and the conveyance would sever the joint tenancy, leaving the co-owners as tenants in common. Thus if either died, there would be no right of

9. *See* Riddle v. Harmon, 162 Cal. Rptr. 530 (Cal. Ct. App. 1980).

10. *Compare* Tenhet v. Boswell, 554 P.2d 330 (Cal. 1976) *with* Alexander v. Boyer, 253 A.2d 359 (Md. 1969).

11. *See, e.g.*, Harms v. Sprague, 473 N.E.2d 930 (Ill. 1984) (adopting the lien theory of mortgages and holding that mortgage did not sever joint tenancy and disappeared on the death of the mortgaging joint tenant).

survivorship, and the mortgage would remain on the mortgaging tenant's interest. Under the newer lien theory of mortgages, the mortgage does not sever the joint tenancy. According to the theory of the joint tenancy, the lien should probably disappear on the death of the mortgaging co-owner, but some courts hold that it survives as a lien on half the property. (Relatedly, courts are divided on whether the death of the nonmortgaging co-owner allows the lien to attach to the entire property.)

Severance simply turns a joint tenancy into a tenancy in common, but sometimes co-owners in either arrangement would like to cease being co-owners altogether. If so, they can agree that one will sell his or her interest to the other, or both will sell to a third party and split the proceeds. Failing that, the parties can petition a court for a *partition*, which is a court order dissolving the co-ownership. Partition is the ultimate form of no-fault divorce; courts will grant partition at the request of either owner, without requiring any justification. Partition can be in kind or by sale. Courts and statutes usually state a preference for in kind partition, which preserves some subjective value for those resources that can be physically split, over partition by sale, which often involves a court in more valuation issues. Nevertheless, there has been a trend toward partition by sale, perhaps because in the case of personal property and urban land, parcels are not as easy to split into viable parts, as was the case with tracts of farm land in an earlier era.

Some states have an additional form of co-ownership, reserved for married couples: the *tenancy by the entirety*. We will return to marital interests below, but the tenancy by the entirety is like the joint tenancy, in that it includes a right of survivorship, but unlike the joint tenancy, the tenancy by the entirety cannot be unilaterally severed. To destroy the tenancy by the entirety, the co-owners must get divorced, or convey the property to themselves (possibly by way of an intermediate "straw" transactor). For the tenancy by the entirety to be created, all the unities for the joint tenancy are required (time, title, interest, possession) plus the unity of marriage. Jurisdictions vary, but the tenancy by the entirety provides if anything a greater protection against creditors than the joint tenancy. Competing policies of protecting spouses and tort victims come into sharp conflict where one spouse commits a tort and the issue is whether the tort victim can reach the entire marital asset.[12]

Marital Interests

Special forms of ownership, such as the tenancy by the entirety, are only the beginning of the special law of marital property, which intersects with family law. Married co-owners are treated like other co-owners during the period of co-ownership, and married co-owners can seek partition or severance of a joint tenancy into a tenancy in common, just like any other co-owners. Property law supplies special rules for married couples on death and divorce. These rules for death and divorce can be modified by prenuptial agreements.

Somewhat controversially, courts are reluctant to supervise the behavior of couples during marriage, adopting a "love it or leave it" approach. This can be because the marriage is a multiplex relationship that is difficult to evaluate from the outside as long as disputes remain in the routine range. (Of course, when there is violence and when couples seek separation or divorce, intervention is called for.) Or it can be an echo of an earlier approach in the common law to defer to the husband's decision-making during the marriage. At common law (but not in equity), the married couple were considered one entity or unified actor. The nineteenth century saw the passage of the Married Women's Property Acts in all the states, which for the first time allowed married women to act as owners at common law during marriage.

---

12. *See* United States v. Craft, 535 U.S. 274 (2002) (discussing Michigan law but declining to insulate assets held in tenancy by the entirety from claims for federal taxes owed by one spouse).

The Married Women's Property Acts and related reforms also changed the implications of marital property law on death. Originally, on the death of the husband, the wife was entitled to *dower*, which gave her a life estate in one-third of the husband's real property, regardless of what the will provided for. When the wife predeceased the husband, he would have a right to *curtesy*, which gave him a life estate in all the real property held by the wife (legally or equitably), again potentially overriding a will that provided for less. Dower and curtesy have now been abolished in all states and replaced with the spousal elective share. This usually gives the surviving spouse the right to elect to take one-third of the deceased spouse's estate, regardless of what the will says. So if *A* and *B* are married, and *A* dies leaving *B* $1 out of a $300,000 estate, *B* can elect to take $100,000.

Aside from the forced share, the other major property issue for married couples is the division of martial property on divorce. Here states can be divided into common law and community property states. Community property is a regime that automatically applies to married couples in certain states, mostly in the West and Southwest, that have Spanish or French law in their backgrounds. Property acquired during the marriage is presumed to be community property, which means that it is subject to fifty-fifty division on divorce. Property belonging to the spouses before the marriage and, in some states, bequests are presumed to be separate but can lose that status if the separate property is sufficiently commingled with martial assets. Property can also be transmuted from separate to community or vice versa by written agreement, but again the presumption is for community property.

Marital property in common law states is subject to equitable division on divorce. Ever since the move to no-fault divorce starting around 1970, fault does not play an official role in property division on divorce. Instead, property division is supposed to reflect a wide variety of contextual factors relating to needs, expectations, and contributions, and is usually but not always limited to the property accumulated by the parties during the marriage. Less emphasis is now put on alimony, which was meant to provide a source of income support for a dependent spouse, traditionally the wife.

The distinction between the community property and common law systems of division on divorce presents yet another example of rules versus standards. Community property uses a rule (the fifty-fifty split) with lots of further rules about what counts and does not count as community property. The modern common law approach is the quintessential standard—fair and equitable division based on all the circumstances. It is difficult to know which approach works better and what the criteria would be for deciding what "better" means in this context. An interesting empirical question would be whether the community property rule, being more predictable, facilitates reaching property settlements upon divorce.

Particularly difficult issues in asset division on divorce surround human capital, which often is the largest asset of the spouses. What if the main economic value generated by a marriage is in the form of human capital in one of the spouses? Some statutes and court decisions call for some valuation of professional degrees and career enhancements, but these decisions are all over the lot.[13] Administration is not easy because the valuation must occur based on the average person in the spouse's field (which may be ambiguous, e.g., physician or surgeon), but the degree-holding spouse's career may work out better or worse than that. A prospective surgeon might break a hand or turn out to lack talent and have to enter a lower-paying specialty. If the court makes the award contingent on the future (by retaining jurisdiction), then the paying spouse may have an incentive not to work hard or to choose a lower-paying but possibly more satisfying occupation or spending time with

13. *See, e.g.*, *In re* Marriage of Olar, 747 P.2d 676 (Colo. 1987) (en banc) (holding degree not to be martial property subject to division but unfairness from sacrifice of career should be considered in maintenance award); O'Brien v. O'Brien, 489 N.E.2d 712 (N.Y. 1985) (degree is property subject to division under statute).

family instead.[14] What if a doctor claims to prefer a career of writing poetry? If the award is lump sum, what should be the measure? Is it one-half the value of the enhancement of the spouse's earnings created by the degree (discounted to present value), or should it be the sacrifices of the nondegree spouse plus a reasonable rate of return? How should value attributable to native talent be treated? What risks do spouses take on entering the marriage in order to gain the surplus from marriage, and how do we wind them up when that surplus is largely gone?

Some commentators analogize the splitting of assets on divorce to the winding up of a partnership. Is marriage a partnership, and if so, what are the implications for asset division? Or does seeing the marriage as at least in part an economic partnership commodify marriage (see Chapter 3)?

Finally, a problem on the borderland between property and contract is the question of contracting among nonmarried people as a potential substitute for marriage. When such arrangements are wound up, should the courts enforce the parties' understanding, to the extent that can be ascertained?[15] Or should such couples be denied access to contract law, to channel them into marriage? Recently, the issue has been whether to extend marriage to gay couples, and if so, to what extent marriage itself should be customizable. Marriage has a third-party aspect in that others must respect the relationship and its associated decision-making powers. Emergency medical personnel cannot be expected to figure out an idiosyncratic marriage substitute or customized marriage with respect to medical decision-making authority. Such issues are compounded when the question turns to plural marriage. Marriage has both customized contract and mandatory property-like aspects,

---

14. *See, e.g.*, Gastineau v. Gastineau, 573 N.Y.S.2d 819 (Sup. Ct., N.Y. Co. 1991) (holding that professional football player wasted marital asset in walking away from professional football contract).

15. Marvin v. Marvin, 557 P.2d 106 (Cal. 1976) (in bank).

and the right mix of them raises many empirical and normative questions.

Further Reading

THOMAS F. BERGIN & Paul G. HASKELL, PREFACE TO ESTATES IN LAND AND FUTURE INTERESTS (2d ed. 1984) (standard reference work).

Jesse Dukeminer, *A Modern Guide to Perpetuities*, 74 CAL. L. REV. 1867 (1986) (surveying various aspects of the Rule Against Perpetuities and related doctrines).

T. P. Gallanis, *The Future of Future Interests*, 60 WASH. & LEE L. REV. (2003) (proposing reforms for the estate system).

Thomas W. Merrill & Henry E. Smith, *Optimal Standardization in the Law of Property: The* Numerus Clausus *Principle*, 110 YALE L.J. 1 (2000) (developing theory of the *numerus clausus* based on information costs).

Elizabeth S. Scott & Robert E. Scott, *Marriage as Relational Contract*, 84 VA. L. REV. 1225 (1998) (analyzing marriage as in part an extralegal commitment that intersects with legal enforcement of property and other arrangements).

SIX

Managing Property

THE FORMS OF OWNERSHIP CONSIDERED in Chapter 5 involve a variety of divisions of ownership over time and among small numbers of persons at a given time. Yet, they all share this common feature: The person who is presently in possession of the asset has full managerial authority over it. Thus, when ownership is divided between a life estate and one or more remainders, the life tenant has full managerial authority over the resource as long as the life estate lasts. Once the life tenant dies, the holders of the remainders take possession, and they assume full managerial authority. At any point in time, the party in possession is the party in control.[1] Similarly, when property is divided among co-tenants, each of the co-tenants—in the eyes of the law at least—has full and equal authority to manage the property. The co-tenants may enter into some formal or informal agreement that confers managerial authority on one of the co-tenants, or prescribes some sharing of authority. But in terms of property rights, the law assumes that each has undivided managerial authority.

In this chapter, we consider some important legal devices that allow management authority over resources to be separated from other incidents of ownership. We will give specific attention to leasing, common interest communities, and trusts, each of which is

---

1. These divisions of ownership can give rise to a variety of conflicts, which, as we saw in Chapter 5 are mediated by a variety of legal doctrines such as waste and partition. But these mediating doctrines also assume that the person or small group that has possession of the property has full managerial authority.

regarded as creating a distinct form of ownership, and each of which plays an important role in modern economic systems.

Importantly, these are not the only legal devices for achieving a separation of management authority from other incidents of ownership. Perhaps the most important device, in terms of the total assets involved, is the business corporation. A corporation owns certain assets in its own name, such as factories, inventories, and intellectual property rights. The corporation is in turn owned by shareholders, who have a claim on the earnings of the corporation (through the payment of dividends), and on the assets of the corporation if it is dissolved. The shareholders, as the ultimate owners of the corporation, appoint directors who hire and oversee managers, who in turn run the corporation. (Directors and managers need not but typically do own shares of the corporation, but even where they do, their interest may be a tiny fraction of outstanding shares, as is typical in large publicly held corporations.) This arrangement allows management of the corporation's assets to be separated from other incidents of the corporation's property—namely, the profits and losses generated by those assets and the liquidation value of the assets.

The law of business organizations allows corporations (and related devices such as partnerships) to serve as pools of assets that creditors of the owners cannot reach: If Joe Shareholder misses a car payment, the corporation's factory is not available to Joe's creditors. And the creditors of the corporation cannot come after the shareholders personally. This "limited liability" means that if the corporation fails, Joe Shareholder's stock might become worthless, but that is all he is on the hook for; his other assets are safe.

These business entities, however, are so important they are studied in separate courses. We will honor that convention here by largely ignoring them. It is important to remember, however, that the separation of management authority from other incidents of ownership can be achieved in multiple ways, including not merely the devices we consider in this chapter but also others, such as forming a corporation.

Why Separate Management Authority from Other Incidents of Ownership?

Property by its very nature tends to concentrate authority over the management of resources. The logic of property is to assign each thing of value to an identifiable owner, who has the right to manage the thing to the exclusion of everyone else. Why then would people ever want to separate managerial authority from other incidents of ownership, such as the rights to possess, consume, or enjoy the profits from some thing? There are several reasons, including those related to financing and avoiding taxes. The most general explanation, however, involves achieving a specialization of functions in the management of resources. This specialization often requires aggregating resources—on some dimensions at least—to achieve the scale needed to support the introduction of specialized management. This aggregation is difficult to achieve solely through contracts among individual owners of smaller scale resources, because of collective action problems such as holdouts and freeriders. Leasing, common-interest communities, and trusts are all forms of property that permit aggregation on some dimensions—which creates the conditions for the introduction of specialized management on those dimensions—while maintaining separation on other dimensions. This explanation is best fleshed out with some examples, which will also serve to introduce the three forms of property we will consider in this chapter.

Consider, first, a shopping center, consisting of a complex of retail stores arrayed in a single building, together with common facilities such as a heating plant, landscaping, a parking lot, and security guards. One way to organize such a shopping center would be to have one person (most likely a corporation) own and manage all the assets in the complex. This single owner-manager strategy has advantages and disadvantages. The principal advantages are that common facilities can be effectively managed and maintained by the single owner. The disadvantages are those characteristic of any large enterprise. It may be difficult to supervise employees, such as retail clerks, in many different shops, and the shopping center may take on a dull homogeneous aspect lacking appeal for many consumers. Another way to organize the shopping center would be to have each store owned and operated independently of the others, the way downtown shopping areas have traditionally been organized. This multiple owner-manager strategy also has advantages and disadvantages. The advantage is that the individual shops can better supervise employees and will exhibit greater variety and responsiveness to consumers. A principal disadvantage is that fragmentation of ownership creates a huge collective action problem. Who will be in charge of providing heat and maintaining the parking lot? Who will provide security services? Who will maintain the landscaping? It would be difficult if not impossible for the individual shop owners to agree on contracts in which they mutually agree to provide such services.

A better solution, which avoids many of the drawbacks of both the single-owner and the multiple-owner strategies, is to use leasing to overcome the collective action problem while retaining individual managerial authority over the individual shops. Under such an arrangement, one party—the owner of the complex as a whole—owns and controls the common facilities, such as the building, the landscaping, and the parking lot, and is responsible for providing security for the whole complex. This solves the collective action problems associated with multiple owners. The individual store spaces are then leased to different shopkeeper-tenants, each of whom is responsible for management of their own individual space. Thus, each individual shopkeeper-tenant decides, independently, how to design the interior space of each shop, what inventory to purchase, and how to compensate and supervise employees. This solves many of the problems of bureaucracy, employee supervision, and homogeneity associated with the single-owner strategy. Given the division of functions permitted by leasing, it is not surprising that this device is almost universally used in the organization of shopping centers.

Our second example is a real estate development consisting of many freestanding single-family homes clustered around some common facility such as a boating marina, a ski resort, a golf course, or an ecological preserve. Here again, we can imagine both centralized and decentralized ways of organizing such a community. One could organize the common interest community under the auspices of a single owner, with the owner managing all the assets and assigning homes to individual families by contract. This would likely tend toward excessive rigidity and homogeneity and would not give individual families control over the design and maintenance of their assigned homes. Alternatively, one could organize the community as a collection of independent homes, relying on contracts among homeowners to support the common facilities. But this would generate potentially insuperable collective action problems if individual homeowners refused to contribute to the common undertaking or otherwise failed to cooperate with each other.

Today, the dominant way to organize such a common interest community is by creating a homeowners' or community association to govern the common facilities, with the individual homes owned as condominiums or in fee simple subject to a package of servitudes running with the land. The homeowners' or community association functions like a private government, with a constitution, laws, an elected governing board, and periodic meetings of unit owners to vote on actions of general interest. Most importantly, the homeowners' or community association is given the power to collect monthly assessments from the homeowners to pay for the ongoing provision of the common facilities. Meanwhile, the individual homes are managed by each individual homeowner, subject to restrictions about exterior decoration and upkeep, and perhaps other matters such as keeping pets. As in the case of the shopping center, we can see that the common interest community is a device for overcoming collective action problems to provide for a specialization of functions.

Our third example involves a problem in the transmission of family wealth from one generation to the next. Suppose the family breadwinner, *B*, is suffering from a fatal disease and does not expect to live much longer. *B*'s spouse, *S*, has limited ability to earn income, and has recently battled with cancer, which is in remission and may or may not return. *B* also has three children from a prior marriage. The eldest, *E*, is independent, has a well-paying job, and is in good health. The middle child, *M*, is still in college and is trying to decide between a low-paying but personally gratifying career and a much higher-paying career. The youngest child, *Y*, suffers from a variety of behavioral problems including drug abuse and has been in and out of group homes for years; it is unclear whether these problems will be resolved. *B* has accumulated substantial savings, and would like to leave the money in such a way as to provide the greatest benefit in the future to the four people *B* cares most about—*S*, *E*, *M*, and *Y*.

If the only options were those presented by the system of estates in land considered in Chapter 5, then none of the options is entirely satisfactory. *B* could leave a will that splits the property into four shares with each survivor owning his or her share in fee simple. But this might leave *S* with insufficient funds for future cancer treatments, or for *M*, if *M* elects the low-paying career option, or for *Y*, if continued treatment for behavioral problems is required. Moreover, *B* is likely to be concerned that some of the beneficiaries, such as *Y*, are not capable of managing the assets, and could fritter the money away or use it for undesirable purchases like drugs. Alternatively, *B* could leave a life estate to *S*, with remainders to *E*, *M*, and *Y*. But *S* might live a very long time, or might remarry, and in either event might not want to devote any of the money for the support of *M* and *Y*, if they need it before *S* dies.

What *B* needs is a faithful and competent manager for the assets, who can invest and dispose of the funds in the future in approximately the way *B* would have done if *B* were still alive. The principal method for doing this today is to create a trust. This allows legal title to the funds to be transferred from *B* to a trustee, *T*, either immediately or upon *B*'s death. If *T* is a corporate trustee, such as a bank trust department, then the funds can be combined with other trust funds and invested in a portfolio of investments, diversifying risk and improving the expected return. Meanwhile, *T* is subject to strict duties of honesty, prudence, and other fiduciary duties in the management of the funds (see below), and can be given detailed instructions about how to distribute the funds among *S*, *E*, *M*, and *Y*, depending on future contingencies. Once again, we can see how the trust overcomes collective action problems in a way that allows for a separation of management authority from other incidents of property and thereby permits a specialization of functions in the use of the property.

Leasing

Let us give closer consideration to the first of these devices for separating management authority from other incidents of ownership—leasing. Leasing is a very old form of ownership and continues to be used in a wide variety of circumstances. It goes by a variety of names: leasing, leaseholds, renting, tenancies, landlord-tenant relations—all are essentially synonymous. We will refer to the relationship between lessor and lessee as "leasing," the specific contractual undertaking between the lessor and lessee that governs their relationship as the "lease," and the property rights the lessee acquires under the lease as the "leasehold."

The essence of leasing is simple. A property owner—the lessor or landlord—agrees to transfer possession of property to another person—the lessee or tenant—for some time period. In return, the lessee agrees to pay the lessor rent, nearly always at periodic intervals. Leasing is similar to bailments in that it entails a temporary transfer of possession of property. It differs in that the purpose of a lease is to convey full economic use of the transferred item to the transferee, whereas in a bailment, the item is transferred for a limited and specific purpose such as repair or safekeeping. Leasing is also similar to the life estate in that the transfer of possession entails temporary but full economic use of the asset. However, the time period in a lease is nearly always described in terms of months and years rather than natural lives as in the case of a life estate.[2]

Leasing also differs from both the bailment and the life estate in that the transferee agrees to make periodic payments of rent to the transferor. Because the lessor expects to receive rental payments, the lessor is inevitably much more involved in monitoring the behavior of the lessee than is typically the case with someone who has entrusted property to a bailee or who has transferred property in a life estate subject to a reversion. The lessor will want to know, at a minimum, if the lessee has abandoned the property, which would have dire implications for future payment of the rent. Moreover, the lessor is likely to keep an eye out for other signs of trouble, such as prolonged illness or unemployment or a closing of the lessee's business. In effect, the lessor's expectation of periodic rental payments will naturally incline the lessor to a more interactive relationship with the lessee than will be the case as between a bailor and a bailee or a life tenant and a holder of a reversion. The continued engagement of the lessor in overseeing the property also allows leasing to be used to achieve a division of functions between lessor and lessee, as previously discussed in connection with the shopping center example.

Leasing covers a wide variety of situations and includes both real and personal property. There are very long so-called ground rent leases of 99 years or more for land on which tenants construct and own their own buildings; leases of agricultural land; leases of commercial space in office buildings or shopping centers; leases of unfurnished houses and apartments; short-term month-to-month leases of furnished apartments; and leases of computers, automobiles, airplanes, and machinery. The fact that leasing

---

2. *But see* Garner v. Gerrish, 473 N.E.2d 223 (N.Y. 1984) (upholding an interest characterized as a lease with a life term and minimizing the distinction between leases and life estates).

occurs in so many different contexts confirms the great utility of this property form.

Leases are sometimes divided into different types depending on the rules for determining when they terminate. A *term of years* terminates at a point in time predetermined in the lease. This can be measured in years, months, or even by a particular day. At common law no notice was required by either party to terminate a term of years on the day appointed, although this has been modified in many states by statute. A *periodic tenancy* rolls over automatically from one time period to the next, unless one of the parties gives notice of termination, usually a month in advance. A *tenancy at will* continues indefinitely, until one of the parties decides to terminate. At common law no notice was required. Finally, a *tenancy at sufferance* is created when a tenant holds over after the termination of a lease. Such a tenant has greater rights than a trespasser, but is obviously subject to eviction by whatever procedures the law allows.

Property and Contract

At the heart of every lease is a bilateral exchange: the transfer of possession of some resource, whether it be land, an apartment, or an automobile, for a designated period of time, in return for a promise to pay rent. Leasing thus includes both a contract—the agreement between the lessor and lessee called the lease—and a transfer of possession of the resource that is the subject matter of the lease. In its contractual aspect, leasing affects primarily the relations between the lessor and the lessee. The contractual aspect is in personam, in the sense that it creates personal rights and duties between the lessor and lessee and does not directly impact the rights and duties of third parties.

Yet the interest of the lessee, although grounded in contract, also has the critical features of a property right: The lease transfers possession and full economic use of the resource to the lessee. As is usually the case, the right of possession includes the right to exclude others from the property possessed. Absent agreement to the contrary, this includes the right to exclude the lessor. Thus, the lessee acquires primary managerial authority over the thing leased during the term of the lease. The lessee can decide who may or may not enter or use the property, how the property will be used, and so forth. Two caveats should be noted about this property right. First, the managerial authority of the tenant can be and often is cabined by provisions in the lease. For example, the lease can say "no pets" or can allow the landlord to enter and inspect the property at certain times. Second, as previously discussed, leasing is often used to achieve a division of functions, so that, in the case of an apartment lease for instance, the tenant has authority over the interior space but the landlord retains managerial authority over common areas such as the building shell, lobby, elevators, and the heating system.

Because the lease transfers possession and economic use of the property to the lessee, the lessee ordinarily assumes the risks and benefits associated with ownership of the leased property, such as crop failure, a surge or decline in profitability, or liability for injury to third parties, during the term of the lease (again, subject to specific modifications in the lease). This is very important in understanding the economics of leasing. The lessor's economic interest during the term of the lease is in receiving the rental payment, which is typically fixed by the contract. The lessee's interest is based on receiving the benefits of possession, which can fluctuate depending on the state of the economy and other external factors, but also on the level of effort and skill the lessee puts into managing the property during the term of possession. The lessee is thus the "residual claimant" in a leasehold arrangement during the term of the lease, meaning the lessee captures the value left over after other obligations are met, including of course the obligation to pay rent to the lessor.[3] The lessee's status as residual claimant

---

3. *See* YORAM BARZEL, ECONOMIC ANALYSIS OF PROPERTY RIGHTS 8–9, 33–54 (2d ed. 1997).

creates a powerful incentive for the lessee to engage in good managerial practices over the leased property during the term of the lease.

After the term of the lease, the landlord reclaims possession of the premises. Thus, in addition to an expectation of the rental payments during the lease the landlord also holds a reversion. As with the temporal split between present possessory and future interest holders we saw in Chapter 5, the tenant's incentives are biased toward present consumption and against investments that produce benefits beyond the lease term. Conversely, landlords are interested less in the present and more in the future. Not surprisingly, the law of waste can be invoked on behalf of the landlord, but because leases are typically of shorter duration than a life estate, the standard in landlord-tenant law is that the tenant must return the premises in the condition at the beginning of the lease except for "normal wear and tear." As was the case with present and future interests, the standard provided by the waste doctrine is a default, and here can be varied in the lease itself.

Most legal issues regarding leasing concern its contractual aspect. As with most contractual relationships, the rules that govern leases are primarily default rules. This means the parties to the lease are free to specify some alternative rule in the lease if they do not wish to abide by the off-the-rack legal rule. Leasing performs so many different functions that it might be sensible to use different packages of default rules for different types of leases. What makes sense as a default rule for agricultural leases does not necessarily make sense for commercial leases, which in turn may not make sense for residential leases. But for better or worse, the common law has sought to identify a single package of default rules for all types of leases. Legislation in many jurisdictions has changed some of the default rules based on the type of leasing involved. For example, in the context of residential leases, but not generally for commercial leases, the default rule regarding risk of destruction of a building during the term of the lease has been shifted from the tenant to the landlord by legislation in most states.

These interventions, however, have been ad hoc and do not reflect a systematic package of defaults that varies by type of lease.

A good example of the contractual nature of leasing law concerns what happens if the leasehold commences, and another tenant (or a trespasser) is in possession of the property. Who is responsible for evicting the holdover tenant or the trespasser at the onset of the leasehold—the landlord or the tenant? Jurisdictions are divided on this issue.[4] Those that follow the so-called English rule imply a covenant requiring the landlord to deliver actual possession. Those that follow the American rule say there is no such implied covenant, and the tenant has the obligation to remove the holdover or the trespasser. A number of jurisdictions adopted the English rule as part of the pro-tenant trend in landlord-tenant decisions in the 1970s, making it the majority rule for residential tenancies today. In either case, the rule is a default, meaning that the parties can override the rule and can specify in the lease which party is obligated to deal with holdovers or trespassers at the beginning of the leasehold.

Following the standard analysis of default rules in the law of contracts, the better default rule is generally the one most parties would want. This "majoritarian" approach minimizes the need for drafting around the rule. Here, the rule most parties would want is probably the one that saves the most on costs spent on evicting holdovers or trespassers. The rule that saves costs means the parties have more joint wealth to share, making them collectively better off. Unfortunately, neither of the contending rules may conserve on eviction costs in every situation. The identity of the cheaper evictor probably depends on the type of leasehold. For rentals of urban apartments, where the landlord is either on the property or has a manager on the property, and where the landlord is familiar with

---

4. *Compare* Hannan v. Dusch, 153 S.E. 824 (Va. 1939) (holding that the default rule is that landlord is not responsible for removing holdover tenant) *with* Adrian v. Rabinowitz, 186 A. 29 (N.J. 1936) (holding the contrary).

the prior tenant and with eviction procedures, the landlord is almost surely the cheaper evictor. For leases of agricultural land, where the tenant is likely to be familiar with the area and the identity of the prior tenant, and the landlord may be an absentee, the tenant may be the cheaper evictor. This illustrates the difficulty of having a single set of default rules that apply to all types of leases. It also may explain why the jurisdictions are divided as to the proper rule.

Models of the Lease Contract

If leases were always construed like ordinary bilateral contracts for the sale of goods or services, there would be little reason to study the contractual aspect of leasing as a distinct topic. Lease law would simply be an application of ordinary contract law. Unfortunately, things are not so simple. Lease law initially developed at a time when contract law was different from what it is today. Perhaps because of heightened respect for *stare decisis* in matters involving property rights, courts have been slow to update the understanding of the contractual aspect of leasing law. One can distinguish three phases in the evolution of the contractual model in lease law.[5]

The first phase conceived of the lease as a bundle of independent covenants or promises. Take a very simple lease in which *L* promises to transfer possession of Blackacre to *T* for three years, and in return *T* promises to pay *L* $100 per year in rent. The promise to provide possession and the promise to pay rent were originally regarded as independent of each other. Thus, if a foreign invader seized Blackacre, ousting *T* from possession, *T* was still obligated to

5. *See generally* Roger A. Cunningham, *The New and Statutory Warranties of Habitability in Residential Leases: From Contract to Status*, 16 URB. L. ANN. 3 (1979); Mary Ann Glendon, *The Transformation of American Landlord-Tenant Law*, 23 B.C. L. REV. 503 (1982).

pay rent to *L*.[6] Or, if *T* stopped paying rent, *L* was still obligated to provide *T* possession. The remedy for breach of any of the independent covenants, as was generally the case in actions at common law, was an award of damages. The one exception to this rule was if the landlord breached the so-called covenant of quiet enjoyment—the promise to provide possession to the tenant—by ousting the tenant during the term of the lease. Ouster by the landlord excused the tenant from further payment of rent, until the ouster was cured.

The model of independent covenants had a number of harsh consequences for both landlords and tenants. If the tenant abandoned the property and stopped paying rent, the model required the landlord to let the property stand idle while periodically suing the tenant for damages—often to no avail if the tenant was insolvent or had disappeared. Or, if the landlord breached covenants regarding the condition of the property, such as a covenant to provide heat, the tenant's only recourse was to shiver and sue for damages.

In the second phase of the evolution of leasing law, which we can call the transitional model, courts and legislatures responded to these sorts of problems by adopting rules and doctrines designed to ameliorate the harshness of the independent covenants model, without abandoning its logic. The transitional model developed several rules that remain important today. To provide relief to the landlord faced with a defaulting and potentially insolvent tenant, courts permitted landlords to insert clauses in leases that allowed landlords to *reenter and relet* property upon default by the tenant. In effect, the landlord could elect to terminate the lease in the event of default. To cut off the tenant's liability for rent when the tenant had abandoned and the landlord took steps to reenter, courts developed the *surrender* doctrine. This treated certain actions by the landlord, such as accepting the keys when proffered

6. *See* Paradine v. Jane, Aleyn 27, 82 Eng. Rep. 897 (K.B. 1647).

by the tenant, as an implied release of further liability for rent. Again, surrender acted as a form of termination of further lease obligations. And to provide some relief to tenants faced with intolerable conditions created by a landlord's breach of a covenant to repair, provide heat, or control the behavior of other tenants, the courts developed the doctrine of *constructive eviction.* This built on the rule that breach of the landlord's covenant of quiet enjoyment would excuse further payment of rent, by holding that landlord breaches that made conditions so intolerable as to require the tenant to vacate were tantamount to an actual eviction. This doctrine, too, effectively permitted early termination of the lease.

Beginning in the middle years of the twentieth century, a third phase developed, in which courts began to conceptualize leases as ordinary bilateral contracts, in which promises are regarded as being mutually dependent. Under modern contract law, a material breach by one party—nonperformance that is significant enough to count as a failure of a condition of the exchange—gives rise to a variety of remedial options for the other party, including rescission of the contract. Applied to leases, this would mean, for example, that if the landlord promised to maintain an elevator in good working order, and it remained broken for some time, the tenant could argue that this was a material breach justifying rescission by the tenant; that is, the tenant could walk away from the lease without liability. Adoption of modern contract law would also mean that a duty to mitigate damages would be implied in all leases. This would mean that a landlord would have a legal duty to seek a substitute tenant in the event of abandonment by the original tenant. Perhaps most significantly, modern contract law might suggest that leased property includes an implied warranty of fitness for the tenant's intended purpose, by analogy to contracts for the sale of goods.

Although the third phase in understanding the contractual aspect of leases has made substantial inroads, it has failed completely to vanquish the rules developed in the first two phases. Adoption of the third model remains selective. For example, in many states the duty to mitigate damages applies to residential leases, but not to commercial leases. Similarly, in most jurisdictions there is an implied warranty of habitability that applies to residential leases, but there is no implied warranty of fitness for intended purposes in commercial leases. Moreover, even where the third model has been expressly adopted, courts tend to allow parties to plead doctrines developed in the second or transitional phase in the alternative. For example, a residential tenant can allege breach of the implied warranty of habitability (a third-phase doctrine) and constructive eviction (a second-phase doctrine) in the alternative. As a result, the contractual aspect of lease law, which in principle could be simple and little different from ordinary contract law, is highly complicated and contains many elements unique to lease law.

Implied Warranty of Habitability

Perhaps the most controversial development in leasing law in recent years has been the widespread adoption of an implied warranty of habitability in residential leases. As noted above, during the transitional period between the model of independent covenants and the modern trend toward adoption of dependent covenants, courts developed the doctrine of constructive eviction. This relieved tenants of all liability under the lease if the conditions of the premises deteriorated so badly that the landlord had in effect ousted the tenant. The doctrine generally required tenants to abandon the property to claim constructive eviction, which obviously posed very severe risks for the tenant. If the courts concluded that constructive eviction had not been established, then the tenant could be held liable for all rent due and owing during the period when the tenant was out of possession. There is also confusion in the case law about whether the tenant must prove the breach of some specific lease provision by the landlord, such as a covenant to repair or provide heat, to establish constructive eviction, or whether it is enough that conditions are so bad that any "reasonable" person would be forced to vacate.

In addition to constructive eviction, other doctrines developed in the transitional period also provided some relief for tenants. If the landlord knew or should have known about some defect in the condition of the property, and failed to disclose this to the tenant before the tenant took possession, some courts permitted the tenant to sue on grounds of fraud or implied misrepresentation.[7] Also, leases of furnished houses or apartments for short terms have long been held to include an implied warranty of habitability.[8] Generally speaking, however, unless constructive eviction or one of these narrow doctrines applied, courts in the transitional phase applied a rule of *caveat lessee*—let the tenant beware.

In a brief period beginning in the late 1960s, nearly all states overturned the rule of caveat lessee and replaced it with an implied warranty of habitability (IWH), at least for residential leaseholds. Two distinct legal theories were advanced in support of this rapid revision in leasing law.[9] One relied on the adoption of housing codes after World War II by most municipalities. Courts reasoned that the codes were intended to define the minimal quality of rental housing in the community, and that every lease is conclusively assumed to incorporate the provisions of the code as implied lease terms. The other theory relied on the development of products liability law and the extension of tort liability to manufacturers for defects in products they sell, even if the product has passed into the hands of someone with whom the manufacturer has no direct contractual relationship. Products liability, in effect, imposes an implied warranty of quality that runs with the product, and courts reasoned that a similar warranty should be implied in residential leases.

---

7. *See, e.g.*, Faber v. Creswick, 156 A.2d 252 (N.J. 1959).

8. *See, e.g.*, Ingalls v. Hobbs, 31 N.E. 286 (Mass. 1892).

9. *See* Javins v. First Nat'l Realty Corp., 428 F.2d 1071 (D.C. Cir. 1970) (seminal decision discussing both theories).

Both theories present a number of unresolved issues, many of which have not been addressed by courts. What exactly does the IWH guarantee? Under the housing code theory, the provisions of the codes would seem to define the duty, but some codes are highly precise, and others are vague and general. Much residential housing, especially in rural and unincorporated areas, is not governed by any code. Does this mean this housing is not subject to the IWH? Courts have said that not every code violation violates the duty, only "material breaches" that affect health or safety, and that judges have "wide discretion" in determining whether the conditions in any given rental unit amount to a material breach.[10] The products liability theory provides even less guidance. As precedents slowly accumulate, the content of the warranty should become clearer, but local conditions (custom again) make variation inevitable, and prevent relying on precedents from other jurisdictions as sure guideposts.

The IWH also fits awkwardly with the modern trend to construe leases as ordinary bilateral contracts. The fit would be good if the IWH were regarded as a default rule, subject to disclaimer in the lease by the parties. In the context of sales of goods, there is generally an implied warranty of fitness for intended purposes. But sellers of goods are permitted to disclaim this warranty by specifying that the good is being sold "as is"; significantly, the same rule applies under the Uniform Commercial Code for leases of personal property (such as cars or equipment).[11] Most courts and legislatures that have adopted the IWH for residential housing, however, have insisted that the warranty is not disclaimable, but rather is binding on landlords and tenants alike. This is in keeping with the housing code and products liability theories, because neither public regulations nor tort

---

10. Jablonski v. Clemons, 803 N.E.2d 730, 733 (Mass. App. Ct. 2004).

11. *See* UCC § 2-315 (implied warranty of fitness for particular purpose); *id.* at § 2-316(3)(a) (permitting warranty to be disclaimed); *id.* at §§ 2A-213, 2A-214(3) (adopting similar provisions in the context of leasing of personal property).

duties to third parties can be disclaimed by contract. Perhaps the best contractual analogy is consumer protection law, where we do sometimes find nondisclaimable terms designed to protect relatively uninformed consumers. But like consumer protection law, nondisclaimability creates a disconnect between leasing law and the law's general treatment of other bilateral contracts.

At a policy level, a number of justifications have been offered for the binding and nonwaivable IWH. Perhaps the one that enjoys the widest support is asymmetric information. In a typical residential tenancy, the landlord knows more about the condition of the property than a prospective tenant, and the landlord ordinarily has better information about the requirements of the law and the meaning of the provisions of the lease (which in residential tenancies is nearly always drafted by the landlord). By guaranteeing a minimal standard of quality, and making this nondisclaimable by fine print in the lease, the IWH corrects for this asymmetric information. The idea is that if both parties were fully informed, the tenant would insist on, and the landlord would agree to, a lease that includes the IWH.

More controversial is the idea that the IWH is justified because of unequal bargaining power between landlords and tenants. Unequal bargaining power is an ambiguous concept, and in many applications it may simply refer to asymmetric information, already discussed. To the extent it goes beyond the idea of asymmetric information, the unequal bargaining power rationale may depend on the vacancy rate in the relevant market. If the vacancy rate is low, then there will be many prospective tenants chasing few available units, and landlords will be in a position to drive hard bargains, including disclaiming any warranties of quality. If the vacancy rate is high, which is not unheard of in cities where developers have overbuilt or population is declining, then landlords will be in a weak bargaining position and may be willing to be flexible about lease terms. Many of the cases and commentaries assume that vacancy rates are always low, especially for low-income tenants. This is probably a safe assumption in cities where new residential housing construction has been restricted—either by limited available land, or strict zoning laws, or rent controls, or some combination of these factors (New York City suffers from all three). But in other cities and towns, such as those experiencing falling population, the assumption is open to question.

Another way to think of unequal bargaining power is to ask whether landlords have market power, in the sense of being able to affect prices by adding or withdrawing units from the market. If so, we would expect them to raise prices to supracompetitive levels. But whether such a monopolist would choose to lower quality as opposed to reducing supply and raising prices is more doubtful, quite apart from the problem of identifying the relevant localized market power in the first place. If regulators had perfect information about such localized market power (if any), they could use devices, such as rent control and conversion control, to prevent artificial supply restriction on the part of the monopolist, or regulate the quality dimensions furnished by the local monopolist under a fine-grained version of the IWH. But the informational assumptions here seem quite heroic.

The most controversial justification for the binding IWH is that it makes low-income tenants better off, and hence produces a more equitable distribution of wealth. This justification is highly debatable if the IWH is introduced in a rental market where landlords are otherwise free to make compensating adjustments, such as raising rents or withdrawing units from the market. If the IWH increases the quality of housing, demand for units may go up, and rents may increase. Alternatively, if coming into compliance with the IWH costs landlords money, the supply of housing may decline, through conversions to condominiums or abandonment, also causing rents to increase. If either or both of these forces is in play, then the question becomes whether the improvement in housing quality is worth more to low-income tenants than the higher rents they must pay. Various elaborate arguments have been advanced as to why ordinary laws of supply and demand may not apply in the rental housing market, but the question in the end is an empirical one.[12] Some tenants may gain from the IWH, but others, who cannot afford to pay more for housing even if the quality is higher, may lose. No one has yet demonstrated that the gainers outnumber the losers—or vice versa. Nor do we have any clear idea how large the relevant gains and losses are.

Perhaps the most unsettling aspect of the IWH is that it is not clear whether the change has had much impact on the welfare of low-income tenants. Appellate decisions interpreting the IWH are few in number, as compared to, say, decisions explicating products liability law. Litigation is expensive, and the amount in controversy in most cases involving an alleged breach of the IWH is small. Given the many uncertainties about the IWH, the absence of appellate decisions suggests either that most cases settle, or tenants do not assert IWH claims very often. If a high rate of settlement is the explanation, then the IWH may have some impact, even if it does not show up in reported appeals. If tenants simply do not assert the IWH very often, then the doctrine is probably not having much impact. Here too, it would be useful to have more empirical information.

Transferring Leasehold Interests

With a few prominent exceptions like the mandatory IWH in residential leases, the modern conception of the landlord-tenant relationship is very much like that of an ordinary bilateral contract. This means the lease can contain virtually any sort of promise the

12. *See* Bruce Ackerman, *Regulating Slum Housing Markets on Behalf of the Poor: Of Housing Codes, Housing Subsidies and Income Redistribution Policy*, 80 YALE L.J. 1093 (1971); Bruce Ackerman, *More on Slum Housing and Redistribution Policy: A Reply to Professor Komesar*, 82 YALE L.J. 1194 (1973); Neil K. Komesar, *Return to Slumville: A Critique of the Ackerman Analysis of Housing Code Enforcement and the Poor*, 83 YALE L.J. 1175 (1973); *see also* RICHARD A. POSNER, ECONOMIC ANALYSIS OF LAW 259–73 (1973).

parties want it to contain: The landlord can promise to shine the tenant's shoes, and the tenant can promise to walk the landlord's dog. If either the landlord or the tenant transfers their interest to a third party, however, we see a significant shift toward standardization of the respective interests.

Suppose the landlord sells the reversion to a third party. The ordinary rule here is that the third party will take "subject to" any unexpired leases. Does this mean that if the original landlord promised to shine the tenant's shoes, the new landlord must continue to shine the tenant's shoes? Probably not: The common law rule is that only promises in the original lease that "touch and concern" the land run to successors in interest. This mysterious requirement is hard to define with any precision; basically what it means in this context is that only those terms in the lease that affect the scope of the property rights or the condition of the land are binding on successors in interest. Promises by the landlord to provide a parking place for the tenant and heat for the building would touch and concern the land; a promise to shine the tenant's shoes probably would be regarded as a personal promise that does not run with the land.

Suppose the tenant decides to transfer the tenant's remaining interest under the lease. The common law rule here is that absent an agreement in the lease to the contrary, the tenant's interest is freely alienable. The landlord will often be concerned about who the tenant might transfer to; at a minimum, the landlord will want assurance that the new tenant is a good credit risk. Landlords are therefore free to include a clause in the original lease providing that the tenant may not transfer without the landlord's permission. Historically, these permission clauses were understood to give the landlord complete discretion in deciding whether or not to permit a transfer, unless the tenant negotiated for additional language stating that consent to transfer will not be "unreasonably withheld." Some jurisdictions have recently rejected this interpretation, however, and have ruled that a permission clause will be construed to mean the landlord must have a commercially reasonable ground for withholding consent, unless the landlord has negotiated for additional language stating that consent can be withheld for any reason.[13] This may well be a better default rule and prevents the landlord from extracting gains in the market value of leases that some tenants legitimately expect to capture. Nevertheless, since most lease transfers involve long term commercial leases where both parties are represented by counsel, it is not clear that tinkering with the default interpretation of permission clauses in this fashion is worth the disruption to settled expectations.

Tenant transfers are subject to a further type of standardization, in that they can be achieved in only two ways: through assignment or a subletting. An assignment occurs when the tenant transfers the entire remaining interest in the lease to a third party, such that the new tenant steps into the shoes of the original tenant. When this happens, the original tenant is still liable to the landlord under privity of contract—for the obligations set forth in the original lease (including the obligation to walk the dog). But the new tenant now holds directly from the landlord, and so is said also to be obligated to the landlord under "privity of estate." This means the new tenant must perform all obligations of the original lease that "touch and concern" the land, in exact parallel to what happens when the landlord sells the reversion to a third party. So the new tenant has to pay the rent to the landlord, but probably does not have to walk the dog.

A sublease occurs when the tenant does not transfer the entire remaining interest in the lease to a third party, but retains some interest for him or herself. For example, if the lease has one year to run, the prime tenant could transfer the summer months to a third party but then retain the last nine months for him or herself. When this happens, the prime tenant remains obligated to the landlord under privity of contract and hence must perform all the provisions of the original lease (including walking the dog). But in a clear echo

13. *See* Kendall v. Ernest Pestana, Inc. 709 P.2d 837 (Cal. 1985).

of feudalism, the subtenant is regarded as holding of the prime tenant, not of the landlord. Consequently, there is no privity of estate between the landlord and the subtenant, and the landlord cannot enforce any of the obligations of the original lease against the subtenant. This includes the obligation to pay rent. If the subtenant defaults on the rent, the landlord's only recourse is against the prime tenant.

Courts have devised a variety of tests for distinguishing between assignments and subleases, but the basic question is whether the original tenant is still in the picture or has transferred everything to the substitute tenant. The more significant point is that there are only two ways to transfer—assignment or sublease—and courts do not recognize any other arrangement. This is another example of the *numerus clausus* principle at work, and can be understood as reducing the information costs about the rights and obligations of the respective parties that third parties (such as creditors or other prospective tenants) would have to bear if a larger menu of options prevailed.

Common Interest Communities

Leasing, as we have seen, is often used to achieve a division of managerial authority between common and separate facilities within a single complex of assets. Common interest communities are also used to achieve a division of managerial authority between common and separate facilities within a single complex of assets. The basic concept of a common interest community is that individual units, whether they be apartments or townhouses or freestanding homes, are usually owned in fee simple by individual owners. The individual unit owners then collectively organize themselves to manage certain common or shared facilities, whether it be the exterior shell, lobby, and heating plant in an apartment building, or swimming pools, driveways, and landscaping in a complex of buildings. Familiar examples of common interest communities include condominiums, cooperative apartments, and gated residential developments. Virtually every common interest community could also be organized by leasing (although leasing has broader applications, as in ground rent leases). Hence, common interest communities are an alternative choice for achieving one of the principal functional ends of leasing.

Common interest communities take one of two legal forms, both of which are expressly authorized by statute. In a condominium, individual units are held in fee simple and common areas and facilities are co-owned by the unit owners (without a right of partition). Unit owners are typically required to be members of a condominium association, which governs the common facilities. In a cooperative, individual units and common facilities are owned by a single entity, the cooperative corporation. Individuals then purchase shares in this corporation, which shares entitle them to a perpetual lease of a particular unit.

Under either of these legal forms, common interest communities function in practice as a kind of private government.[14] Such communities are nearly always created by a single person or entity, typically a real estate developer (analogous to the founders of a new political entity). The developer will incorporate the plan for the common interest community in promises that are included in the deeds to the land and that run with the land (more on promises running with the land in Chapter 8). These deed promises are sometimes called covenants, conditions, and restrictions (CCRs). These promises provide the basic framework for the management of the common interest community (analogous to a constitution or city charter), and are binding on the managers of the common or shared facilities and the individual unit owners alike. The CCRs will typically provide that the individual unit owners constitute a

---

14. *See* Robert C. Ellickson, *Cities and Homeowners Associations*, 130 U. PA. L. REV. 1519 (1982); Clayton P. Gillette, *Courts, Covenants, and Communities*, 61 U. CHI. L. REV. 1375 (1994).

homeowners' association (HOA), which will gather periodically or on special occasions to vote on matters of common concern to the community (analogous to the electorate of a state or city participating in elections or referenda). The CCRs will also typically provide for a governing board, which is in charge of managing the common or shared facilities and enforcing rules and regulations that control the behavior of the individual unit owners (analogous to a legislature or city council). Typically, the board consists of individual unit owners elected at a meeting of the HOA. The board may hire a manager (analogous to a city mayor or manager) and other employees to manage the common or shared facilities, or may enter into contracts with outside firms to provide these services. Importantly, the HOA will have the power to impose periodic assessments on the unit owners to cover the costs of providing common or shared facilities and services (analogous to taxes).

Given these organizational features, it is possible to describe the differences between leasing and common interest communities as being similar to the differences between dictatorship and democracy. Consider a residential complex consisting of a number of buildings containing multiple units, along with common facilities such as a swimming pool, recreation center, parking lot, and landscaping. If the complex is organized by leasing, the landlord has exclusive managerial authority over the common or shared facilities. The landlord can dictate what hours the swimming pool is open, whether free aerobics classes will be held in the recreation center, how often the parking lot will be resurfaced, and so forth. If the complex is organized as a common interest community, the common or shared facilities will be managed by the HOA or the governing board elected by the HOA. The HOA or the board will decide, typically by majority rule, what hours the swimming pool is open, whether free aerobics classes will be held, and how often the parking lot will be resurfaced.

The distinction between dictatorship and democracy must be qualified, however, because there are other important constraints that operate in both contexts. The landlord is constrained by the terms of the leases entered into with individual tenants and by legal duties such as the IWH. If the landlord agrees in the leases to keep the swimming pool open until midnight and to provide free aerobics classes, then the landlord will be contractually bound by these commitments. And the landlord cannot allow the property to descend into unsafe and unsanitary conditions without running the risk of liability under the IWH. Similarly, the CCRs in the common interest community may include promises that run with the land and constrain the discretion of the homeowners' association and the board. If the CCRs include promises about the hours of the swimming pool, aerobics classes, and so forth, then the HOA and the board will be bound by these promises.

Also, both the dictatorial landlord and the majoritarian HOA will be constrained by market forces. If the landlord refuses to resurface the parking lot, and huge potholes develop, tenants may decline to renew their leases and the landlord may have trouble attracting new tenants. Similarly, if the board in a common interest community refuses to raise assessments to pay for resurfacing the parking lot, unit owners may suffer damage to their cars and the market value of their units may decline. Once a majority of the unit owners decides the board has been too stingy about the parking lot, this will predictably lead to a change in policy by the HOA or the election of new board. In short, the persons who occupy individual units in a leased complex have exit options, and the persons who occupy individual units in a common interest community have voice options.[15] The explicit or implicit threat of exercising these options constrains whoever is exercising managerial authority over the common or shared assets.[16]

---

15. *See generally* ALBERT O. HIRSCHMAN, EXIT, VOICE, AND LOYALTY: RESPONSES TO DECLINE IN FIRMS, ORGANIZATIONS, AND STATES (1970).

16. Exit from polities is often more inconvenient, and sometimes nearly impossible as in the case of actual dictatorships.

The percentage of residential property in common interest communities has increased steadily in recent decades, to the point where in many states today, more than one-half of new residential construction is organized in this fashion. What accounts for the surging popularity of this mode of dividing managerial authority over residential housing? The most general explanation is that people increasingly want the advantages of a division of managerial authority. Whether it be common facilities such as swimming pools or golf courses, or the economies of scale involved in sharing expenses for exterior maintenance, landscaping, and security services, the division of functions made possible through the use of a common interest community provides many benefits that plain ownership does not. Given that such a division of authority can also be achieved by leasing, however, this leaves a further puzzle: Why hasn't the demand for a division of authority between common and separate functions been satisfied by leasing individual units in a rental complex? Why do we have common interest communities at all, given the leasing option?[17]

One possible explanation is tax law. The tenants in a leased residential complex cannot themselves deduct any portion of their rental payments against their income. In contrast, in a common interest community the owners of the individual units are allowed to deduct against income mortgage interest expense and the portion of their monthly assessments that reflects property taxes (subject to certain limits). Many real estate professionals believe that a significant part of the demand for housing in common interest communities is driven by these perceived tax advantages.

The matter is more complicated, however. Investors in rental properties can deduct mortgage interest payments and property taxes, and can also deduct other expenses, such as depreciation, that ordinary homeowners cannot. To the extent that the market

---

17. *See* Henry Hansmann, *Condominium and Cooperative Housing: Transactional Efficiency, Tax Subsidies, and Tenure Choice*, 20 J. LEGAL STUD. 25 (1991).

for residential rental property is competitive, these tax deductions should be reflected in lower monthly rental payments, offsetting or perhaps exceeding the tax benefits from owning an individual unit.[18] Furthermore, the use of common interest communities has spread to contexts such as gated communities of freestanding houses, where the use of the common interest community provides no tax advantage, because the individual units would almost certainly be owned rather than leased whether or not there is a common interest community. So in this context at least, taxes cannot explain the popularity of the common interest device.

Another explanation might be that people prefer to live in a self-governed community rather than in a community run by a dictator-landlord. It is undoubtedly true that some people are attracted by attending meetings of HOAs and serving on governing boards. But there is also significant anecdotal evidence that many people find these duties tiresome and are irritated by the often petty politics associated with disputes over assessment levels and pet policies.[19] Given the difficulties of managing property by majority rule, the "transaction costs" of daily life in a common interest community are probably higher than in a rental community. Also, common interest communities can impose significant restraints on the ability of unit owners to exit, insofar as board approval is required for transfers of units (this is especially common with cooperative apartments). Thus, it is doubtful that governance advantages can account for the growing popularity of common interest communities, except perhaps for a subset of persons who find participatory governance structures a positive attraction.

---

18. As covered in courses on tax law, there is an additional advantage to owner-occupancy. A tenant must pay rent to the landlord out of after-tax income, whereas an owner enjoys the benefits of occupancy without have to pay tax on this "imputed income." This may be the most important tax benefit of owner-occupancy.

19. *See* Nahrstedt v. Lakeside Vill. Condo. Ass'n, Inc., 878 P.2d 1275 (Cal. 1994) (recounting a major squabble over three cats).

A third explanation, which is consistent with the general theme of this chapter, is that, at least in the residential context, people increasingly find that common interest communities provide a better dividing line in the allocation of managerial authority between the common and separate facilities. We can call this the "designer kitchen" phenomenon. If the individual units in a residential complex are leased, then the tenants have general managerial authority over their individual units. They can decide what kind of furniture will be put in the unit, what the window treatments will look like, and of course they will have authority over who can enter the unit as a guest, whether the TV or the stereo is on at what hours, and so forth. But if the unit holders want to undertake a more dramatic change in the interior space, such as installing a designer kitchen, leasing presents problems. The landlord will be reluctant to pay for a designer kitchen, if the landlord has doubts about whether future tenants will be willing to pay higher rents to defray the costs of this improvement. The tenant will be reluctant to pay for the kitchen (assuming the landlord consents to this), because the improvements would be fixtures that would belong to the landlord when the lease terminates. So an individual who craves a designer kitchen will have difficulty getting one in a leased unit. (In many commercial tenancies, leases last much longer and each tenant is expected to remodel interior space according to its needs.)

In contrast, if the complex is organized as a common interest community, the designer kitchen presents few problems. The interior space is understood to be owned by the unit holder in fee simple. Thus, if the unit holder wants a designer kitchen, and is willing to pay for it, the unit holder can have the designer kitchen. The effect of the designer kitchen on the future value of the unit, for better or worse, will be borne entirely by the unit owner, not the other owners with interests in the complex. The point of course is not limited to designer kitchens, but applies also to remodeled bathrooms, tearing down or moving walls, combining two units into one, and so forth.

As society grows wealthier, and more people become interested in personalizing the space in which they spend their daily lives, more people will be interested in a property arrangement in which they have unilateral control over the design of their personal living space. If people also want the advantages of a division of managerial authority between common facilities and individual units, then common interest communities permit people to have the advantages of this division of authority, while also conferring a much stronger degree of individual control over interior spaces than is generally possible with leasing. This may be the best explanation for the growing popularity of common interest communities relative to leasing, given the weaknesses in the other explanations.

Trusts

Even more clearly than leasing and common interest communities, trusts are designed to separate management authority from other incidents of resources. Unlike leasing and common interest communities, trusts are typically not used to divide physical assets into common and separate components, with different management regimes devoted to each. Instead, trusts tend to be used for the management of assets held for investment purposes. Management of the assets is separated from the use and enjoyment of the income and capital gains generated by those assets, allowing different persons to manage and to consume the fruits of the assets. This arrangement is extremely useful. It is the principal mechanism today for managing the transmission of wealth within families. It is also widely used in the management of charitable foundations and nonprofit associations, in the organization of pension funds, and in the creation of certain kinds of investment vehicles.

The trust is one of the great inventions of English law (and the equity courts in particular), widely adopted or emulated by other legal systems. It involves three legal personas and some assets, sometimes called the trust *res* or corpus. The first persona is the settlor, who creates the trust out of assets that the settlor owns, typically in fee simple. The settlor makes a declaration, either by a deed of trust during the settlor's life (an inter vivos trust) or by will (a testamentary trust), that the assets are subject to a trust. The declaration of trust conceptually splits the assets into two components, legal and equitable. Legal title to the trust assets is given to the second persona, the trustee, who typically retains possession of the assets and is charged with their protection and management. Equitable title to the trust assets belongs to the third persona, the beneficiary, who is entitled to enjoy the benefits of the trust corpus. Thus, once the trust takes effect, the trustee becomes the manager of the assets, while the beneficiary gets the beneficial use and enjoyment of the assets.

The different personas involved in the creation of a trust can be either natural or artificial persons (e.g., corporations). Corporate trustees are especially common. Most banks have trust departments, which specialize in the management of trusts. It is also possible for one person to function as more than one persona. The settlor can also be the trustee (if the settlor is still alive), and the trustee can also be a beneficiary. The only limit traditionally recognized is that one cannot create a trust in which one is both the sole trustee and the sole beneficiary.[20] But even this restraint is breaking down in some jurisdictions.

Trust law is the one area where the system of estates and future interests discussed in Chapter 5 continues to play an important role. Legal title to the trust assets is typically held by the trustee in fee simple. Hence the trustee can manage the property largely the way any owner of a fee simple could. The trustee can sell the property, use the proceeds to acquire different property, rent

---

20. *See* RESTATEMENT OF THE LAW THIRD, TRUSTS § 3, cmt. d (2003) ("The settler or the trustee, or both, may be beneficiaries; but a sole trustee may not be the sole beneficiary.")

the property, use the property as collateral for a loan, and so forth. With respect to the equitable title of the beneficiaries, however, title is often divided. For example, there may be a surviving spouse, one or more children with spouses, and one or more grandchildren. Lawyers naturally looked to the system of estates in land to describe the different equitable interests of the different beneficiaries. Hence, beneficiaries will have equitable estates for life, equitable vested or contingent remainders, and occasionally equitable executory interests. Lawyers who practice trust law, at least in the context of family wealth transmission, need to be fluent in manipulating the categories of estates in land and future interests.

As in the case of leasing and common interest communities, contracts play a large role in the formation and implementation of trusts. The identity and duties of the trustee, the identity and interests of the beneficiaries, and the nature and extent of the trust property are all matters that can be spelled out in written agreements between the settlor and the trustee. These issues largely concern only the three personas involved in the trust—the settlor, the trustee, and the beneficiary—and do not affect the world at large. Most rules of trust law are therefore default rules that can be modified by contract.[21]

The principal exception to the purely contractual nature of the trust concerns the identity of the trust property, which can affect third parties, such as individual creditors of the trustee and the beneficiaries. In particular, it is important that the creditors of the trustee not be able to reach trust assets to satisfy the individual debts of the trustee. Trustees will also want assurances that creditors of the trust will not be able to reach the individual assets of the trustee to satisfy their claims. Consequently, for the trust to function properly, the trust assets must be sequestered from the other

---

21. *See* John H. Langbein, *The Contractarian Basis of the Law of Trusts*, 105 YALE L. J. 625 (1995).

assets of the trustee.[22] Title to the assets of the trust must be registered as trust property, and the trustee *T* must indicate whether *T* is acting in *T*'s capacity as trustee when *T* undertakes actions such as buying and selling securities for the trust. Also, owners of beneficial interests receive a degree of protection against transfers to third parties with notice of the trust.

Many trusts in the United States also have *spendthrift clauses*, meaning that creditors of the beneficiaries cannot reach the trust assets before they are distributed to the beneficiary. These clauses provide an additional reason why trust assets have to be sequestered and separately marked off from other assets of the trustee and the beneficiaries.

Much of trust law consists of an elaboration of what are called the fiduciary duties of trustees. These can be broadly subdivided into duties of loyalty, duties of impartiality, and duties of prudence. Duties of loyalty preclude trustees from self-dealing or engaging in transactions that create a conflict of interest with their obligations to the settlor and the beneficiaries. Duties of impartiality require that trustees act fairly toward all beneficiaries, not favoring one class of beneficiaries at the expense of others. Duties of prudence require that the trustee invest and manage the trust assets in a fashion that entails an appropriate degree of risk, given the circumstances of the beneficiaries and the nature of the trust property.

One interesting issue that arises in trust administration concerns the problem of changed circumstances not anticipated by the settlor. This is particularly an issue in the creation of charitable trusts, which can last for a very long time. Suppose, for example, the settlor leaves money in trust to create a foundation for the support of polio victims. Some years after the settlor dies, Dr. Jonas Salk develops the polio vaccine, with the result that over time there are

---

22. *See* Henry Hansmann & Urgo Mattei, *The Functions of Trust Law: A Comparative Legal and Economic Analysis*, 73 N.Y.U. L. REV. 434 (1998).

progressively fewer victims of the disease who need support. Must the trustee continue to use the trust funds for the support of diminishing numbers of polio victims, or can the trustee seek to have the trust modified to devote the funds to some other purpose? This question is governed by the *cy pres* doctrine ("cy pres" is Norman French for "so close" or "as close"), which permits courts in some circumstances to revise trusts in light of changed circumstances. American courts, reacting to abuses of cy pres doctrine by English courts, initially applied a very restrictive version of the doctrine. They required that the specific charitable purpose be impossible or illegal, and that the instrument of trust reflect a "general charitable intent" in addition to the specific purpose. More recently, courts have become more willing to invoke the doctrine, with the *Restatement of the Law Third, Trusts* going so far as to say that cy pres should be available when carrying out the original trust would be "wasteful."[23]

Further Reading

Richard Craswell, *Passing on the Costs of Legal Rules: Efficiency and Distribution in Buyer-Seller Relationships*, 43 STAN. L. REV. 361 (1991) (explaining the complexities in determining whether mandatory quality rules like the IWH benefit consumers).

Robert C. Ellickson, *Cities and Homeowners Associations*, 130 U. PA. L. REV. 1519 (1982) (advancing the model of common interest communities as private governments).

Henry Hansmann & Renier Kraakman, *The Essential Role of Organizational Law*, 110 YALE L.J. 387 (2000) (providing a general theory of organizational law based on partitioning assets).

---

23. 2 RESTATEMENT OF THE LAW THIRD, TRUSTS § 67 (2003).

Mary Ann Glendon, *The Transformation of American Landlord-Tenant Law*, 23 B.C. L. REV. 503 (1982) (describing the evolution of the contractual model in lease law).

Thomas W. Merrill & Henry E. Smith, *The Property/Contract Interface*, 101 COLUM. L. REV. 773 (2001) (developing a model explaining the mixture of contract and property elements in leasing and trust law).

SEVEN

Land Transactions and Title Records

WHENEVER AN OWNER CONCLUDES that someone else would make better use of some or all of the owner's property, a transfer is likely to occur. Alienation—by gift, sale, will, or intestacy—is one of the normal incidents of ownership, and is critical to the overall functioning of a system of property rights because it allows assets to be reallocated until they end up in the hands of the person who can obtain the highest value from their use. Even some of the lesser interests such as bailments and leases are created by some kind of transfer. In this chapter, we mainly focus on sales—transfers of property for valuable consideration—but will make sideways glances at gifts and inheritance. After considering some aspects of the contractual process as it relates to property, we will consider ownership records, which generally facilitate transfers but cause certain complications in particular settings. The focus throughout will be on land, in part because the transfer process for land involves high stakes and has the most elaborate systems of transfer and record-keeping. In part, this is because land is used to ground other related transactions, especially by serving as security for mortgages. We end the chapter with a look at security interests and mortgages in particular.

Land Sale Contracts

Property and contract come together when property interests are transferred for consideration, usually for some combination of cash and debt. In the case of personal property, issues of the timing and quality of performance are handled under contract law, and the Uniform Commercial Code (UCC) in particular. Land sales differ from sales of personal property in many ways, not least in the length of time over which they stretch. Putting aside efforts related to searching for prospective buyers and sellers, which can entail entering into contracts with real estate brokers, a land sale has three phases. The process begins with the land sale contract and ends with the closing, when a deed passes from the seller to the buyer. The period in between, the executory period, can last for several months, and has a number of features unique to land transactions.

A land sale contract, to be enforceable under the Statute of Frauds, must be in writing and signed by the party against which enforcement is sought. The writing need not be terribly formal, but must identify the parties and the land, express an intent to convey it, and state the price. Because land is considered unique, land sale contracts are enforceable by the equitable remedy of specific performance. This is an order directing the party found to be in breach of the contract to carry out that party's promises under the contract. Usually it is purchasers who seek specific performance, requiring sellers to go forward with the promised transfer of the property. Given its uniqueness, the buyer may not have any good substitute for the land subject to the contract. So an award of expectation damages will not provide the buyer complete relief. But even sellers, who are expecting only money out of the deal, can enforce a sale on a buyer with cold feet, as long as the requisites for enforcement are met. The availability of specific performance on both sides of the transaction provides more than symmetry (which may appeal to the sense of fairness at the heart of equity); it also may reflect the fact that land's uniqueness means that being unable to rid oneself of unwanted land is difficult to measure in damages. Courts can avoid the thorny question of what damages would make a disappointed seller indifferent to retaining the land by simply enforcing the deal and having the sale go through.

Land sale contracts usually contain a number of express and implied promises. One of the most important is the seller's promise to provide marketable title. (This is a default rule; sellers can contract around this by promising only insurable title.) "Marketable title" is a term of art around which a great deal of precedent has built up. The concept refers to certain risks that the buyer (most likely, the buyer's attorney) discovers during the executory period before the closing. Basically a title is unmarketable if the buyer finds an undisclosed defect or cloud on the title during this period that presents a likelihood of litigation. A buyer is not required to "purchase a lawsuit." So, for example, a disclosed easement would not be a defect. The disclosed easement is presumably already reflected in the agreed upon price. But an undisclosed easement, which would not be reflected in the price, would be a defect that presents a likelihood of litigation. Any substantial risk that the seller does not have title (which risk has not been removed during the executory period by the seller) makes title unmarketable. But a potential claim that would be barred by the statute of limitations would not render title unmarketable. Slight defects of title can be remedied (again, equitably) through a reduction in the purchase price, thus avoiding the more drastic result of undoing the entire deal. At closing, all the promises, such as the warranty of marketable title, must be fulfilled, and the land will be transferred with a deed and consideration changing hands.

The land sale contract governs the relationship between the seller and the buyer during the executory period, which runs from the signing of the contract to the closing. During this period, the state of the title is in a curious intermediate state: The seller is treated as having a personal property interest in the land and the buyer as having a real property interest. This is called *equitable conversion* because the seller is still the legal owner (as reflected in the land records) but is treated as the equitable owner of a personal property interest—the right to receive the proceeds of the sale. Conversely, the buyer is the equitable owner of a real property interest in the land and is the legal owner of the cash or the anticipated proceeds of the loan that will be used to purchase the land. In the executory period, both parties have an insurable interest in the property, but the default rules as to who gets insurance proceeds in the event the property is destroyed or damaged vary greatly by jurisdiction. In many jurisdictions risk of loss tracks the equitable real interest, and thus the buyer would be the recipient of any insurance proceeds. Wise parties will allocate these risks explicitly in the land sale contract, especially if they prefer a different allocation of insurance payments and proceeds than the law provides.

Another important consequence of equitable conversion is what happens if either the buyer or seller dies between the contract and the closing. If the seller dies in the executory period with a will leaving personal property to relative *A* and real property to relative *B*, relative *A* will receive the equitable interest in the sale and eventually the proceeds at the closing. (In our example, *B* may receive the legal title but be obligated to turn the proceeds over to *A*.) For purposes such as insurance and inheritance, equitable conversion matters greatly to certain classes of third parties. Although parties are free to override some of the effects of equitable conversion by allocating insurance payments and proceeds or by writing a specific will, they are not free to alter the basic ground rules for what counts as equitable personal and real property in the executory period. The number of options are limited, and their effects are kept simple in a fashion reminiscent of the *numerus clausus* (see Chapter 5), with enough flexibility so as to avoid frustrating many of the ends that informed parties would want to pursue.

After the closing, the land sale contract becomes largely irrelevant; it is said to "merge" with the deed so that only those undertakings expressed in the deed bind the seller. Although there are exceptions to this doctrine of merger, sellers are mostly off the hook at this point unless the deed contains future warranties. Deeds are of three main types. A deed that does not warrant title, but passes only whatever interest the seller had, is called a *quitclaim deed*. If the seller warrants title, the seller can either warrant title against all defects, making it a *general warranty deed*. Or the seller can take responsibility only for defects arising during the seller's period of ownership, which is called a *special warranty deed.*

Warranties of title typically vary in terms of when they give rise to liability and who can invoke them. Sellers giving warranty deeds may include any of six covenants in their deeds, which fall into two classes, present covenants and future covenants. Present covenants include the covenant of seisin, which provides a warranty of title in the grantor; the covenant of right to convey, which warrants the authority of the grantor to alienate; and the warranty against encumbrances, which, like the implied promise of marketable title in the executory period, warrants against undisclosed easements, clouds on the title, and so forth. If there is a violation of any of these present covenants, it occurs at the moment of the closing. By contrast, future covenants can be violated at the closing or any time thereafter. They are the covenant of warranty, which commits the seller to defend the title against lawful claims against it; the covenant of quiet enjoyment, which warrants that no one with superior title will challenge the buyer; and the covenant of further assurances, which obligates the seller to defend the buyer's title in litigation and execute needed documents to remedy any defects in title documents. There is no violation of these covenants until a problem arises and the seller fails to perform on the covenant.

The immediate buyer may enforce any of these covenants at the time they are breached (within the statute of limitations). The present covenants may be enforced as of closing and the future covenants when and if the seller fails to act as required by the relevant covenant. In all states, the future covenants run to remote purchasers—as where *A* sells to *B*, and *B* sells to *C*, and *C* wishes to enforce against *A*. In this respect, these contractual promises take on a property-like aspect, analogous to the covenants running with the land we will consider in Chapter 8. Some states allow present covenants to run to remote grantees, but because they are violated, if at all, at the closing (here the *A*-to-*B* transfer), the statute of limitations starts running then. So if *A* sells to *B* at Time 1 with a warranty deed, and *B* sells to *C* at Time 2, *C* could sue *A* for a violation of a present covenant within the statute of limitations from Time 1 or on a future covenant if the suit is filed within the statutory period after the alleged violation.

There has been some trend toward leaving the seller on the hook after the closing. Under the common law, sellers were not permitted to make fraudulent representations, but otherwise the doctrine of caveat emptor (buyer beware) prevailed. In particular, sellers did not warrant that the land or buildings were free from defects or were fit for any particular purpose. Some states have changed the common law rule to require sellers of residential real estate to disclose material latent defects, that is, those that a reasonable inspection would not disclose. In a sense, this post-closing liability creates a more lasting in personam relationship between sellers and buyers. The tendency is to hold sellers of new homes to a higher standard than other sellers, with many courts consciously adopting a products liability theory that would allow even subsequent purchasers to sue the builder.[1] Like the implied warranty of habitability we saw in landlord-tenant law (see Chapter 6), the warranty of quality in the sale of new homes is a consumer protection measure. Probably even more so than the implied warranty of habitability (IWH), it is aimed at asymmetric information in the contracting process, because in most (but not all) jurisdictions, it can be disclaimed by the seller or waived by the purchaser. Consistent with the notice-giving rationale, such disclaimer or waiver has to be specific and explicit.

Deeds in general have a notice-giving effect. Much of this effect is achieved by recording, to which we turn shortly, but the requirements for a valid deed and a conveyance have also been shaped by the problem of notice. As noted above, the Statute of Frauds requires a description of the land sufficient to identify it. Such descriptions are of two main types. In the eastern United States and in formerly independent Texas, land descriptions use

---

1. *See, e.g.*, Schipper v. Levitt & Sons, Inc., 207 A.2d 314 (N.J. 1965).

the "metes and bounds" system under which parcels are identified by geographical features or landmarks (for example, stones, and less reliably, trees), lengths and directions, in a description of a trip around the boundary of the parcel (as in "start at the big stone by Lake Lemon and then proceed North 25 Degrees East for 150 rods . . ."). In the rest of the country, a rectangular survey system, which originated with the Land Ordinance of 1785, provides the parameters for identification of interests in land.[2] This system features six-mile square townships oriented with respect to principal base lines and principal meridians (for example, "the Northwest quarter of the Southwest quarter of Section 29, Township 3 South, Range 4 West, ____ Base and Meridian"). Each township is further divided into 36 one-mile square sections (640 acres) that can be further divided. (Corrections are needed at regular intervals to account for the roughly spherical shape of the Earth.) Two main advantages of the Public Land Survey System are the regular rectangular shape of plots and the ability to locate them from standard starting points. With GPS systems rapidly making their way into surveying, the advantage of the rectangular survey in terms of locating and describing boundaries is probably less than it used to be, but surveying still benefits from regularly shaped, especially rectangular, parcels that come neatly together across much of the country.

Surveys and land descriptions are but a part of the information of which purchasers and others need notice. The conveyancing process itself is also designed to furnish some notice. In feudal times the transfer of a freehold interest had to be accompanied by "livery of seisin," which could take the form of a transfer of a clod of earth, a twig, or a set of keys. These days a conveyance by deed must include delivery of the deed. Delivery provides some assurance that the transfer has occurred, which is of great importance to anyone

2. Much of the country west of the Appalachians is covered by this public survey, with exceptions—including, interestingly, the Virginia Military District in southern and central Ohio, which was granted to Revolutionary War veterans from Virginia as compensation for their service.

who wants to know who the current owner is. So when *A* grants to *B*, *A* must transfer a deed to *B*'s control. Borderline cases become interesting, as where *A* puts a deed in a place where *B* will find it after *A*'s death, as a substitute for a will devising the land to *B*. If the location is under *B*'s control, and *A* cannot easily get the deed back, it is probably a delivery. Conditional deliveries can receive very different treatment in different jurisdictions because two policies come into conflict. As we saw with gifts causa mortis (see Chapter 4), courts do not look with favor on parties' attempts to evade the formal requirements for wills, which give an assurance of the testator's intent and a lack of coercion, and so on. However, it is well known that probate is cumbersome, and the well-advised can avoid it by using trusts. So *A*'s delivery of a deed to a trusted person with conditional instructions for delivery (e.g., after the grantor's death) might be regarded as a "poor man's trust," and if so, giving effect to the deed makes sense.

Title Records

The most elaborate notice-giving devices of modern times are the systems of title records. The most widespread title records are for property in land. Because land is fixed in location, valuable, and used for secured lending, it has lent itself to systematic record keeping, in America since Colonial times. Some types of personal property such as cars, boats, airplanes, lost artwork, and some intellectual property also have registries. But most personal property is not registered except in connection with its use as collateral for security interests (see below).

Land records in the United States are highly decentralized. Although the rectangular survey is national, and titles to much private land trace back to a grant from the federal government, title records are typically kept at the county level. Most land in the United States is covered by recording systems or *recordation*, in which records relating to title (deeds, mortgages, etc.) are filed in an office, and indexed by grantor and grantee. (A few jurisdictions also have tract indexes in which all the documents relating to a given parcel are referenced.) The other major type of system is *registration*, in which land records are typically arranged by parcel, and the land office inspects each document to be filed and guarantees the validity of titles. The Torrens system and the systems of many civil law countries exemplify registration, which has a higher start-up cost and requires better trained personnel (the more so the more definitive the title documents are meant to be).

Registration provides a more definitive answer to ownership questions than does recordation. Registration avoids more errors, and those errors that do occur are insured through registrar liability with compensation funded through registration fees. In recording systems, this insurance function is provided by private companies, which typically maintain their own version of the title records (called "title plants"). Title insurance provides a level of assurance that probably is sufficiently effective to make a shift from recordation to title registration not worthwhile once a system of recordation is established. However, countries setting up land records for the first time, as in former communist countries, tend to opt for registration, whether out of its advantages in terms of accuracy or its association with civil law, especially of the German type.

In a recording system, there is no certification of title by public authorities. The only function of the public records office is as a repository of records, organized by indexes. It is the responsibility of prospective buyers and lenders (and their attorneys) to examine these records and figure out for themselves whether the seller is offering a sufficiently good title. The central concepts in conducting these examinations are the title search and the chain of title. A title search involves going backward in the *grantee* index to find the links in the chain of title (for example, *C* received from *B* who received from *A*). This is less than half the story, however. The real worry is that any one of the people in the sequence might have done something untoward such as convey the same land twice. So one must go back down the *grantor* index to find out what these people have done. The most thorough conceivable search would involve figuring out what each person in the chain of title might have done at any time. This would be costly and largely pointless. Instead, buyers are only responsible for knowing what each link in the chain did from the time that link *received a deed* until the time the next person *recorded*. Why is that? Because in certain circumstances, persons who fail to record may lose their interest in the property to persons who acquire interests later in time.

How is it possible for *C* to receive good title from *A* when *A* had already conveyed the land away to *B*? In a world of no title records, the answer would be that *C* could not. The foundational principle of property transfer is *nemo dat quod non habet* ("one cannot give what one does not have"), and as we saw in Chapter 5, a grantor is presumed to give all that the grantor has unless specified otherwise. That is, the transferee steps into the transferor's shoes except to the extent that a lesser interest is being carved out for transfer. If the shoes are already on some other transferee's feet (metaphorically speaking in all cases except for shoes), then *A* has nothing left to transfer. The effect is like first-in-time. If *A* transfers to *B* and then to *C*, there was something to transfer to *B* the first time but not to *C* the second. (If *A* purports to transfer to *B* property *A* does not have and then later acquires it, *B* can sue to force a transfer to *B* under the equitable doctrine of estoppel by deed.)

Recording acts are superimposed on the basic *nemo dat* regime. Thus, if a recording act does not apply, *nemo dat* does. The main effect of a recording act is to cause someone—typically a later transferee—to win who would otherwise lose under *nemo dat*. There are three types of recording acts. The earliest type, which is still found in North Carolina, is the *race statute*, under which the first claimant to record wins. Thus if *A* sells to *B*, and then *A* sells to *C*, but *C* records before *B*, *C* has better title than *B*. (If *B* had recorded immediately, the recording act would not change the result from *nemo dat*, that *B* beats *C*.) What can *B* do? *B* can sue *A*, if *A* can be found and is not judgment-proof.

Courts were none too pleased when people in the situation of *C*, the later transferee, took the deed knowing of the earlier conveyance. For *C* to win under such circumstances seemed unfair, and there could be many reasons why losing the property might seem a disproportionate punishment for *B*'s lack of timely recording. So courts began to make exceptions, which culminated in *notice statutes* under which *nemo dat* is only overridden in favor of subsequent good faith purchasers for value (GFPVs). A purchaser for value is someone who gives consideration for the property. Thus, a person taking by gift or inheritance would not be able to take advantage of the statute. Someone is in good faith if they have no notice, actual or constructive, of a prior inconsistent interest. Thus in our example, if *C* pays consideration and has no notice of the prior *A*-to-*B* transaction, then *C* will win. If *C* had actual notice of the deed to *B*, even if it is unrecorded, *C* cannot benefit from the statute. More importantly, a properly recorded deed furnishes *constructive* notice of *B*'s interest, thereby preventing *C* from being a GFPV. (Constructive notice can be record notice as here, or inquiry notice, i.e., knowledge of a fact that would put a reasonable person upon an inquiry that would result in actual notice. For example, seeing a ditch with running water on the land would put someone on inquiry notice to find out about an easement for the ditch.) As in the case of the race statute, *B* can protect *B*'s interests by recording as quickly as possible, which will prevent *C* from winning under the notice statute, because the recording provides constructive notice.

Some states, especially those of the mid-Atlantic and the old Northwest, have adopted *race-notice* statutes, under which a GFPV must win both the race to record and be without notice of the earlier transaction. Thus in our example, if *A* sells to *B*, and then *A* sells to *C*, who has no notice, and after that *B* records before *C*, *nemo dat* would still apply in favor of *B*. Why? Because although *C* would win under the "notice" prong of the test, *C* fails to win under the "race" prong because *B* recorded first. Of course as always, *C* can sue *A*, if that is feasible. Again, a transferee's best bet, besides doing a title search, is to record as soon as possible. That way, the deed will be in subsequent purchasers' chain of title and will furnish record notice to them.

The purpose of the recording acts in limiting the rights of owners vis-à-vis GFPVs is ultimately to make property more alienable. Prospective purchasers, who will be the new true owners, will be discouraged if they cannot be assured at reasonable cost that their grantor's title is good. In general it is advantageous to owners that prospective purchasers have such assurance.

The recording acts also make a major exception to promote the alienability of property by someone who has won under the act. Consider the situation under a notice statute, in which *A* sells to *B*, and then *B* sells to *C*, who was without notice, and then *D* purchases from *C* knowing of the *A*-to-*B* transaction. Should *D* beat *B*? Taken literally, because *D* had notice of the *A*-to-*B* transaction, *D* is not a GFPV and so would not prevail under the act against *B*. But *D*'s grantor, *C*, who did not have notice, *would* beat *B*. The idea of the so-called *shelter rule* is that *D* should be able to shelter under *C*'s rights: Once *C* wins under the recording act, *C* can then transfer these rights to anyone without the transferee losing the protection of the act. So *D* wins against *B* by virtue of *C*'s rights. The shelter rule protects *D* by letting *D* step into *C*'s shoes. Otherwise *C* would have a hard time finding a buyer. (There is one exception to the shelter rule: If *C* transfers to *A*, the original grantor, then *A* cannot take advantage of the shelter rule, because a *C*-to-*A* transfer carries with it a danger of collusion. And discouraging someone like *C* from selling to someone like *A* does not diminish *C*'s potential market much).

In thinking about the chain of title, it is worthwhile to take the perspective of one searching the title records. Although it is true that adverse possession and some liens may not appear on the land records, the chain of title is meant to limit the search that grantees are responsible for. Consistent with this purpose, a deed needs to be not only recorded but also linked up with the rest of the chain of title. Consider the situation in which *A* sells to *B* who does not record, *B* then sells to *C* who records, and then *A* sells to *D*.

What happens under any of the types of statutes (assuming there is no tract index)? If *D* uses the grantee index to work backwards, *D* will find *A*, but working forward in the grantor index, *D* has no way to find *C*, because the intermediate link through *B* is absent. As far as the records are concerned, *B* is a "stranger to the title." Again, *D* is not required to search the entire land records, which would be prohibitively expensive. Instead *C* is not counted as having recorded until *C*s deed is linked up to *A*'s through a recorded chain. Otherwise *C*s deed is termed a *wild deed*, and does not count as recorded vis-à-vis *D*. (Relativity applies, though, meaning that *C*s deed is recorded for purposes of anyone claiming under *C* such as *C*s successors in interest.) Again, the goal of the recordation system is to furnish cost-effective notice, even though, as we will see, problems do remain.

For personal property the exception to *nemo dat* in favor of GFPVs generally comes in through the Uniform Commercial Code (UCC) as enacted in all the states except Louisiana (which is a civil law jurisdiction). For example, if an owner entrusts a chattel to someone who deals in goods of that kind—for example, leaving a watch at a watch shop in a bailment for repair—a person purchasing the watch from the shop in the ordinary course of business will obtain good title even as against the original bailor-owner.[3] This is probably a situation where the owner clearly can do more to avoid the problem than the subsequent good faith purchaser—the owner picked the bailee. But in many scenarios, deciding between innocent owners and GFPVs is very difficult in terms of comparative fault. By and large, U.S. law (of the various states) favors original owners more than does civil law or even English law, which tend to be relatively more solicitous of good faith purchasers. In U.S. jurisdictions, someone, even a GFPV, purchasing from a thief will lose to the original owner, unless enough

3. UCC § 2-403(2)–(3).

time has passed, and the other requirements for adverse possession have been met.

Otherwise the UCC provides for limited circumstances in which a good faith purchaser for value can acquire title when the transferor has what is called "voidable title."[4] Suppose *S* sells a watch to *P*, who in turn sells to *G*. If *P* obtained the watch from *S* by fraud or using a check that bounces, *P* has a title that is voidable, because *S* can bring an action to have the transaction undone. (By contrast, "void" title is invalid for all purposes, without any need for one side to act to set it aside.) Under these circumstances, if *P* sells to *G* before *S* finds out about the defect in the *S*-to-*P* transaction, and *G* purchases from *P* in good faith (without notice of the problem) and for consideration, *G* obtains good title even against *S*.[5] Of course, *S* can go after *P*, if possible. *G* must qualify as a GFPV in order to win; otherwise *S* beats *G*. Thus, if *G* had notice of the bad check, or if *G* did not pay consideration, *G* would not keep the watch. Sometimes a very low price in the subsequent (here, *P*-to-*G*) transaction can be evidence of bad faith on *G*'s part. In these voidable title situations of fraud and the like, it is harder to say in general who is more at fault: *G* and *S* are both innocent parties, but *P* (who is truly at fault) is typically not available, so one of them must bear the loss. Conceivably the loss could be split between the two, but this option is almost never used. Rather than try to allocate the loss based on fault or even a fifty-fifty split, the property-like all-or-nothing approach is used instead. Here clarity and predictability are usually at a premium.

Whether transactors qualify as GFPVs is largely governed by statutes such as the recording acts or the UCC. Occasionally, equitable principles fill in interstices left by these fairly

---

4. UCC § 2-403(1).

5. *See* Kotis v. Nowlin Jewelry, Inc., 844 S.W.2d 920 (Tex. Ct. App. 1992) (illustrating the operation of the UCC and upholding determination that *G*, to use our symbols, did not purchase from *P* in good faith).

comprehensive systems. Courts sometimes hold the original owner responsible for negligence for succumbing to a fraud, as where a fraudster tricks the owner into signing documents that turn out to be a deed.[6] Some courts will allow a subsequent GFPV to prove that the original owner was negligent so as to estop the owner from denying the GFPV's title. If the owner's negligence led to justified reliance on the part of the GFPV, they hold that it would be unfair for the original owner to prevail against the GFPV. In economic terms, the original owner in such situations was the cheapest cost avoider—as determined on a relatively individualized basis. The application of estoppel here operates as a more fine-grained balancing of relative fault between the original owner and the GFPV and allows the GFPV to win even though the deed was a void one. This ex post approach is reminiscent of the equitable exceptions that courts first made to the original race-type recording acts. What the division of labor should be between hard-and-fast rules with ex ante clarity and ex post standards couched in terms of individualized justice runs throughout property law and beyond.

Not everything relevant to title is reflected in the land records. Some types of liens, such as "mechanic's liens" for tradespeople who have worked on a building, and tax liens, might qualify the title without having to be recorded. And problems such as the incapacity of the grantor might invalidate the title, without any sign on the face of the records.

Adverse possession, which we encountered in Chapter 2, can also affect title without appearing in the record chain of title. If *A* acquires title by adverse possession against *O* and does not record, and then *O* sells the land to *P* who records, who owns the land? Even if *P* does a thorough search of the land records, *A*'s interest will not appear. Although it might seem that the policy of the recording acts should require that *P* win in such a case, nevertheless courts hold that *A* wins by adverse possession. *P* is required to protect *P*'s

6. *See, e.g.*, Hauck v. Crawford, 62 N.W.2d 92 (S.D. 1953).

interest against adverse possession by inspecting the land itself, in a form of inquiry notice. If someone with no apparent connection to the prospective grantor is occupying the land, the would-be purchaser must inquire further to find out whether the occupier has a claim based on adverse possession. If the statute of limitations has run, there can be no valid sale by the record owner. If the statute has not yet run, the record owner must remove the adverse possessor to provide marketable title: Remember that no one is expected to purchase a lawsuit. (Similar considerations of inquiry notice apply to easements by prescription, which we will take up in Chapter 8.)

Adverse possession also occurs in boundary disputes, which can cause special headaches for purchasers. Suppose *A* fences in a strip of *B*'s land and meets all the requirements for adverse possession (open and notorious, adverse, etc.) for the requisite period. Years go by, and the fence disintegrates. *B* then sells the land to *C*. As in our previous example, *C* is expected to inspect the land, but the fence is not there, so *C* has no way of knowing about the loss of the land to *A*. Nevertheless, adverse possession is robust enough that *A* still wins in such a situation, even though the idea of inquiry notice here is far-fetched.[7] The law shows great solicitude that title by adverse possession is as valid as any other title, and successful adverse possessors like other owners are not required to mark their boundaries. One possible solution would be to require adverse possessors to record their interests. But notice that the only adverse possessors likely to do so would be those in bad faith (and those who have recently discovered the adverse possession). Depending on the purpose of adverse possession, this could be quite perverse.

Another method of preventing ancient history from being relevant in title disputes and searches is to cause them to be beyond the chain of title. Marketable title acts make unenforceable those interests that have not been recorded (or re-recorded) within a given time period working back from the present, typically the last forty years. This has the effect of eliminating constructive notice of

7. Mugaas v. Smith, 206 P.2d 332 (Wash. 1949).

any inconsistent unrecorded claims more than forty years old, so the old claims are eliminated by a transfer to a GFPV. And as noted earlier, title insurance is used to cover certain risks of defects in the title. These usually do not include adverse possession, which despite the fence example above, is usually best discovered by the purchaser inspecting the land.

Whether the problems of notice and the state of title are solved with bright line rules or vague standards or some combination of the two, it is important to remember that they raise the issue of relativity of title we saw in Chapter 2. Property rights are distinctively in rem, but questions of ownership are often presented in litigation between two identified parties. Such litigation can have what amounts to an in rem effect, however. If a GFPV or an adverse possessor (AP) "beats" the record owner, the GFPV or AP has title good against the world. But note that this does not mean that the original owner has nothing: The owner's title still trumps everyone else's. By the same token, relativity of title tells us that in the situation in which owner *A* is defrauded of real or personal property by *B*, who "sells" to *C*, and estoppel or the UCC tells us that *C* beats *A*, *A* still has better title than *B*, which leaves *A* with a claim for damages against *B*. Even when quiet title actions are brought to remove known clouds on title or resolve known problems (e.g., adverse possession), these actions, although in theory in rem, tend to involve identified competing claimants. Only in registration systems does a registrar give conclusive title against all claims both known and unknown. For this reason the registrar can be thought of as standing in for the (in rem) public and correspondingly, registration countries (notably but not exclusively those following the German system) tend to have a strict *numerus clausus* (Chapter 5). Registrars can pronounce on title more easily if they need not incur the information costs of figuring out how idiosyncratic interests fit into the array of interests relating to the land in question.[8]

---

8. *See* Benito Arruñada, *Property Enforcement as Organized Consent*, 19 J.L. ECON. & ORG. 401 (2003).

Mortgages

Another device closely related to land transfer and records, and in which equity has played a major role, is the mortgage, as well as security interests more generally. Mortgages on real estate are familiar examples of security interests. A security interest is a conditional property right in an asset that secures the payment of a debt. The mortgage is evidenced by a document separate from the promissory note or the debt contract. The security interest gives its holder the right to seize the asset in the event of nonpayment of the debt, as well as the right to be paid ahead of other junior creditors, which is very relevant in bankruptcy. The filing of a bankruptcy stays proceedings to seize an asset but maintains the security interest holder's seniority. Whether inside or outside bankruptcy, priority means that secured creditors are to be paid before general creditors, who are to be paid before equity holders (shareholders in a corporation, the landowner in the case of a real estate mortgage). Various secured creditors are paid in the order of their priority, which is usually first-in-time according to when their interest was perfected. Mostly perfection is effected by recording or filing, but some security interests can receive their priority through possession or other special rules. (Note that all these devices for perfection, whether it be recording, filing, or taking possession, have a notice effect.) A house worth $200,000 might be subject to a first mortgage of $100,000 and a second mortgage of $50,000. The homeowner then has equity of $50,000. (As we will see, this term derives from the "equity of redemption," which is the right of the owner to save the property by paying off the debt.) Suppose the value of the house declines to $130,000, and the owner defaults. The holder of the first mortgage is paid in full ($100,000), the holder of the second mortgage gets $30,000, and there is no equity. If the loan is a recourse loan, the second mortgage holder might be able to get a deficiency judgment against the borrower for $20,000. If the loan is nonrecourse, the borrower is not personally liable.

Why would a lender and borrower agree on a security interest? The borrower can get a lower interest rate if the debt is secured, because the lender runs less risk of not getting its money back. Of course the interest rate on other debt incurred by the borrower should adjust upward, because the borrower will have fewer assets available to satisfy other debts. Sophisticated lenders dealing with borrowers will ask to inspect the borrower's books and put covenants against pledging borrower assets into their loan agreements. But in the case of tort creditors and other small creditors, no upward adjustment in rates may happen. Some have theorized that secured debt is thus problematic, because it harms tort creditors and other nonadjusting creditors, but there is scant empirical evidence that this is a major problem.[9] (To some extent, the problem is handled by mandatory insurance requirements in certain industries, such as taxi cabs.) Others argue that secured debt allows for specialization in monitoring the activities of the borrower, who as an equity holder prefers risk more than is optimal overall. (As residual claimants, equity holders get all the upside after fixed claims are paid but suffer no losses beyond their investment.) Where security interests fit into the overall picture of financing both descriptively and normatively is still an active area of inquiry.

We saw in Chapter 4 how security interests in personal property are governed by the UCC and leave a large scope to self-help by the holder of the security interest in the event of nonpayment. Mortgagees (the holders of real estate security interests) are not allowed to use self-help against defaulting mortgagors (borrowers giving mortgages). Instead they must go through an elaborate process of foreclosing on the mortgage. Traditionally, in a strict foreclosure the lender-mortgagee would go into equity court to set a time limit on the mortgagor's exercise of the equity of redemption, thereafter "foreclosing" that possibility forever and leaving the

---

9. Yair Listokin, *Is Secured Debt Used to Redistribute Value from Tort Claimants in Bankruptcy? An Empirical Analysis*, 57 DUKE L.J. 1037 (2008).

property with the mortgagee. In almost all states the strict foreclosure has been replaced with judicial foreclosure, in which the mortgagee files an action seeking a foreclosure sale. These days the procedures for judicial foreclosures and foreclosure sales are governed by statute. At any time during the process, the debtor has the right to pay the debt and keep the property. States vary also in whether the lender-mortgagee can seek a deficiency judgment where the proceeds from the foreclosure sale are insufficient to cover an outstanding recourse debt. The foreclosure sale is not necessarily the end of the story. In roughly half the states, the borrower-mortgagor has a time period (up to two years) to exercise a statutory right of redemption by paying the price paid by the purchaser at the foreclosure sale. Over time, there has been some oscillation in terms of how much extra leniency to provide for defaulting borrower-mortgagors. Some see a tendency for legislatures to favor bright line rules, which are then muddied up by courts, whereas others have argued that the system is relatively stable except in periods of widespread financial distress during which both courts and legislatures try to rescue borrowers who are in trouble.

A judicial foreclosure sale is administered by a court, but some states allow parties to include a provision for a private foreclosure sale in the mortgage. As with judicial foreclosure sales, there is a concern that the price the property fetches in such sales will be on the low side (often the lender-mortgagee is the only bidder), and in a private foreclosure sale courts must also scrutinize the procedure adopted by the mortgagee administering the sale.[10] Often it makes sense for a defaulting borrower-mortgagor if possible to sell the property him or herself and use the proceeds to pay the lender.

The equity of redemption and the more recent statutory right of redemption act like call options held by the mortgagor, that is, the right but not the obligation to purchase the property for the outstanding debt (in the case of the equity of redemption) or the

10. *See, e.g.*, Murphy v. Fin. Dev. Corp., 495 A.2d 1245 (N.H. 1985).

foreclosure sale price (in the statutory right of redemption). Because the borrower-mortgagor retains this stick in the bundle of rights, one can expect the price a bidder would pay to be correspondingly depressed. Although this is clearly a benefit to a defaulting borrower ex post, whether this helps borrowers (or which ones at the expense of which others) ex ante depends on the adjustment in interest rates and any cross-subsidies involved. In a nonrecourse debt, the borrower-mortgagor has the opposite type of option. Because the borrower is not on the hook beyond the value of the security, the borrower in effect has a put option whose exercise price is the outstanding amount of the debt. Thus in our example above, if the property is worth only $125,000, the nonrecourse borrower has the right to force a sale (like the exercise of a put option) to the lender for the value of the loan, here $150,000.

Lenders have used other mortgage-like devices, sometimes to get around the procedural requirements of a foreclosure. A deed of trust is structured like a transfer of ownership of the land to the lender-mortgagee who holds the land in trust for the mortgagor until the debt is paid. As option theory would indicate, this is an equivalent structure to the regular mortgage lien in which the mortgagor is considered the owner. From a legal point of view, the equivalence has led courts to treat deeds of trust the same as mortgages, including providing for procedural safeguards and the right of survivorship (see the discussion of severance in Chapter 5). Another method, which was originally designed to give the lender maximum protection, is the installment sales contract, in which the lender retains ownership until all the payments (over time) are made. In the old days, the lender could retain the land even if the buyer defaulted after paying almost all the purchase price. Equity courts, not surprisingly, intervened to allow late payment or restitution of amounts paid when a forfeiture appeared unfairly excessive or unfair. (Courts often point to the maxim that "equity abhors a forfeiture.") The same equitable tradition is at work here as with the penalty doctrine in contract law, according to which liquidated damages clauses providing for damages greatly in excess of actual damages will not be enforced unless they are a reasonable ex ante forecast of damages. Given the general policy of freedom of contract, a flat ban on penalties has long been treated as a puzzle in need of explanation. Although it is true that high liquidated damages in the general contractual context can be used to deter entry into an industry (reducing competition and increasing market power), it is doubtful that installment sales contracts may be used for such purposes. Perhaps, as with the related (and again equitable) unconscionability doctrine, courts use the antiforfeiture reasoning in cases in which some other type of hard-to-prove overreaching or opportunistic behavior has infected the deal. By their nature, these considerations are difficult to tease out of appellate opinions. These days, installment sales contracts and other similar devices are often treated as mortgages, with the full redemption rights that mortgagors enjoy.

The tendency to treat other mortgage-like devices as mortgage liens, with all that that entails, can be regarded as yet another instance of the *numerus clausus* at work. Rather than let parties create new and possibly idiosyncratic variants on security interests, the law mandates a standard package of rights, duties, and procedures for this special property interest. In a particularly dramatic recent example, the Federal Communications Commission (FCC) tried to achieve the effect of a security interest by cancelling a broadband personal communications service (PCS) license for failure to pay after a spectrum auction. The U.S. Supreme Court held that under the Bankruptcy Code, the FCC could not do this without actually taking a security interest, which it had failed to do.[11]

Finally, it is worth recalling that mortgages on land go a long way toward explaining the continued importance of land to property law. Although it is true that personal property and intellectual property are increasingly important, and land is less central to advanced economies than in the formative years of the estate system, land is

11. FCC v. NextWave Pers. Commc'ns Inc., 537 U.S. 293 (2003).

a convenient security for loans, often for loans that have little to do with real estate. Think of a chip manufacturer giving a mortgage in its land and factory, or a publishing house mortgaging its headquarters. Because land is valuable, long-lasting, and stationary, it is easy to document and to lend against—two considerations that are tightly connected. Indeed in emerging economies there is a school of thought that giving informal occupiers formal title to land, which they can then use as collateral on impersonal markets, is the way to unlock the economic potential of land and the enterprises that land-based financing could foster.[12]

Further Reading

Douglas Baird & Thomas Jackson, *Information, Uncertainty, and the Transfer of Property*, 13 J. LEGAL STUD. 299 (1984) (arguing that information costs are critical in understanding property transfer and the title security system).

Quintin Johnstone, *Land Transfers: Process and Processors*, 22 VAL. U. L. REV. 493 (1988) (providing a good summary of real estate transfer issues).

Saul Levmore, *Variety and Uniformity in the Treatment of the Good-Faith Purchaser*, 16 J. LEGAL STUD. 43 (1987) (surveying different treatments of good faith purchasers in different legal systems).

ANDRO LINKLATER, MEASURING AMERICA (2002) (providing history of the rectangular survey system).

Carol M. Rose, *Crystals and Mud in Property Law*, 40 STAN. L. REV. 577 (1988) (developing thesis that recordation and mortgage law cycle between ex ante rules and ex post standards).

Robert H. Skilton, *Developments in Mortgage Law and Practice*, 17 TEMP. U. L.Q. 315 (1943) (arguing that complexities in mortgage law largely stem from legislative intervention during economic crises).

---

12. HERNANDO DE SOTO, THE MYSTERY OF CAPITAL (2000).

EIGHT

Neighbors and Neighborhood Effects

PROPERTY SOLVES A GREAT MANY PROBLEMS about the assignment of responsibility over resources and creates incentives for the management of resources that generally assure good custodial practices. Owners of houses have incentives to make sure that the roof does not leak and the plumbing functions properly. Owners of businesses have incentives to assure that shops are clean, safe, and attractive to customers. But the private-property strategy, which entails chopping up the world into small units of resources, each governed by its own owner-manager, also creates problems. The little boxes of owner-sovereignty can create bottlenecks or barriers to access for neighbors, which prevent property from being used to its highest potential. And owner-sovereigns do many things on their property that will have indirect effects on neighbors. Economists call these neighborhood effects "spillovers" or "externalities." As discussed in Chapter 3, externalities are the effects of actions taken by one property owner that impose involuntary benefits or costs on others. The qualifier "involuntary" is important: If an action by one property owner has the consent of another property owner, then the action should not be considered an externality. Our focus in this chapter is on how the law regulates these neighborhood effects or externalities, which are in a real sense created by the exclusionary strategy of property.

Neighborhood effects can be either positive or negative. Lawn care provides a simple illustration. If I am highly conscientious about tending to my lawn—keeping it neatly cut, free of weeds, and watering it to maintain a nice shade of green—then I enjoy certain benefits, whether it be pleasure at looking at my lawn, pride in seeing the effects of my labors, or an increase in the market value of my home as a result of "curb appeal." But these efforts also produce positive spillover effects for my neighbors. They too will obtain some pleasure from looking at my lawn, and the market value of their homes may increase (slightly) because they are situated near someone with a fine-looking lawn. These are "free goods" to them that I have provided without any explicit payment for my efforts.

Conversely, if I am not conscientious about tending to my lawn—if I let it go to seed, let the crab grass proliferate, and so forth—then this will produce negative spillover effects for the neighbors. They will incur some displeasure from viewing my unsightly lawn, the market value of homes in the neighborhood may decline (slightly), and there is even some evidence that unkept or poorly maintained property may encourage other types of anti-social behavior in the neighborhood (this is the "broken windows" thesis—that poorly maintained property can cause an increase in criminal activity in a neighborhood[1]). These are also free—but unwanted—"bads" created by my lack of effort.

In this chapter we explore various strategies for regulating impediments to access by neighbors and neighborhood spillovers. We will consider strategies based on tort liability, modification of property rights, contracts running with the land, and public regulation. These strategies are both substitutes and complements to each other. The question in each case is which strategy or combination of strategies makes the most sense. All things being equal, we want to encourage positive externalities and discourage negative externalities. But of course, all things are never equal. Legal mechanisms are costly, both in terms of the costs of the mechanisms

1. James Q. Wilson & George L. Kelling, *Broken Windows: The Police and Neighborhood Safety*, ATLANTIC MONTHLY, Mar. 1982, at 29, 31–32; *see also* Hope Corman & Naci Mocan, *Carrots, Sticks, and Broken Windows*, 48 J.L. & ECON. 235 (2005); *but see* BERNARD E. HARCOURT, ILLUSION OF ORDER: THE FALSE PROMISE OF BROKEN WINDOWS POLICING (2001).

themselves—legal fees, for example—and because they restrict the discretion of property owners as to how they manage or use their individual units of property. These restrictions represent opportunity costs, in the sense that property owners may no longer be able to put their property to certain uses that they may value more highly than the uses permitted by the legal mechanism. It is always necessary to weigh the gains from adopting particular legal mechanisms or combination of mechanisms, in terms of more positive and fewer negative externalities, against the costs of these mechanisms. The need to consider these tradeoffs is one of the lessons of the most famous article about neighborhood effects ever written, to which we turn next.

The Coase Theorem

The modern analysis of neighborhood effects or externalities has been strongly influenced by the work of Ronald Coase. Coase wrote a pathbreaking article in 1960 that focused on simple negative spillovers, such as a confectioner whose machinery causes vibrations that disrupt a doctor's examining room next door, or a rancher whose cattle wander onto a farmer's land and trample the crops.[2] Coase engaged in a thought experiment, in which he asked how these problems would be resolved if it were costless for the neighbors to enter into contracts with each other over the use of their respective properties. The conclusion he reached was that the neighbors would always agree on the use of the land that maximizes the joint value of their respective properties. If the law favors the more productive use, then the neighbors will agree to continue that use, because the owner of the less productive use will not be able to muster a side payment sufficient to induce the more productive user to desist or modify the more productive use. If the law

2. R. H. Coase, *The Problem of Social Cost*, 3 J.L. & ECON. 1 (1960).

favors the less productive use, then the owner of the land with the more productive use *will* be able to muster a side payment that will induce the owner of the less productive use to desist or modify that use. If contracting were costless, the neighbors would contract for modifications in their respective activities until they reached the point at which further gains would not induce additional modifications in the use of either property.

A simple numerical example illustrates the argument. Suppose there are two neighboring landowners, a factory and a laundry. The factory uses a production process that emits soot. The soot penetrates into the laundry, so that the more soot the factory emits, the more difficult it is for the laundry to produce clean clothing. Assume the problem can only be controlled by the factory installing various types of soot arrestors. The more effective the arrestor, the more expensive it is to install and operate. But the more effective the arrestor, the cleaner the clothing produced by the laundry, which increases its sales and its profits. The schedule of costs and profits looks like this:

A	*B*	*C*	*D*
Pounds of soot	*Cost to factory*	*Profit to laundry*	*Sum of B & C*
10	$0	($2000)	($2000)
8	($200)	($1300)	($1500)
6	($900)	$600	($300)
4	($1400)	$1800	$400
2	($2500)	$2700	$200
0	($4000)	$3500	($500)

Under Coase's thought experiment, it doesn't matter whether the law says the factory has a right to emit as much soot as it likes, or if it says that the laundry has a right to be free of soot, or if it prescribes some intermediate position. If contracting is costless, the parties will trade away their rights in return for side payments until they reach the outcome that maximizes their joint wellbeing. Obviously, neither of the extreme results—complete freedom to emit soot or complete prohibition on emitting soot—represents a stable solution. If the entitlement goes to the factory, the laundry will be willing to make side payments to the factory if it will install arrestors. At least for the less expensive arrestors, the laundry gains more in profits than it would cost to install arrestors. Conversely, if the entitlement goes to the laundry, the factory will be willing to pay the laundry to let the factory emit some soot. At least for the most expensive arrestors, the costs to the factory exceed the profits lost by the laundry. The proposals will go back and forth, but with zero transaction costs, the bargaining will continue until the parties settle on four pounds of soot. At this level, the joint wealth of the factory and laundry is maximized at $400, and neither party can make an offer to the other that will make both of them better off. For example, if the laundry tries to convince the factory to reduce emissions to two pounds, this will increase the laundry's profits by $900 ($2700 – $1800) but will cost the factory $1100 (by increasing its cost from $1400 to $2500). No deal. Similarly, if the factory tries to convince the laundry to let it increase emissions to six pounds, this will save the factory $500 (by reducing the cost from $1400 to $900), but the laundry will lose $1200 in profits ($1800–$600). Again, no deal.

What are the lessons to be drawn from this thought experiment? Coase did not believe that contracting is costless. To the contrary, he thought it always consumes significant resources. So, what's the point?

One point often drawn from Coase—the so-called reciprocity of causation—sits rather uneasily with property law. Coase was at great pains to point out that there would be no use conflict if either party were absent. So when there is a conflict between cattle and crops, confectioners and doctors, or factories and laundries, Coase thought it is incorrect to say that the cattle, the confectioner, or the factory causes harm to the crops, the doctor, or the laundry, respectively. Without the crops, the doctor, or the laundry there would be no conflict. The economic question is which activity is more valuable if we cannot have both, and in a zero-transaction-cost world the opportunity cost will be reflected in the size of the payment that would be offered by the one who lacks the entitlement.

Coase's agnosticism about causation does not accord with widespread moral intuitions. The owners of damaged noses do not cause punches in the sense that the owners of overactive fists do. And when we get to questions of murder and rape in criminal law, Coasean causal agnosticism is a nonstarter. With respect to property, too, causal agnosticism does not square with the structure of entitlements. When someone owns Blackacre, the exclusion strategy protects the owner against an open-ended set of invasions, ranging from intrusions by persons and large objects to interferences with use from unusual odors and sounds. When the conflict between cattle and crops, or confectioners and doctors, or factories and laundries arises, we are not writing on a blank slate. The owner has a presumptive right against such invasions. In high-transaction-cost settings, we may sometimes have to overcome these transaction costs in the interest of mutual accommodation and maximizing the value of resources—think of airplane overflights. But the basic structure of entitlements is inconsistent with Coasean causal agnosticism in important respects. Whatever the exact source and justification of our moral intuitions against force and theft, the basic structure of property entitlements sounding in exclusion makes the system easy to understand and use, among all the far-flung parties who are expected to respect owners' rights.[3] In other words, there are transaction-cost reasons—as Coase would be the first to appreciate—for *not* treating causation in resource disputes as symmetric.

Notwithstanding these reservations about the conception of property implicit in Coase's article, his emphasis on the importance of transaction costs and the possibility of exchange of rights offers

3. *See* Thomas W. Merrill & Henry E. Smith, *The Morality of Property*, 48 WM. & MARY L. REV. 1849 (2007).

valuable lessons for courts and lawyers. One lesson is that if high transaction costs make contracting impossible, then perhaps the law should mimic the result the parties would agree on if they could contract. If we assume that all parties are rational maximizers, that is, that they always want more of whatever it is they value, and if we assume that all values can be expressed in terms of money, then this suggests that the law should try to achieve the result that maximizes the joint wealth of the affected parties measured by their willingness to pay. Obviously, these are debatable assumptions. Irrationality is not uncommon. Many would strenuously insist that all values cannot be cashed out in dollars. And setting the entitlement (to emit or prevent emissions) will have distributive consequences in that having the initial entitlement will make that party better off. But the Coase theorem is widely cited by those who think that efficiency is an important value in the design of legal institutions, and the thought experiment seems to provide intuitive support for the importance of trying to achieve efficient results.

A second lesson is that lawyers should think about possible contractual solutions to externality problems when they are feasible. Litigation and regulation are not the only or even usually the best solutions to problems about access over neighboring property or regulating spillovers. Neighbors can negotiate contracts to modify their property rights by easements or can enter into contracts governing the use of land that run with the land. (Many problems are solved by more informal understandings, including norms of live and let live.) These "Coasean bargains" may provide a better solution than litigation or public regulation.

A third possible lesson is that the law should be designed so as to facilitate contractual solutions to externality problems. Here, two lines of inquiry have emerged in response to Coase. The first and less-developed line of inquiry picks up on his suggestion that the initial delimitation of rights must be clearly established to permit market transactions to transfer and recombine rights. This perhaps suggests that bright line rules will facilitate contractual exchanges of rights.[4] But this conclusion, if correct, is in considerable tension with first point above about the desirability of having the law mimic the outcome the parties would reach if transaction costs were zero, which seems to require highly discretionary entitlement rules. It may be that the law can either encourage ex ante bargains or can provide an ex post substitute for bargains, but cannot easily do both.

The second line of inquiry, which has consumed a tremendous amount of intellectual energy, asks whether entitlements should be exchanged only with the consent of the parties or should be allowed to be taken by one party on payment of a judicially determined price. This is the famous distinction introduced by Calabresi and Melamed between "property rules" and "liability rules."[5] An entitlement protected by a property rule must be purchased through a voluntary exchange of rights. An entitlement protected by a liability rule can be taken unilaterally in return for a payment of just compensation, as when the government uses its power of eminent domain to acquire property (see Chapter 9).

Commentators, including Calabresi and Melamed, initially assumed that property rules should prevail in low-transaction-cost settings where Coasean bargains are possible. Coasean bargains assure efficiency; at least the affected parties who agree to the exchange must be better off, or else they would not enter into the agreement. And requiring the consent of all the owners protects subjective values in circumstances where owners place a higher value on their property than the market does. In high-transaction-cost settings, however, it was thought to be preferable to switch to liability rules. Because the party forcing the exchange

---

4. *See* Thomas W. Merrill, *Trespass, Nuisance, and the Costs of Determining Property Rights*, 14 J. LEGAL STUD. 13 (1985).

5. Guido Calabresi & A. Douglas Melamed, *Property Rules, Liability Rules, and Inalienability: One View of the Cathedral*, 85 HARV. L. REV. 1089 (1972).

must pay just compensation, which is usually set at fair market value, the party forcing the exchange will do so only if the new use is more valuable than the present market value. Thus, compelled exchanges (liability rules) were thought to promote efficient solutions in the presence of high transaction costs—in the sense of maximizing market-measured wealth. Of course, compelled exchanges are not necessarily efficient in the broader sense that asks whether the welfare of the parties is enhanced, because such exchanges will sometimes result in a sacrifice in subjective values not captured by markets. For liability rules to begin to reflect subjective values, they need to be more complicated than simply a judicial estimate based on market prices, but perhaps because such schemes would add to administrative costs we rarely see them in practice.

The Calabresi and Melamed analysis, building on Coase, tends to view the problem of externalities ex post, after a particular problem of access or a spillover has developed. From this perspective, high transaction costs can appear to be ubiquitous. Even if there are only two parties, once they are locked in a dispute they stand in a bilateral monopoly relationship that may lead to bargaining breakdown. The ex post perspective therefore tends toward the conclusion that liability rules are always superior to property rules on efficiency grounds.

More recently, scholars have shifted from the ex post to the ex ante perspective, asking what incentives these different modes of protection create for future behavior. Here, the case tends to shift back toward property rules, or, according to some, more elaborately tailored liability rules designed to tweak incentives. Because property rules protect subjective values that are not reflected in the market's valuation of property, they protect reliance interests and encourage investment. Property rules are also relatively simple for duty-holders to interpret (keep off, or else) and for courts to administer. And property rule protection creates an incentive for owners to generate new information about the uses to which their property can be put.[6] So from a dynamic or ex ante perspective, it would seem that property rule protection should remain the norm, and liability rules the exception.

Tort Liability: Nuisance

One way the law seeks to control externalities is through tort liability. The tort of trespass to land plays a role here, insofar as some access issues or negative externalities may give rise to an action for trespass. For example, if *A* engages in blasting that causes rocks to block *B*'s driveway, or if *A* engages in slant drilling to extract oil from underneath *B*'s land, these activities would give rise to a claim for trespass. By far the most important form of tort liability for regulating neighborhood effects or externalities, however, is nuisance.

Two different types of legal action bear the name "nuisance": public nuisance and private nuisance. The *Restatement of the Law Second, Torts* classifies both as a type of tort. It is not clear that this is correct. Torts are typically interferences with some private right, such as bodily integrity, reputation, or property. A public nuisance is defined as an unreasonable interference with a right common to the public as a whole. A public nuisance is thus perhaps more accurately regarded as a public action, akin to a criminal prosecution or an action to enforce the public trust doctrine (discussed in Chapter 3), rather than a tort.

The classic example of a public nuisance is blocking a public highway or a navigable waterway. Public nuisance actions are usually brought by public authorities, such as the state attorney general or the county prosecutor. The relief sought is usually an order of abatement—in effect, an injunction requiring the defendant to cease interfering with the public right. Sometimes, however, private parties are allowed to bring public nuisance actions, if they can

---

6. Henry E. Smith, *Property and Property Rules*, 79 N.Y.U. L. Rev. 1719 (2004).

show that they have suffered "special injury" from the interference with the public right. An example would be a landowner who has been barred from reaching his or her home by the blockage of a public highway. Here, the landowner is allowed to act as a "private attorney general," seeking to vindicate the public right, which will also redress the special injury suffered by the landowner.

Private nuisance clearly is a form of tort liability. A private nuisance is defined as an unreasonable interference with a private right: the use and enjoyment of land. Nuisance differs from trespass in that nuisance protects use and enjoyment rather than possession. Thus, trespass applies when there has been an intrusion by an object large enough to interfere with some portion of a person's right to possession of land. An intrusion by another person, a vehicle, a building, an animal, or a body of standing water would be examples. Nuisance applies to any thing that affects the use and enjoyment of land. Thus, intrusions of the sort covered by trespass can be claimed as a nuisance insofar as they too impair the use and enjoyment of land. (The actions are not mutually exclusive with respect to these intrusions, although some definitions of nuisance exclude anything that could be a trespass.) In addition, however, nuisance covers all sorts of others kinds of intrusions that cannot be said to displace a person from possession of land but nevertheless can be annoying or debilitating: smoke, odors, vibrations, sound waves, pollution of streams, radiation, beams of light—all these things are potentially subject to liability as nuisances.

An intentional trespass—one that the defendant knew or should have known would occur—is governed by a standard of strict liability. Liability attaches whether or not the intruder exercised reasonable care. And liability attaches whether or not the intrusion caused harm. Thus, a person who can establish an intentional trespass by the defendant is always entitled to an award of nominal damages, even if the plaintiff cannot prove actual damages. And if there is a likelihood that the intrusion will continue or will be repeated in the future, the court may enjoin the trespass, even if actual harm cannot be shown.

In sharp contrast to trespass, the standard of care for determining when an intrusion will give rise to nuisance liability is difficult to define or pin down. An intentional nuisance—an intrusion that the defendant knew or should have known would interfere with the plaintiff's use and enjoyment—is subject to liability only if the intrusion causes "substantial" harm and is "unreasonable." Exactly what these terms mean, and how they will be applied in any particular circumstance, is difficult to say. About the only safe generalization is that nuisance liability is very context-dependent and is determined in a case-by-case fashion.

The requirement of substantial harm is generally understood to eliminate liability for what English courts called "trifling inconveniences." Smoke from your neighbors' backyard barbecue and the yelps from their dog may irritate you, but a court is not likely to find that these sorts of intrusions reach the "substantial harm" threshold. Context is clearly relevant here. Erecting a huge neon sign does not impose substantial harm in Times Square, but it very likely might in a residential neighborhood.

In addition to imposing substantial harm, the intrusion must be unreasonable. What this means is even more elusive. The *Restatement of the Law Second, Torts* says that unreasonableness is determined by a balancing test: One asks whether the "the gravity of the harm outweighs the utility of the actor's conduct."[7] This suggests a kind of back-of-the-envelope cost-benefit analysis. Courts do not seem very comfortable with this suggestion, however. At least it is hard to find many decisions that engage in an explicit balancing of harms and benefits in determining whether particular intrusions are reasonable or unreasonable.

Several other factors seem to play a role in guiding courts in nuisance cases. Invasiveness is one. The *Restatement*'s cost-benefit definition of unreasonableness suggests that anything done on neighboring property that will affect the use and enjoyment of the

7. RESTATEMENT OF THE LAW SECOND, TORTS § 826(a) (1979).

plaintiff's property can give rise to a nuisance claim. But courts seem uncomfortable with claims that aesthetic blight by itself can constitute a nuisance. Garish paint jobs, junked cars, or poorly kept lawns will usually escape liability. Courts are much more likely to find a nuisance when the defendant is responsible for some invasion of the plaintiff's column of space, as by air pollution, water pollution, or loud noise. In this sense, nuisance seems to reflect the structure of trespass, where a physical invasion is required.[8] But there are exceptions to this generalization. Funeral homes and halfway houses for paroled prisoners and recovering drug addicts are often challenged as nuisances, with some success. And if the defendant does something on the defendant's land for the specific purpose of irritating a neighbor, such as erecting a "spite fence," there is a high probability that courts will find this to be a nuisance, at least if the action has no obvious utilitarian purpose other than imposing harm.

The nature of the locality is another important contextual factor. As the Supreme Court once stated, "A nuisance may be merely a right thing in the wrong place, like a pig in the parlor instead of the barnyard."[9] Thus, a smoky factory is less likely to be found to be an unreasonable use of land in a district comprised of smoky factories, than it would be in a residential neighborhood. Nuisance law in this regard functions like zoning, encouraging different uses of property to be clustered together in different neighborhoods, where spillover effects are less likely to impose substantial harm on neighbors.

Temporal priority is yet another factor, although somewhat weaker than invasiveness or the nature of the locality. Courts naturally look more skeptically on a defendant who seeks to

---

8. *See* Richard A. Epstein, Nuisance Law: *Corrective Justice and Its Utilitarian Constraints*, J. LEGAL STUD. (1979); Henry E. Smith, *Exclusion and Property Rules in the Law of Nuisance*, 90 VA. L. REV. 965 (2004).

9. Vill. of Euclid v. Ambler Realty Co., 272 U.S. 365, 388 (1926).

introduce a new and unsettling use into an established neighborhood, than they do when long-established uses are challenged by those who want to upgrade the area. Nevertheless, "coming to the nuisance" is usually rejected as an affirmative defense. Temporal priority is a factor to consider in the balance, but is not decisive, especially because, as we saw in Chapter 2, encouraging a race to be the first is quite undesirable in some contexts. A strong coming to the nuisance defense would encourage people to use their parcels as intensively and as early as possible, in order to establish the right to engage in such activities in the face of a new more sensitive use. The result would be like a prescriptive easement (see below) without the necessity of meeting the requirements for acquiring rights by prescription. Likewise under a strong version of coming to the nuisance, someone with a sensitive use in mind would also want to engage in it earlier than may be optimal, in order not to lose to someone else with an inconsistent use.

The question of remedy, and in particular the debate over the propriety of property rules versus liability rules, also looms large in nuisance cases. The discussion here is often framed in terms of the New York Court of Appeals decision in *Boomer v. Atlantic Cement Co.*[10] In *Boomer*, a cement plant located near Albany emitted dirt, smoke, and vibrations, and the trial court found this conduct was a nuisance to a group of neighboring property owners. The sole question on appeal was whether the court should issue an injunction against the nuisance, or should instead order some other relief, such as temporary or permanent damages. Enjoining the nuisance would in effect recognize a property rule: The cement plant would then have to purchase the consent of the neighbors to continue operating. An award of permanent damages would protect the neighbors with a liability rule: The cement plant could acquire their rights in a compelled exchange in return for the payment of damages.

---

10. 257 N.E. 2d 870 (N.Y. 1970).

The court acknowledged that prior New York decisions indicated an almost automatic presumption in favor of injunctive relief to protect the subjective values associated with property ownership. But it decided that an injunction should be denied, provided the cement company agreed to pay permanent damages to the property owners. The court was clearly concerned that an injunction might result in shutting down the plant, which cost $45 million to build and employed more than 300 people. It regarded this as an unacceptable cost to the community. The dissent pointed out that this was the functional equivalent of giving the cement company a private right of eminent domain to condemn a permanent easement to commit a nuisance.

The analysis in *Boomer* is entirely ex post. The court took the decision to build the cement plant in a neighborhood with many residents as a given, and balanced the benefits to the plaintiffs of being free of the nuisance against the investment and jobs that might be lost if the nuisance were abated. Adopting a liability rule, which allowed the cement company to coerce an exchange of entitlements, seems correct from this perspective. If we view the problem from an ex ante perspective, however, it is much less clear that this is right. Perhaps we want cement plants to take greater care in determining where they locate, assuring that they leave enough space between the plant and neighboring property owners to minimize negative spillover effects. Adopting a property rule, that is, awarding an injunction against the nuisance, would have provided a powerful incentive for cement plants in the future to acquire the necessary rights to prevent such problems from arising. Alternatively, the dire ex post situation could be avoided and the residents given more protection, if the cement company had to justify its choice of prospective location for the plant in a proceeding at which the residents had notice and an opportunity to be heard. Such requirements are commonly built into environmental statutes and requests for variances or special exceptions to zoning regulations (considered below). They are also a feature of statutes providing for private eminent domain for easements of road access and to water.

In a sense, what is at stake between the cement plant and the residents is an *easement* allowing the plant to create a nuisance, another land use device to which we will soon turn.

The *Boomer* situation is prime grist for analysis of property rules versus liability rules, and there is another sense in which the Calabresi and Melamed perspective is ex post: its view of the nature of entitlements. To Calabresi and Melamed, a collective decision over who gets the entitlement—polluter or resident—intersects with the question of how it is protected—property rule or liability rule. This gives four logical possibilities. Under Rule 1, the resident has the entitlement to be free from pollution, and the polluter must bargain in a consensual transaction with the resident or residents who hold this entitlement. Under Rule 2, the resident still has the entitlement, but the remedy is an award of damages. So if the polluter causes $100 of damage a day, the resident can sue multiple times to collect $100 a day or once to collect the discounted stream of daily $100 payments from now on, called "permanent damages." But under Rule 2, the resident cannot stop the pollution: The polluter can keep on polluting as long as the officially determined damages are paid. In effect, the polluter can take an easement for the "price" of the permanent damages. When there are many residents, any one of whom might hold out, there is a tendency, as in *Boomer* itself, to consider Rule 2 protection.

As for Rules 3 and 4, Calabresi and Melamed apply a twist on the Coasean notion that causation is reciprocal: If the harmful interaction is caused either by the polluter or the resident, either one in principle could have "the entitlement" to prevail in the situation of conflict. So under Rule 3, the polluter has the entitlement to pollute, protected by a property rule, in the sense that the resident is going to have to bribe the polluter to stop if that is to be the result. Finally, under Rule 4 the polluter has the entitlement to pollute, but the resident can take this entitlement—and shut the pollution down—upon payment of officially determined damages. Strikingly, at around the same time as Calabresi and Melamed's article came out, in *Spur Industries, Inc. v. Del E. Webb Development Co.*, the

Arizona Supreme Court, facing a case in which a retirement community had expanded close to a cattle feedlot, allowed the developer to obtain an injunction upon payment of the damages to the feedlot for the costs of shutting down.[11]

Spur is virtually the only nuisance case in which this "Rule 4" approach has been adopted. Why? For one thing, from the point of view of property, the symmetry between Rules 1 and 2 on the one hand and Rules 3 and 4 on the other, is illusory.[12] Consider Rule 3. When does a polluter have the "right" to pollute? This is controversial enough in the first place, but a closer look reveals that the common law provides for rights to pollute in only very narrow circumstances. One can have an easement to pollute either by grant or prescription—we will return to easements in the next section. But the common law emphatically does not include a right to pollute in the basic package of rights associated with fee simple ownership. Owning Blackacre gives the right to be free from a wide range of intrusions—not all spelled out in advance—but not the right to commit invasions. In the Rule 3 scenario as envisioned by theorists like Calabresi and Melamed, the polluter, on closer inspection, may not have such a right at all. Imagine the resident erecting a giant fan to blow the pollution back onto the factory grounds. If the polluter cannot get an injunction against the fan, this suggests that the polluter may have been able to get away with pollution but did not have the right to commit it. This understanding is very important when the polluter becomes subject to environmental regulation: Such regulation is not regarded as a taking of any preexisting right. More generally, the need for a simple, lumpy package of rights against sundry invasions breaks the symmetry. We are not writing on the Coasean blank slate assumed by the Calabresi and

11. 494 P.2d 700, 708 (Ariz. 1972) (en banc).

12. *See* Henry E. Smith, *Self-Help and the Nature of Property*, 1 J.L. ECON. & POL'Y 69, 70–76 (2005). Also, courts may be less likely to require a payment if the residents rather than the developer are asking for an injunction.

Melamed framework. Although we sometimes move from injunctions to damages in the law of nuisance (Rule 1 to Rule 2) as in *Boomer*, there is no "right to pollute" that is symmetric to the right to be free of pollution, and hence there is no need to soften the "right to pollute" (Rule 3) with a liability rule that allows such a "right" to be taken in a coerced exchange (Rule 4). Small wonder then that examples of Rule 4 are so hard to come by.

Modification of Property Rights: Easements

A second, and very different, strategy for handling certain kinds of neighborhood effects or externality problems relies on a modification of property rights known as an easement. Easements carve out particular uses of property and transfer control over those uses to someone other than the owner of the property from which the carve-out occurs. Easements are very commonly used to overcome impediments to access to land that can limit development and use and enjoyment of land. Familiar examples are right-of-way easements and utility easements. But easements are also used to control particular uses of land. For example, conservation easements, which are becoming increasingly popular, prohibit certain kinds of development of land in order to enhance ecological resources, which provide positive externalities for other landowners in the neighborhood and society more generally.

Let us start with some vocabulary. The property from which the easement is carved out is called the *servient* estate. The property whose owner has the right to engage in or prohibit the use that is singled out is called the *dominant* estate. If the easement permits the owner of the dominant estate to perform some act on the servient property, it is called an *affirmative* easement. If the easement requires the servient property owner to desist from engaging in certain activities or uses on the servient property, it is called a *negative* easement. Most easements are *appurtenant* to the ownership of land, meaning that the benefit of the easement is attached to a particular parcel of land, and runs with the ownership of the benefitted land (the dominant estate). Some easements, at least in the United States, are held *in gross*, meaning that the benefit of the easement is not linked to ownership of any particular land, but rather is owned by some person or entity without regard to whether they own any particular land or dominant estate.

Some illustrations may help clarify these distinctions. Suppose *A* and *B* own adjacent parcels of land. *A* grants *B* the right to drive motor vehicles across *A*'s land to reach a public road. *A* owns the servient estate, and *B* owns the dominant estate. *B* has an affirmative easement in *A*'s land; the easement is appurtenant to the ownership of *B*'s land, meaning that whoever owns *B*'s land in the future will also own the easement allowing access by motor vehicles to the road. Now, suppose *C* decides to grant a conservation easement to the *D* foundation, in which *C* promises not to fill, drain, develop, or otherwise disturb fifty acres of wetlands on *C*'s land. *C*'s is the servient estate, and *D* is the dominant property owner. *D* has a negative easement in *C*'s land; the easement is in gross because it is not attached to any particular land owned by the *D* foundation.

An easement is generally regarded as a property right, and hence it is proper to speak of easements as a strategy for managing externalities through modifications of property rights. It is instructive in this regard to contrast easements with licenses. As discussed in Chapter 4, a license, in its simplest form, is a waiver of the right to exclude. Suppose *A* says to *B*: "Go ahead and drive your car across my land to reach the road." This means *A* cannot use self-help or legal means to stop *B* when *B*, in response to this statement, starts to cross *A*'s land. But the permission is understood to be revocable, in the sense that *A* can change *A*'s mind tomorrow and deny further permission to cross. It is also understood to create no rights good against third parties. Thus, if *B* starts to cross and finds the way blocked by *C*, *B* has no legal claim against *C*.

A and *B* could also sign a contract that says *A* will allow *B* to cross *A*'s land for one year, provided *B* pays *A* $10 for each crossing. This would be enforceable as a bilateral contract between *A* and *B*, and *B* would have an action for breach of contract if *A* decided after six months to refuse further crossings by *B*. But it would still be regarded as a contract right. The right is personal to *A* and *B* and would not necessarily run to any successor to ownership of *B*'s land. And the right would not necessarily create any rights against third parties.

An easement is a more robust right than either a license or a contract. An easement is typically irrevocable, either for a designated period of time or in perpetuity. Although one can purchase easements, they are often granted gratuitously or as part of a more general exchange of property rights; periodic payments are rarely required. Easements do not depend on the personal identity of the grantor and grantee. Easements attach to ownership of land and follow the ownership of land into whoever's hands it may fall. This is always true of the servient estate. It is also true of the dominant estate, at least with respect to appurtenant easements (which are more common). Finally, although authority for this is relatively thin, easements appear to be regarded as rights in rem, in the sense that all the world is subject to a duty not to interfere with an easement. Given the relative permanence, impersonality, and in rem effects of easements, it is not surprising that they have been regarded as property rights.

How does one create an easement? There is the right way, and there are a bunch of legal doctrines that bail out people who have failed to create an easement the right way. The right way to create an easement is by a written grant. This is a writing that includes all the elements required to make a valid transfer of real property by deed from one person to another (see Chapter 7). The writing should include the identity of the servient and dominant lands (or of the benefitted owner in the case of an easement in gross), a description of the easement, and whatever formalities are required by state law for a valid transfer of land, such as attestation of signatures. To assure that the easement is not wiped out by a future good-faith purchaser without notice (see Chapter 7), it should be recorded. To ensure that the easement appears in the chain of title of the properties that are benefitted and burdened, it should not be created by reservation in a grant to some other party. In other words, if *A* wants to convey an easement to *B*, *A* should not try to create the easement by reservation in a deed to *C*, since the attempted grant to *B* will not appear in *B*'s chain of title.[13]

With distressing frequency, parties neglect to create an easement the right way, that is, by written grant. Instead, they behave as if the dominant estate has certain use rights with respect to the servient estate, and then something happens, such as a transfer of one of the properties to a stranger, which causes the owner of the servient estate to deny the existence of any use rights in the dominant estate. Litigation then ensues. The courts could respond to this common situation by saying "tough luck," and denying dominant claimants any rights absent a written grant. But, perhaps not surprisingly, courts have generally taken an ex post view of the problem. Once there has been a falling out, the parties are in a bilateral monopoly situation, and negotiation of a written grant may be out of the question. Courts have accordingly created a number of doctrines that allow easements to be created as matter of law.

Two of these doctrines are based on implied intent. Where there is some sort of preexisting use, such as a driveway or a utility line, and the owner subdivides the property, courts will sometimes declare that an *easement by implication* exists. The required elements are said to include (1) severance of title to land held by one owner; (2) an existing use, which was visible and continuous at the time of the severance; and (3) reasonable necessity for continuation of the use after severance. The doctrine apparently rests on the assumption that the parties must have intended an easement permitting continuation of the use but neglected to reflect this intent in a written instrument.

13. *But see* Willard v. First Church of Christ, Scientist, 498 P. 2d 987 (Cal. 1972) (allowing an easement to be created by reservation, without discussing the chain of title problem).

Even absent a preexisting use, if an owner subdivides property in such a way as to leave it landlocked, courts will sometimes declare an *easement by necessity*. The required elements are said to be (1) severance of title to land held by one owner and (2) strict necessity at the time of the severance. Again, the rationale is said to be that the parties would not want to create a subdivision in which one or more parcels were landlocked, because this would severely impair the value of the property. Some states take the idea of an easement by necessity in a different direction, allowing a landowner with insufficient access to petition a court or other official to allow it to condemn an easement and pay damages. This use of what Calabresi and Melamed would call a liability rule promotes access but can be quite threatening to the target of the condemnation. These statutes typically allow the condemnee to object on the grounds that the easement is not necessary for access, for example, because alternative means of access exist.

A third way to create an easement as a matter of law is by *prescription*. This is the analogue of adverse possession, considered in Chapter 2, with the twist that here the running of the statute of limitations creates an adverse right of use rather than possession. The difference turns on the behavior of the adverse user. If the adverse user acts like an owner, exercising a general right to exclude others and manage and control the property, then adverse possession governs. If the adverse user merely engages in a particular use of the property—such as crossing it or using it as a ditch to drain water—then prescription governs. Otherwise, the same elements that apply in determining whether someone has established title by adverse possession also apply in ascertaining whether an easement by prescription exists: The use must be open, notorious, continuous, exclusive, and under a claim of right for the period of the statute of limitations. With adverse use, as opposed to adverse possession, the continuous and exclusive elements apply somewhat differently. The touchstone in resolving these elements is what a normal holder of an easement would do. This feature is nicely captured in old English cases, which justified prescription on the fiction that the servient owner had long ago granted an easement to the dominant owner, but the grant had been lost.

The fourth and final way to create an easement as a mater of law is by the doctrine of *equitable estoppel*. This doctrine is grounded in general principles of equity. The required elements are (1) the giving of an express license to use property, (2) the reasonable expenditure of significant money or labor by the licensee in reliance on this license, and (3) circumstances indicating that revocation of the license would be unjust. Technically, equitable estoppel does not create a property right. It merely reflects the judgment of a court that it would be inequitable for the owner to revoke the license; hence the court enjoins the servient owner from revoking the license. Given that the theory does not technically create a property right, questions may arise about how long an easement by estoppel lasts, and whether it is transferable and descendable.

The four devices for creating an easement as a matter of law only work for affirmative easements. Some actual use on the servient land is required. This is in significant part a matter of notice. If there is some actual physical activity on *A*'s land, then *A* can be expected to be aware of this fact. In contrast, if the claim is that *A* should be required to desist from engaging in some use, perhaps because this is what *A* or *A*'s predecessor did in the past, it is not obvious that *A* would have ever thought about the possibility of a legal claim for an easement being advanced based on *A*'s having done nothing. The problem of notice is so severe that English courts refused to recognize any negative easements outside four narrow categories.[14] U.S. courts are more tolerant—at least when the negative easement is created by grant. But U.S. courts have refused to allow negative easements to be created by prescription,[15] and as a practical matter

---

14. These were an easement against blocking sunlight from falling on a window, against blocking the flow of air in a defined channel, against blocking the flow of water in a defined channel, and against removing lateral support for a building.

15. *See* Fontainebleau Hotel Corp. v. Forty-Five Twenty-Five, Inc., 114 So. 2d 357 (Fla. Dist. Ct. App. 1959).

do not allow negative easements to be created by implication, necessity, or estoppel either. A few U.S. courts have created what amounts to a negative easement by prescription in ruling that constructing a building that casts a shadow on a neighbor's solar collector can be a nuisance.[16] But in addition to the problem of notice discussed above, this creates an enormous incentive to be first to capture the sun's rays, either by putting up a building or a solar collector, and thus could give rise to wasteful racing behavior, analogous to what we see with the rule of first possession (see Chapter 2). In some states, solar access is now governed by statute, usually through a system of permitting or prior appropriation along the lines of water law (see Chapter 3).[17]

The multiple ways of creating an easement are mirrored by multiple ways of terminating easements. The orthodox method, again, is by grant. The parties can execute a written instrument that terminates the easement, following the formalities of a real estate deed. Easements can also be terminated by abandonment, if the servient owner can show that the dominant owner has failed to use the easement for some time or has made statements indicating an intention no longer to use it, and has taken some affirmative act reflecting the intent to abandon. Distinct, but somewhat similar, is termination by prescription. If the servient owner blocks the easement, for example, by putting up a fence across a right of way, and the dominant owner fails to take action to reopen the easement before the statute of limitations runs, the servient owner may be able to claim termination by prescription. Finally, an easement will be terminated by merger, if the dominant and servient tracts come under ownership by the same person. No one can have an easement over one's own land.

How can a servient owner ensure that the dominant owner does not overuse or misuse an easement? The law here reflects a mix of

---

16. *See* Prah v. Maretti, 321 N.W.2d 182 (Wis. 1982).

17. Sara C. Bronin, *Solar Rights*, 89 B.U. L. Rev. 1217 (2009).

bright line rules and rules of reason, analogous to the trespass-nuisance divide. If the dominant owner acquires additional land and attempts to use an existing easement to reach the new land, this will always be condemned as a misuse of the easement, even if the increased burden is trivial.[18] On the other hand, if the dominant owner's business grows, with the result that the volume of traffic using an existing easement increases significantly, this will be permitted as long as the increased traffic does not impose an unreasonable burden on the servient owner. Some commentators have expressed frustration with the formality of the distinction.[19] Perhaps the difference in treatment simply turns on the specificity of the underlying rights. Easements are usually clear about the identity of the dominant parcel; thus, in the case of newly added land, there is an unambiguous violation of a clear limitation on the right. Easements are much less likely to be clear about the permitted intensity of use. There is, if you will, a gap in the specification of rights in this case, which must be filled in by the court for the parties, making a standard of reasonableness appropriate. The parties are always free to specify in the easement what volume of use is permitted, and a violation of such a limitation would similarly be subject to automatic condemnation by a court.

Contract: Covenants Running with the Land

Closely related to easements are covenants running with the land. Sometimes covenants and easements are lumped together as "servitudes." We have described easements as modifications of property rights. Covenants could be described the same way. But covenants

18. *See* Penn Bowling Recreation Ctr., Inc. v. Hot Shoppes, Inc., 179 F.2d 64 (D.C. Cir. 1949).

19. Lee J. Strang, *Damages as the Appropriate Remedy for "Abuse" of an Easement: Moving Toward Consistency, Efficiency, and Fairness in Property Law*, 15 Geo. Mason L. Rev. 933 (2008).

have a stronger contractual flavor than easements. Covenants always originate in written promises between a grantor and grantee of interests in land. There are no doctrines that provide for covenants as a matter of law, as there are with respect to easements. Covenants typically apply to questions about permissible uses of property, whereas easements more typically involve questions of access. And covenants are much more likely to impose negative rather than affirmative obligations, whereas the obligations of an easement are nearly always affirmative. Indeed, one could say that covenants are simply contracts about the permissible uses of land with one feature not otherwise found in contracts: Covenants "run with the land," meaning that the benefits and burdens of the promises roll over automatically when the interests of the original promisor and promisee are transferred.

Suppose a developer subdivides a tract of land. The developer requires that every purchaser of a lot in the subdivision take a deed that includes a promise that the purchaser will use the property as a single-family residence only. There is no doubt that such a deed restriction is enforceable as a contract between the developer and the purchaser. Thus, if a purchaser who has signed such a deed attempts sometime later to turn the single-family house on the lot into a duplex, the developer can sue the purchaser for breach of contract. Unless the purchaser can establish one of the standard defenses to such an action (e.g., lack of contractual capacity), the developer should win, and the court would either award damages or enter an injunction to prevent the breach.

Whether or not such a contractual promise is a covenant running with the land comes into play only if the original promisee (the developer) or the original promisor (the purchaser) has transferred the property to someone else. The law has developed two tests for determining whether such promises run with the land: equitable servitudes and real covenants. It is important to stress that equitable servitudes and real covenants do not refer to two different interests in property, like a fee simple and a life estate. They are the *same thing*. These are simply two different legal tests for establishing whether a contractual promise respecting the use of land runs to successors in interest, as opposed to being merely a personal obligation between the original promisor and promisee. To state the matter differently, we start with the same thing, which is a promise between *A* and *B*. The question then becomes, is the promise binding on A_1 and/or B_1, their successors in interest? To determine the answer to this question, we apply one of two legal tests, the equitable servitude test and the real covenant test. If the promise passes either one of these tests, it is enforceable against the successors. If it does not pass either test, it is only a personal promise between *A* and *B* and is not binding on their successors.

Which test do we apply? The *equitable servitude* test originated with the court of equity in England (Chancery). Hence, if one is seeking an equitable remedy for violation of a promise respecting the use of land by a successor in interest, such as an injunction, one would ordinarily apply the equitable servitude test. The *real covenant* test originated with American courts that held that certain grantor-grantee promises respecting the use of land run to successors in interest in an action at law. Hence, if one is seeking to recover damages for a breach of a promise respecting the use of land by a successor in interest, one would ordinarily apply the real covenant test. Because, in most jurisdictions, the courts of law and courts of equity merged long ago, and the old forms of action are no longer supposed to limit the authority of courts of general jurisdiction, this differentiation based on whether one is proceeding "at law" or "in equity" seems artificial and outmoded. Perhaps one day it will break down. But for now, the safest assumption is that the type of relief being sought by the plaintiff (injunction or damages) will dictate which legal test will be used to determine if the promise "runs."

The equitable servitude test was invented by the English Chancery in the famous case of *Tulk v. Moxhay*.[20] Tulk owned Leicester Square and several houses surrounding the square

20. 2 Phillips 774, 41 Eng. Rep. 1143 (Ch. 1848).

in London. Tulk sold the square to one Elms, by a deed in which Elms promised for himself, his heirs, and assigns, to keep the square in good condition and to allow the residents in the houses surrounding the square to use it as a "garden and pleasure ground." Ownership of the square passed by several conveyances into the hands of Moxhay, whose deed said nothing about this promise, although Moxhay admitted he was aware of Elms's original promise because he had seen it in the deed from Tulk to Elms. When Moxhay threatened to build on the square, Tulk sued for an injunction, and won.

The court in *Tulk* acknowledged that such a promise would not run to a successor in interest in an action at law. In England, covenants run with the land only when they are contained in leases between a landlord and tenant. But the court said this did not preclude a court of equity from issuing an injunction when the successor took with actual notice of the promise. According to the court, because the original promise by Elms no doubt affected the price he paid, "nothing could be more inequitable than that the original purchaser should be able to sell the property the next day for a greater price, in consideration of the assignee being allowed to escape from the liability which he had himself undertaken."[21] (Is this true? What if Elms assumed the promise was good only until he sold the property to someone else?) The key was that Moxhay had acquired the property with actual notice of the promise: "[I]f an equity is attached to the property by the owner, no one purchasing it with notice of that equity can stand in a different situation from the party from whom he purchased."[22]

Based on *Tulk* and following decisions, the equitable servitude test has come to be understood to have three elements. (1) The parties must intend that the promise will be binding on their successors. This was satisfied in *Tulk* because Elms had promised on

21. 41 Eng. Rep. at 1144.

22. *Id.*

behalf of himself and his "heirs and assigns." (2) The successor must have notice of the promise to be bound by the burden of the promise. In *Tulk* the successor (Moxhay) had actual notice; later decisions established that constructive notice through the recordation of the original deed will also suffice. (3) The promise must be one that "touches and concerns the land." More on this mysterious phrase in a moment.

Meanwhile, American courts ventured forth beyond what English courts had allowed in enforcing promises against successors in interest in actions at law. English courts allowed covenants respecting the use of land to run to successors only if the original covenant was between a landlord and tenant. If the landlord sold the reversion, or if the tenant assigned the lease, the covenants in the original lease would bind their successors if certain conditions were met (see Chapter 6). American courts took this doctrine and extended it to the context of real estate developments. If the original promise was contained in a deed between a real estate developer and a purchaser of property in that development, the original promise would also run, provided the same conditions developed in the landlord-tenant context were met. The courts described the general condition between the original promisor and promisee that would permit this doctrine to apply as "privity of estate."

In its full-blown form, the real covenant test has come to be understood to have the following elements. (1) The parties must intend that the promise will be binding on successors. Usually this will be established by language indicating that the parties are promising on behalf of their "heirs, successors, and assigns" or words to that effect. Intention can also be established, however, by a more general consideration of context. (2) The original promise must have been made between grantor and grantee, landlord and tenant, or others who are in "privity of estate." This type of privity is often called "horizontal," and it is rarely of much importance in American cases, as nearly all the cases involve promises imposed by real estate developers on original grantees in a new development (grantor-grantee relationship). (3) For the burden of a promise to run, the successor must have acquired the entire interest of the original promisor, in what is known as "full vertical privity." For the benefit of a promise to run, the successor must have acquired at least part of the interest of the original promise, in what is known as "partial vertical privity." (4) The promise must be one that "touches and concerns the land."

As this brief summary suggests, the main differences between the equitable servitude test and the real covenant test are as follows. The equitable servitude test requires that a successor in interest must have notice of the promise, real or constructive; the real covenant test does not. The real covenant test requires privity of estate between the original promisor and promisee and full or partial privity of estate between the successors and the original parties to the promises; the equitable servitude test does not. Both tests require that the original parties intend the promise to bind successors, and that the promise touch and concern the land.

What does the mysterious phrase "touch and concern" mean? The purpose of this requirement is relatively clear. It is designed to differentiate between promises that it makes sense to impose on successors in interest and promises that it makes sense to limit to the original promisor and promisee only. Suppose the original parties include in the deed a promise that the purchaser, a barber, will cut the hair of the seller, a real estate developer, once a month. If the barber subsequently transfers the property to a law professor, obviously it makes no sense to hold that the promise runs with the land. The developer (or the developer's successor in interest) would not want a haircut by a law professor. Conversely, if the original parties include in the deed a promise that the property will be used for a single-family residence only, this will certainly have an impact on future successors, both of the promisor and the promisee. This kind of promise is clearly one that it makes sense to impose on successors in interest.

Why not simply rely on the parties to the original promise to signal whether they intend the promise to run? The problem seems to be that parties generally fail to attend to this issue on a carefully considered, promise-by-promise basis. The tendency, all too often, is to make lots of promises, and say they all are intended to run. Courts have generally been skeptical that this should be taken literally. The *Restatement of the Law Third, Property* would reverse this skeptical attitude, and substitute what amounts to a presumption that promises will run, unless they violate public policy.[23] But so far, courts have been reluctant to abandon the touch-and-concern screen for when promises run.

Although unwilling to give up on touch and concern, courts have been stymied about how to specify exactly what this means. Perhaps some progress could be made by reverting to the general reason for having a legal mechanism like servitudes that run with the land: the need for a governance regime to regulate positive and negative neighborhood effects or externalities. Promises that regulate externalities, either by encouraging positive externalities (taking care of the lawn) or discouraging negative externalities (no boarding houses), would be deemed to touch and concern the land. Promises that have no discernible neighborhood effects (cutting the developer's hair, agreeing to finance a loan from a company affiliated with the developer), would be deemed not to touch and concern the land. To be sure, whether or not something is an externality is often debatable. So asking courts to decide whether a promise regulates externalities would not resolve all the borderline cases, such as whether a promise to buy water from a common well runs with the land.[24] But it might at least point courts in the right direction.

Because servitudes running with the land often involve fairly specific promises about land uses, these promises run a significant risk of becoming obsolete. A classic example is a promise to limit all

---

23. Restatement of the Law Third, Property: Servitudes §§ 2.1, 3.1 (2000).

24. *See* Eagle Enterprises v. Gross, 349 N.E.2d 816 (N.Y. 1976) (holding that promise to purchase water from a common well did not touch and concern the land).

lots in a subdivision to single-family homes: Years later, the area changes such that the highest and best use of all or part of the land is for commercial use such as retail. In the face of such changed circumstances, it may be very difficult or impossible to amend the promises, because all persons owning property in the development would have to agree to the change. Unanimous consent will be very hard to achieve, given that one or more owners may hold out. Perhaps the holdouts could be induced to relent by side payments from the owners who desire change, in a "Coasean bargain." But free-rider problems may prevent the owners who desire change from raising enough funds to induce the holdouts to relent, and after all, the main point of the Coase theorem is that in the real world, transaction costs will sometimes block wealth-increasing deals.

A well-designed package of servitudes will anticipate this problem. It may include specific time limits on different promises, or the entire package may expire after a certain period of time, such as forty years. More recently, well-advised developers have incorporated into packages of servitudes some mechanism for amending the original promises by something less than unanimous consent. Modern condominium developments, for example, make extensive use of servitudes that restrict the use of individual units and the common facilities in a variety of ways (see Chapter 6). But they also typically include some mechanism, such as a supermajority vote of the homeowners' association, which allows abrogation or amendment of the original promises. Because a supermajority is hard to muster, this allows purchasers to rely on the original package of promises. It also allows for change when a strong consensus develops that change is appropriate.

Absent such an amendment procedure, the primary safety valve for overcoming problems created by changed circumstances is judicial abrogation under what is called (appropriately enough) the *changed circumstances* doctrine. Courts generally apply a very demanding standard in determining whether to refuse enforcement of covenants running with the land because of changed circumstances. They require evidence that the restriction will be of "no benefit" to property owners who desire to keep it in place.[25] Obviously, if one or more owners object to abrogation, they will usually be able to make some argument that the restriction provides a benefit to them. Other grounds for seeking abrogation include abandonment, laches, and violation of public policy. The difficulty of obtaining judicial modification or abrogation underscores the desirability of including an amendment mechanism in the original package of covenants.

Public Regulation: Zoning

The legal mechanisms for regulating neighborhood effects or spillovers previously considered—nuisance suits, modifications of property rights by easements, and covenants running with the land—are all subject to severe limitations. Nuisance suits are expensive and unpredictable, easements require difficult negotiations or legal action, and covenants running with the land, as a practical matter, can only be imposed by developers in new subdivisions. In light of these limitations, it is not surprising that the law has turned to public regulation as a way of encouraging positive and discouraging negative externalities. A wide variety of laws are designed to regulate land use externalities. Environmental laws limiting air and water pollution, regulating and remediating hazardous waste disposal, and assuring the quality of water supplies are examples. Laws like the National Environmental Policy Act (NEPA),[26] and its many state analogues, seek to control the impacts of new government projects by requiring a careful consideration of effects and alternatives in an environmental impact statement before the project is undertaken.

25. *See, e.g.*, Bolotin v. Rindge, 41 Cal. Rptr. 376 (Cal. Ct. App. 1964).

26. 42 U.S.C. §§ 4321–4335 (2000).

By far the most common form of public regulation designed to regulate neighborhood effects and externalities, however, are local zoning laws. Zoning laws are of two broad types: Euclidean zoning and planned unit developments.

Euclidean zoning (so named for the Supreme Court case that upheld the constitutionality of local zoning ordinances[27]) starts with a map of the local community. On the map, neighborhoods are marked off in zones having different types of land uses, such as "industrial," "commercial," "residential," and so forth. Individual parcels of property are restricted to the uses that are permitted in their zone. The permitted uses can be either cumulative or noncumulative. Under *cumulative zoning*, uses are ranked in a hierarchy from most to least intensive, in accordance with their presumed incompatibility with single-family residences. Within any zone, one can devote one's land to the designated use plus any less intensive uses. Thus, in a zone designated "commercial," the owner could build a retail store but could also engage in less intensive uses such an apartment house, a two-family house, or a single-family home. Under *noncumulative zoning*, only the designated use is permitted. If a zone is designated "commercial," only commercial buildings are permitted in that zone.

The theory behind Euclidean zoning is that separation of uses will enhance positive spillovers and minimize negative spillovers. Industrial plants will be segregated in one zone, commercial operations in another, apartment houses in yet a third, with single-family homes shielded from all these other uses. In upholding this kind of zoning against constitutional attack, the Supreme Court expressly recognized that zoning was designed to minimize nuisance-like incompatibilities, and that the protection of the single-family home was the dominant objective.

Euclidean zoning works best if it is adopted on a clean slate, before a community is developed. The zoning map, at least implicitly, is deemed to reflect a *comprehensive plan* for the community, and

---

27. Vill. of Euclid v. Ambler Realty Co., 272 U.S. 365 (1926).

all development is supposed to unfold in accordance with this plan. When zoning became popular in the early decades of the twentieth century, however, it was adopted by many cities that were already largely developed. Layering the zones on top of existing neighborhoods was difficult, because often land uses were extremely intermixed. Courts ruled that municipalities could not "downzone" properties that had already been developed and devoted to a use that was incompatible with the zoning scheme. In some states, such "nonconforming uses," as they are called, have been held to be constitutionally protected as vested rights.[28] In some communities, nonconforming uses are permanently grandfathered. In others, they have been given a finite period of time to continue operating, after which they had to be converted into a conforming use or abandoned. Either way, these nonconforming uses inevitably compromised the purity of the comprehensive plan. Interestingly, nonconforming use protection applies only to developed property. Raw land that has not been developed can be subject to severe zoning restrictions that impair its market value, without running afoul of constitutional limitations.

The judicial protection of nonconforming uses highlights the preventive nature of zoning regulation. When a court determines that some land use is a nuisance, or when a legislative body determines that a particular land use is a public nuisance, it is well established that the use can be eliminated, without any need to provide compensation to the owner of the property for losses associated with such action.[29] Zoning is designed to prevent nuisance-like interferences, but does not rest on any finding that the owner actually is committing a nuisance. Courts have concluded that this

28. *See, e.g.*, Valley View Indus. Park v. City of Redmond, 733 P.2d 182 (Wash. 1987) (en banc).

29. *See, e.g.*, Hadacheck v. Sebastian, 239 U.S. 394 (1915) (owner of brickyard shut down by local ordinance not entitled to compensation); *cf.* Lucas v. South Carolina Coastal Council, 505 U.S. 1003 (1992) (property owner not entitled to compensation for regulation that destroys all economically beneficial value if the regulation tracks the common law of private or public nuisance).

preventive rationale is not sufficiently powerful to justify shutting down existing nonconforming uses, at least not with some kind of transitional relief.

Zoning, like covenants running with the land, frequently encounters problems associated with changed circumstances. What was once thought to be an ideal location for single-family homes comes to be an area more appropriate for multifamily homes, or perhaps for commercial development. Changes can be made in zoning rules either through obtaining a variance or special exception, or through an amendment to the zoning plan. Variances and special exceptions are usually relatively small changes that affect only one or a small number of properties. Variances are more discretionary and can often be granted by administrators or by zoning boards of appeals. Despite their name, special exceptions are given as of right as long as the landowner satisfies the criteria in the zoning ordinance. If a larger change is required, the zoning plan must be amended. Such amendments require action by the local legislature, and thus are harder to obtain.

Is zoning beneficial overall? This is hard to answer in the abstract. Zoning carries with it the costs of rigidity and artificial scarcity of land but may be more effective than nuisance or covenants in dealing with severe spillover problems—although nuisance and covenants have their defenders. The fact that incumbent homeowners favor zoning is not dispositive on the question of overall welfare: People squeezed out of the housing market because of zoning's contribution to scarcity and higher cost do not have votes in local politics. At best, they are represented by developers who would like to cater to their demand. Recent empirical work suggests that in California and the urban Northeast, zoning increases housing prices significantly through artificial scarcity. In other areas, housing more directly reflects the costs of construction.[30]

---

30. Edward L. Glaeser & Joseph Gyourko, *The Impact of Building Restrictions on Housing Affordability*, 9 Econ. Pol'y Rev. 21 (June 2003).

As zoning laws have grown older, problems of changed circumstances have become more acute. Frequent recourse to variances and amendments eventually led to a second conception of how zoning might work, which has come to be known as the planned unit development (PUD).

In contrast to Euclidean zoning, which is grounded in the idea of a comprehensive plan for the entire community devised by experts, the PUD is based on the idea of a negotiated bargain between developers and local political authorities.[31] Typically, a developer will approach a city with a proposal to build a new subdivision or shopping center, or to redevelop an existing neighborhood. City authorities and the developer will then negotiate a plan for the development, including not just private spaces such as houses, apartments, and commercial areas, but also open spaces, public parks, streets and sidewalks, and even schools and other community facilities. The city authorities are understood to have the power to veto the development, and they use this leverage to obtain promises that will provide benefits to the community. The developer, of course, can always back out of the project, and will use this leverage to try to maximize the economic return from the development. The result is a negotiated compromise, which generates the plan that governs the development, but does not affect other areas of the municipality.

PUDs reflect a very different philosophy about how to regulate externalities than the one reflected in Euclidean zoning. Whereas Euclidean zoning is based on a philosophy of separating uses into discrete zones, a PUD typically incorporates a mixture of different uses in one area. This is thought to generate a more vibrant, diverse community than Euclidean zoning, which tends toward homogeneity. Whereas Euclidean zoning is driven by a desire to achieve comprehensive and rational planning, imposed from above, PUDs

---

31. *See* Carol M. Rose, *Planning and Dealing: Piecemeal Land Controls as Problem of Local Legitimacy*, 71 Cal. L. Rev. 837 (1983).

are individually negotiated and yield a series of idiosyncratic projects that may or may not sum to a coherent whole. Whereas Euclidian zoning maintains a sharp distinction between public and private, with land use planning regarded as a public function governed by elections, laws, administrative rules, open meeting requirements, and judicial review, PUDs entail a mixture of public and private decision making, with some inevitable loss of transparency and public participation. Critics of Euclidean zoning hail PUDs as more flexible, realistic, and responsive to public needs. Critics of PUDs condemn them as a sell-out to interest-group influence at the expense of the general interest. The debate goes on, although the trend is clearly in the direction of greater use of PUDs.

Because zoning is a form of local regulation, there is nothing to ensure that the interests of outsiders are factored into the process. A particularly troubling claim is that zoning rules are designed, either deliberately or inadvertently, to exclude racial minorities and poor persons from locating in particular communities. For example, suburban communities often adopt zoning rules that require large minimum lot sizes for single family homes and impose extensive open space requirements, with little space allocated for apartments or multifamily units. The effect of such rules is to limit development to large, expensive homes that few minorities and no poor households can afford. The New Jersey courts have sought to combat these effects by holding that exclusionary zoning violates the state constitution, and by requiring communities to amend their ordinances to include more generous allocations for low- and moderate-income housing.[32] These efforts at judicial reform have led to a prolonged tussle between the courts and the legislature over the proper remedy, with the result that the issue still remains unresolved. A few other states have made milder

---

32. S. Burlington County NAACP v. Twp. of Mount Laurel, 336 A.2d 713 (N.J. 1975).

attempts to police exclusionary zoning,[33] but most have ignored the issue.

One solution to the problem of exclusionary zoning would be to relocate land use planning functions from local governments to regional or state governments. This would allow a wider range of interests to be represented in the planning process. Such a shift in the level of regulation, however, would come with a sacrifice in detailed knowledge about local conditions and preferences. Moreover, there is little prospect that local communities will voluntarily relinquish their "right to exclude" any time soon, any more than individual property owners willingly give up their right to exclude, which is why the problem of externalities is so intractable.

Further Reading

R. H. Coase, *The Problem of Social Cost*, 3 J.L. & ECON. 1 (1960) (pioneering study of the role of transaction costs in situations with externalities and propounding what later came to be known as the Coase theorem).

Guido Calabresi & A. Douglas Melamed, *Property Rules, Liability Rules, and Inalienability: One View of the Cathedral*, 85 HARV. L. REV. 1089 (1972) (seminal article introducing the distinction between property rules and liability rules).

Robert C. Ellickson, *Alternatives to Zoning: Covenants, Nuisance Rules, and Fines as Land Use Controls*, 40 U. CHI. L. REV. 681 (1973) (offering a comparative analysis of different legal mechanisms for regulating neighborhood effects).

WILLIAM A. FISCHEL, THE HOMEVOTER HYPOTHESIS (2001) (arguing that the political power of local landowners is the key to understanding land use regulation).

33. *See, e.g.*, BAC, Inc. v. Bd. of Supervisors, 633 A.2d 144 (Pa. 1993).

James E. Krier & Stewart J. Schwab, *Property Rules and Liability Rules: The Cathedral in Another Light*, 70 N.Y.U. L. REV. 440 (1995) (emphasizing the importance of the ex ante versus ex post perspectives in considering the choice between property rules and liability rules).

A. MITCHELL POLINSKY, AN INTRODUCTION TO LAW AND ECONOMICS ch. 1 (3d ed. 2003) (offering a clear introduction to the Coase theorem and the choice between property rules and liability rules).

NINE

Government Forbearance

THE GOVERNMENT HAS MADE an appearance at various points in this book, as an enforcer of property rights, a creator of different property forms, a recorder of property rights, and an arbiter of disputes between neighbors, among other functions. But the government can also pose a threat to property rights, either by seizing property or by changing the rules of the game in ways that are destabilizing to owners. The most general question here is how far the government should forbear from undermining the expectations of owners about what they can and cannot do with their property. Complete vindication of expectations is impossible. Change is inevitable, and as new problems emerge, adjustments in property rights are often the response. Consider, for example, how changing attitudes about racial discrimination resulted in laws that limit the right of owners to refuse to rent or sell their property to persons based on their race (see Chapter 4). But too much change in government policy toward property, including in the extreme case outright expropriation, can undermine the ability of owners to plan for the future and may discourage them from undertaking needed investments. Striking the right balance between accommodating change and forbearing from frustrating expectations has always been, and will continue to be, difficult.

In this chapter, we consider some of the important ways in which governments are constrained to forbear from upsetting the expectations of property owners, thereby enhancing the security of ownership and the value of the institution of property.[1]

The General Form of the Problem

The difficulty in striking a balance between demands for change and protecting reliance interests is nicely illustrated by a famous Supreme Court case, *Charles River Bridge v. Warren Bridge*.[2] In 1785, Massachusetts granted a charter to the Proprietors of the Charles River Bridge to build a private toll bridge across the Charles River between Boston and Charlestown. The charter, after one extension, was to last 70 years, or until 1855. As population and economic activity in the Boston area grew, the bridge became highly profitable. In 1828, the legislature was persuaded to charter a second bridge, the Warren Bridge, which would roughly parallel the Charles River Bridge. The new bridge was to collect tolls for a short time and then become a free bridge. Not surprisingly, once the Warren Bridge stopped collecting tolls, the value of the Charles River Bridge franchise was destroyed. The proprietors of the Charles River Bridge sued, claiming that their charter was impliedly exclusive, and that by chartering the second bridge to compete against the first, the legislature had impaired the obligation of contract, in violation of Article I, section 10 of the Constitution.[3]

1. For econometric studies suggesting the importance of secure property rights and government forbearance to economic performance, *see, e.g.*, Daron Acemoglu et al., *The Colonial Origins of Comparative Development: An Empirical Investigation*, 91 AM. ECON. REV. 1369 (2001); Simon Johnson et al., *Property Rights and Finance*, 92 AM. ECON. REV. 1335 (2002); Paul G. Mahoney, *The Common Law and Economic Growth: Hayek Might Be Right*, 30 J. LEGAL STUD. 503 (2001).
2. 36 U.S. (11 Pet.) 420 (1837).
3. Stating that no state shall pass any law "impairing the obligation of Contracts." U.S. CONST. art. I, § 10, cl. 1.

In the Supreme Court, all the justices agreed that the original charter was a contract between the Commonwealth of Massachusetts and the proprietors of the Charles River Bridge, and hence was protected by the Constitution. But they disagreed sharply about whether the original charter should be interpreted as including an implied promise of exclusivity.

Chief Justice Taney, writing for the majority, adopted the rule that corporate charters should be strictly construed in favor of the government. Because the charter was silent on whether it precluded a competing bridge, the proprietors' claim failed. Taney noted the great difficulty that courts would have in determining the scope of exclusive rights if such a provision were implied. How far up and down the river would the original bridge have the right to operate as a monopoly? He also stressed how an implied term of exclusivity could interfere with economic growth and technological change. Many ferry charters had been replaced by bridge charters, and many charters for turnpike roads had been superseded by charters for railroads. If charters for bridges and roads always include an implied term of exclusivity, then innumerable old charters would awake "from their sleep," and their promoters could call upon the courts "to put down the improvements which have taken their place."[4] In other words, affording too much protection for the reliance interests of the original charter holders would stifle progress.

Justice Story wrote a long and impassioned dissent. He said the rule of strict construction applied only to government charters given by donation, not to charters supported by consideration. Charters given for a promise of some return benefit, such as the one for the Charles River Bridge, should be liberally construed in favor of the grant recipients to ensure that the charters achieve their intended purpose. He rhetorically asked whether the original proprietors would have built the bridge, at considerable expense and

4. 36 U.S. at 477.

risk, if they had been told that the state reserved the right to build a free bridge immediately next door. The rule adopted by the majority would discourage investment in enterprises designed to promote the public interest. Such a rule, he said, did not preclude modification of charters if technological or social change rendered the original promise obsolete. But the proper way to repeal or modify a charter was by using the power of eminent domain and paying just compensation for the value of the rights taken.

Charles River Bridge raises enduring questions about how far the government should forbear from interfering with expectations of property owners. The general question here is how much risk property owners should be expected to assume based on changes in government policy. Chief Justice Taney did not believe that property owners assume all risks of change in public policy. He acknowledged that explicit takings are prohibited without compensation, and that government must keep its express promises. But all other risks from government action he would treat as no different from the risks associated with natural disasters or changes in consumer preferences. Implicit in this view is the assumption that the government can generally be trusted to do the right thing.[5]

Justice Story believed that the government should provide a more robust form of insurance against risks associated with the government's own actions. At the very least, when the government has taken action specifically designed to induce parties to invest in some enterprise, the government has an obligation to forbear from undermining reasonable expectations associated with that investment. In effect, Justice Story would impose a duty of good faith on the government in dealing with persons who have acted in reliance on its promises. His view implied a more skeptical attitude about whether government can be trusted without court supervision.

---

5. *See also* Louis Kaplow, *An Economic Analysis of Legal Transitions*, 99 HARV. L. REV. 511 (1986).

What is at stake here? Justice Story is probably correct that requiring the government to forbear from frustrating reasonable expectations would induce higher levels of investment in new enterprises. The risk of making such investments would be reduced, and hence the expected return would be higher. Justice Taney may be correct that a general policy of forbearing from interfering with reasonable expectations would significantly tie the hands of the government. If the government always had to pay just compensation to those whose reasonable expectations were frustrated, politicians might hesitate before adopting otherwise desirable changes in policy, because of the additional cost of compensation.

The matter is complex, however, because it is not clear how government actors respond to forbearance requirements.[6] With private actors, the requirement to forbear or pay internalizes the cost of interfering with others' rights to the private actor, who can then weigh it against the benefit from the action in question. With governments, things are less clear. If governments must forbear or pay, the cost of compensation ultimately comes out of taxpayers' pockets. Politicians seek to maximize their political support and, in particular, their chance of reelection, which may or may not correlate closely with taxpayer welfare. The incentives of government officials are especially likely to be skewed if the linkage between government action and the need for higher taxes is not very transparent.

Another way to view the problem is to ask whether or how far one generation should be allowed to tie the hands of the next. Government forbearance presents a more specific application of the problem of "dead hand control" that raises its head in many areas of the law of property. Just as we ask whether an owner should be allowed to dictate who should get the owner's property

6. *See, e.g.*, Daniel A. Farber, *Public Choice and Just Compensation*, 9 CONST. COMMENT. 279 (1992); Daryl J. Levinson, *Making Governments Pay: Markets, Politics, and the Allocation of Constitutional Costs*, 67 U. CHI. L. REV. 345 (2000).

after the owner's death, or whether an owner should be allowed to enter into a servitude that limits the use of the property after it has been sold to someone else, we also must ask whether one generation of lawmakers should be allowed to make promises to forbear from interfering with property that are binding on succeeding generations of lawmakers. One perspective is that it is inherent in the concept of democratic government that each generation should be able to decide what laws it will be governed by.[7] Values and social problems change, and it makes no sense that people living today should remain slaves to the vision of those long dead. A rival perspective is that the ability to entrench certain expectations is vital to achieving the goals of democratic government; to deny this tool to lawmakers would impair their ability to govern.[8] Certainly, we hold governments to their contracts, and one way of viewing the problem of government forbearance is to ask whether an additional precommitment device analogous to a government contract is useful or possible.[9]

In practice, neither of the extreme positions—never permit entrenchment or always permit entrenchment—prevails. Our legal system has gradually become more committed to the principle of majority rule, for example, by expanding the franchise to include previously excluded groups such as racial minorities and women, providing for direct election of the Senate, and choosing Presidential electors by statewide elections. Yet many features of entrenchment remain, such as requiring the approval of both houses and the President before a law is passed—which is in practical effect a supermajority requirement—and subjecting legislation to review by life-tenured judges to assure compliance with the Constitution.

---

7. *See, e.g.*, David Dana & Susan P. Koniak, *Bargaining in the Shadow of Democracy*, 148 U. PA. L. REV. 473 (1999).

8. *See, e.g.*, Eric A. Posner & Adrian Vermeule, *Legislative Entrenchment: A Reappraisal*, 111 YALE L.J. 1665 (2002).

9. Kyle D. Logue, *Tax Transitions, Opportunistic Retroactivity, and the Benefits of Government Precommitment*, 94 MICH. L. REV. 1129 (1996).

As is reflected in the competing positions of Justices Taney and Story in *Charles River Bridge*, our legal system seeks to strike a balance between majoritarianism and entrenchment, as well as between change and stability.

Sources of Forbearance

From the perspective of a property owner, the problem of government forbearance is largely one of minimizing the risks associated with changes in government policy that impair the value of property. Property owners do not want to abolish government. After all, this would leave property at the mercy of trespasses, nuisances, and conversions committed by others, and would almost certainly result in a severe undersupply of public works such as roads and sewers that greatly enhance the value of property. Nor do property owners necessarily even favor minimal government. Zoning appears to be highly popular with owners of single-family residences, perhaps because zoning has been designed to protect single-family homes against potential adverse effects from commercial or multifamily development (see Chapter 8). What most owners want is to be able to predict with some confidence what the government is likely to do in the future that could have an impact on the use and enjoyment of their property. Will the government prohibit certain uses previously permitted, or dramatically change tax rates, or embark on a takeover of property by public authorities? Forbearance means, above all, predictability about future government policy.

There are multiple sources of government forbearance, in the sense of predictability about government policy toward property. Lawyers are most interested in constitutional constraints on government, such as the protection against uncompensated takings of property. But these are not the only sources of forbearance, or even the most important ones. Among the other sources of constraint are democratic politics, social norms that encourage respect for property, and rule of law values. We will return to the rule of law momentarily. But first, a few words about democratic politics and social norms.

As should be obvious, one very important source of government forbearance is ordinary politics. In a democracy, government is unlikely to take action that would affect large numbers of property owners in an adverse way. Consider, for example, the tax deduction for home mortgage interest. There is no constitutional or other legal impediment to abolishing this deduction, and it has been widely criticized as an unwarranted subsidy for homeownership. But the home mortgage interest deduction enhances the value of millions of homes throughout the country (and its supporters cite the greater involvement of homeowners in their communities). Notwithstanding repeated calls to eliminate the deduction, or phase it out for higher-income taxpayers, the political outcry that would greet any attempt at repeal probably insures against any such adverse action taking place in the foreseeable future.

The political support that property enjoys depends not only on how widespread the form of ownership is, but also on whether owners have a credible threat to exit from the jurisdiction. Property that is immovable, such as land and fixed-plant investment, is generally more vulnerable to changes in government policy. Many railroads learned this lesson the hard way in the nineteenth century. State and local governments made lavish promises to induce the construction of new rail lines. But after they were built, many governments reneged on their promises, or attempted to impose new taxes and regulations that restricted the profitability of the investments that had been made. This kind of "bait and switch" behavior is one interpretation of what happened in *Charles River Bridge*.

The importance of political constraints is reflected in the fact that property is generally much less secure in authoritarian regimes than in democratic ones. Outright expropriation is rare in democracies. It is much more common in authoritarian and one-party regimes. In the extreme cases of Soviet Russia and Maoist China, expropriation became celebrated as official policy. There seems to be a loose associational relationship between widespread property ownership and political democracy, in that widespread property ownership supports democracy, and democracy helps support widespread ownership of property. One reason for this is that democracies tend to promote government forbearance from interfering with property.[10]

Social norms provide another important source of government forbearance. The relevant norms range from general customs of society to internal bureaucratic habits. In countries with strong traditions of respect for property rights, government officials—whether elected or not—are likely to act with restraint in taking action that affects owners. This will be true whether or not constitutional or other formal laws require this, and whether or not owners have access to courts to call officials to account—although formal legal constraints and judicial enforcement will no doubt reinforce social norms of respect. In effect, in a society with strong norms supporting ownership, elected politicians and bureaucrats will internalize these norms, so it is unlikely they will take action that deeply upsets owner expectations, even if such opportunism might be in their short-term interests.

The history of post-Maoist China provides a possible illustration of the importance of social norms in fostering forbearance.[11] Reflecting its communist heritage, all land in China is owned by the state or by rural collectives. Buildings and other improvements can be held privately, in the form of time-limited ownership rights, and the Chinese constitution has been amended to stipulate that these rights cannot be taken by the government except in the public

---

10. *See* MANCUR OLSON, POWER AND PROSPERITY: OUTGROWING COMMUNIST AND CAPITALIST DICTATORSHIPS 25–43 (2000); Douglass C. North & Barry R. Weingast, *Constitutions and Commitment: The Evolution of Institutions Governing Public Choice in Seventeenth-Century England*, 49 J. ECON. HIST. 803 (1989).

11. *See generally* KENNETH W. DAM, THE LAW-GROWTH NEXUS: THE RULE OF LAW AND ECONOMIC DEVELOPMENT 233–78 (2006).

interest and for compensation. Nevertheless, there is little tradition of judicial enforcement of these rights. Moreover, China engages in frequent takings of rural land and of urban land that was developed before China opened itself up to foreign investment.[12] There are many complaints about the lack of procedures and the adequacy of compensation for these takings. Yet notwithstanding the weak legal and political checks on government interference with property rights, China has had little difficulty in recent years attracting large amounts of capital from foreign investors. This investment has fueled an enormous construction boom, especially in major cities along the coasts.

The intriguing question presented by China is: What is the basis for the apparent confidence on the part of foreign investors that they will get their money back from the fixed-plant investment projects they have funded? How do they know the Chinese government will forbear from directly or indirectly expropriating these investments? Formal legal guarantees cannot be the answer, because judicial enforcement is too weak. Legislative checks on administrative opportunism cannot be the answer, as China is a one-party state. The best answer would seem to be that Chinese administrators in the post-Mao era have developed a strong norm against interfering with the expectations of foreign investors. Chinese officials have "compartmentalized" their behavior toward property, with one set of attitudes about old property—rural land and older Mao-era urban buildings—and a different set of attitudes about new property developed in the post-Mao era. Foreign investors have been able to observe the consistent behavior generated by these compartmentalized norms, and have become confident that Chinese officials will forbear from interfering with foreign investment. The conditions of repeat play with current and future foreign investors and the practice of partnering with local government

12. *See* Katherine Wilhelm, *Rethinking Property Rights in Urban China*, 9 UCLA J. Int'l L. & Foreign Aff. 227 (2004).

entities may also serve as a constraint on government behavior. Whatever the explanation, the recent history of China suggests that caution is in order before concluding that strong legal rights enforced by courts are a necessary precondition for creating the degree of government forbearance needed for investment in property to flourish.

The Rule of Law

The most general legal strategy for achieving a significant degree of government forbearance is a commitment to the rule of law. Like other concepts in political theory, there is considerable dispute about what "rule of law" means. For present purposes, we can define the rule of law as a strategy for promoting forbearance by requiring that the government act in accordance with rules that are generally applicable, knowable in advance, and enforced by an impartial judiciary. The objective, again, is to enhance the predictability of the government's behavior, so that owners have greater confidence about what the government is likely to do in the future that could affect their property. The predictability here is supplied by the expectation that courts will require the government to obey existing laws that protect property, and that the government will obey the courts.

There is no freestanding rule of law norm in American law. Instead, the rule of law is supported by a variety of doctrines and understandings. We will briefly consider four: procedural due process, the doctrine of vested rights, *stare decisis*, and waivers of sovereign immunity to permit suits against the government.

Procedural Due Process

One very important doctrine reinforcing the rule of law is procedural due process. The Due Process Clauses of the Fifth and

Fourteenth Amendments to the U.S. Constitution provide that the government may not deprive individuals of "life, liberty, or property, without due process of law." These words have been interpreted to mean many things. The most important from the present perspective is a commitment to the principle of legality. Individuals who have entitlements to "life," "liberty," or "property" may not have these things taken away by the government unless the government demonstrates it has complied with all requirements of existing law that protect these interests. For example, assume the law provides that the government may not seize an individual's real property for nonpayment of taxes unless the government proves that the taxes are owed and have not been paid. Under the Due Process Clauses, the individual is entitled to demand a hearing before any seizure takes place, to challenge the legal proposition that the taxes are owed and/or the factual claim that the taxes have not been paid. In effect, due process guarantees that the individual be given an opportunity to challenge the legality of the seizure before it occurs, both as to its legal and its factual basis.

This is a powerful reinforcement of government forbearance. Procedural due process provides a weapon for the property owner to assure that the government does not ignore the rules on the books, either because of hostility to the owner, a mistake about the relevant law or facts, or just plain sloppiness. To be sure, procedural due process does not protect property owners against prospective changes in the rules that have an effect on property. The government can change the rules, and in any future dispute the new rules will be applied, not the rules that were in effect at some time in the past such as when the property was acquired. Still, the due process guarantee makes the government's behavior more predictable, and thus enhances the security and value of property rights.

One important question that arises in the due process context is how we define the "property" that is subject to this guarantee. (Similar questions are presented about the meaning of "life" and "liberty," but this would take us too far afield.) The basic answer is that just about everything we have covered in this book qualifies as property for procedural due process purposes—and more besides. In a series of controversial decisions in the early 1970s, the Supreme Court held that property includes all entitlements grounded in law upon which people rely in their daily lives.[13] Under this "new property" definition, not just conventional property—such as houses, cars, and securities—is included in the category of due process property, but also welfare benefits, disability benefits, government employment protected by civil service laws, publicly supplied utility services, professional licenses, and even public schooling.[14] This goes well beyond the common-law idea of property as based in large part on a right to exclude others from specific resources. If a central reason for wanting to secure government forbearance is to enhance incentives to develop and invest in property, it is not clear that welfare benefits, utility services, or the right to attend public school should be regarded as property, as these benefits are not things in which individuals invest. They may use the stream of benefits to invest in something else, for example, in developing their own human capital. But the benefits themselves are not subject to individual control and direction. Arguably, therefore, the Court's "new property" definition is overbroad.

The overbreadth of the definition of property would not matter, and might even be considered a good thing in terms of expanding the scope of the rule of law, except for one concern: the broader the definition of property, the greater the pressure on the courts to dilute the procedural protections afforded for the protection of property. There is some evidence that this has occurred. Before the Court embraced the "new property" conception, it was understood that the government must generally afford a person a hearing on the legality of a taking of property *before* the deprivation takes

13. *See* Bd. of Regents v. Roth, 408 U.S. 564 (1972); Goldberg v. Kelly, 397 U.S. 254 (1970).

14. Charles A. Reich, *The New Property*, 73 YALE L.J. 733 (1964).

place, subject to some narrow exceptions for public emergencies and the like.[15] After the expansion of coverage reflected in the new definition, the Court announced that the procedures appropriate in any given context should be determined by a balancing test, in which courts weigh the significance of the private interest, the marginal value of additional procedures in protecting that interest, and the cost to the government of providing the additional procedure.[16] This balancing test has allowed the Court to declare that many interests are adequately protected by hearings held after, rather than before, the deprivation occurs,[17] as well as to scale down the required procedures to include in some cases mere notice and an opportunity to voice objections before a nonjudicial officer.[18] If these dilutions spill over to traditional property rights, this would represent a serious erosion of protection against unlawful government interference with property.

Vested Rights

A second and much less well-defined rule of law constraint is the doctrine of vested rights. Roughly speaking, rights are vested when there are no contingencies of law or fact that might stand in the way of their enjoyment. Thus, a future interest is considered vested either when it becomes possessory ("vested in possession") or when any conditions precedent that must be resolved before it can take effect have been satisfied ("vested in interest"). (See Chapter 5.) The core example of a vested right is full ownership of tangible property,

---

15. *See, e.g.*, N. Am. Cold Storage Co. v. Chicago, 211 U.S. 306 (1908).

16. Mathews v. Eldridge, 424 U.S. 319 (1976).

17. *Id.*

18. *See, e.g.*, Goss v. Lopez, 419 U.S. 565, 576 (1975) (student entitled to brief face-to-face hearing and statement of reasons from school official before being suspended from public school, assumed to be a property right).

for example, a fee simple in land. But the concept has a broader signification as well. In the famous case of *Marbury v. Madison*,[19] William Marbury's commission to serve as a justice of the peace was described as a vested right, because his appointment papers had been signed by the President and sealed by the Secretary of State and all that remained was for the commission to be delivered, which the Court concluded was a purely ministerial act that entailed no discretion. So the concept of vested rights can include things such as public offices as well as more conventional property rights.

Protecting vested rights was once described as the central concern of American constitutional law.[20] In its strongest form, the doctrine of vested rights provided that neither courts nor legislatures could interfere with rights once they were vested. In a weaker form, the doctrine proclaimed that all retroactive interferences with vested rights were prohibited. Both forms of the doctrine have faded considerably over time. One reason is the lack of any express textual basis for the doctrine of vested rights in either the federal or most state constitutions. A second problem is the difficulty of defining the key concepts of "vesting" and "retroactive." A third problem is the accumulation of counterexamples, whereby demands for social change have led to the overturning of vested rights. The freeing of slaves, who were regarded as property under earlier law, and the prohibition movement, which rendered distilleries and liquor stocks worthless, are examples. In both cases the "de-vesting" of rights was authorized by a constitutional amendment, but these and other upheavals nevertheless produced major cracks in the edifice of vested rights.

Notwithstanding its weakened status, the concept of vested rights continues to play a role in promoting government forbearance.

---

19. 5 U.S. (1 Cranch) 137 (1803).

20. Edward S. Corwin, *The Basic Doctrine of American Constitutional Law*, 12 MICH. L. REV. 247 (1914).

A particularly striking example is the protection of nonconforming uses under zoning laws. Uses established before the imposition of zoning have generally been allowed to continue, with some state courts requiring compensation for their abolition. Since 1950, many zoning ordinances have attempted a gradual phase out ("amortization") of such nonconforming uses.[21] In addition, retroactive legislation continues to be disfavored. The Supreme Court has held that retroactive laws that interfere with property rights require a double justification under the Due Process Clause—one justification for the interference, and a separate justification for making the law retroactive.[22] And the Court has held that ambiguities about whether a statute applies retroactively are generally to be resolved in favor of the statute applying only prospectively.[23] These understandings, cumulatively, provide additional security for property rights.

Stare Decisis

The understanding that courts should follow previous decisions unless they have a strong justification for overruling—known generally as *stare decisis*—serves also to protect expectations about property rights. It has long been held that "[c]onsiderations in favor of *stare decisis* are at their acme in cases involving property and contract rights, where reliance interests are involved."[24] Whether courts in fact are more faithful to precedent in matters implicating property rights is difficult to say. Certainly during the "rights revolution" of the 1970s, courts overturned a number of older

---

21. *See, e.g.*, William B. Stoebuck & Dale A. Whitman, The Law of Property § 9.17 (3d ed. 2000).

22. *See, e.g.*, Usery v. Turner Elkhorn Mining Co., 428 U.S. 1, 15–16 (1976).

23. Landgraf v. USI Film Products, 511 U.S. 244 (1994).

24. Payne v. Tennessee, 501 U.S. 808, 828 (1991).

property doctrines as "vestiges of feudalism." Landlord-tenant reforms, such as the adoption of the implied warranty of habitability, the duty to mitigate damages, and increased freedom for tenants to sublet or assign are examples of judicial reforms of this era. Still, the perpetuation of old forms of ownership, like the defeasible fees, as well as the resistance to *Restatement*-inspired reforms in the law of servitudes, suggest an enduring judicial caution about upending property law too much.

Note that the doctrine of *stare decisis* applies only to the courts, not other branches of the government. The functional significance of strong adherence to precedent in matters of property (assuming it exists) is that this channels law reform toward the legislature, where change can be made prospective. Such a channeling, of course, furthers general rule of law values of predictability and notice.

Waivers of Sovereign Immunity

Common law courts were originally royal courts, answerable to the King. Perhaps out of prudence, the courts decided the "King could do no wrong," and hence could not be sued without his consent. Modern courts have perpetuated this understanding in the form of the doctrine of sovereign immunity: The government cannot be sued without its consent, which must be clearly given. If we are interested in promoting government forbearance through a rule-of-law strategy, sovereign immunity is potentially a serious barrier. The government cannot be held to account for the legality of its behavior unless it can be haled into a court of law, where a judgment directing the government to comply with the law can be rendered.

Fortunately, enough inroads have been made into sovereign immunity to allow the rule-of-law strategy to take hold. Under the Administrative Procedure Act, the federal government has broadly waived sovereign immunity for claims against government agencies for other than money damages.[25] This allows courts to review and potentially set aside a broad array of government actions alleged to be contrary to law. Claims for money damages can be brought against the federal government under the Tucker Act either for breach of contract or a taking of property without just compensation.[26] The waiver for contract claims has been held to include claims for reliance damages based on the government's breach of a promise to forbear from certain kinds of regulations.[27] The recognition of this cause of action could evolve into an important check on government policy reversals that undermine property rights. The waiver for takings claims has allowed the Takings Clause (considered below) to be given teeth insofar as it applies to the federal government.

State governments also enjoy sovereign immunity; indeed, the Supreme Court has held that the states enjoy a particularly powerful form of sovereign immunity that cannot be abrogated by Congress under its general Article I powers such as the Commerce Clause.[28] Nevertheless, express constitutional limits on state power, such as the Contract Clause and the Takings Clause (which applies to the states through the Fourteenth Amendment) are recognized as overriding any sovereign immunity that subordinate state units, such as municipalities, might claim,[29] and possibly even the immunity of states themselves. The Court has diluted the accountability of states under the Takings Clause by imposing an elaborate set of requirements of exhaustion of state remedies before plaintiffs can turn to federal courts for relief.[30] Still, these exhaustion requirements shield the states only to the extent that they have

---

25. 5 U.S.C. § 702.

26. 28 U.S.C. § 1346.

27. United States v. Winstar, 518 U.S. 839 (1996).

28. Seminole Tribe of Fla. v. Florida, 517 U.S. 44 (1996).

29. *See* First English Evangelical Lutheran Church v. County of Los Angeles, 482 U.S. 304 (1987).

30. *See* San Remo Hotel v. San Francisco, 545 U.S. 323 (2005).

subjected themselves to a legal regime that provides protection for property, so even here we see that the rule of law strategy has room to work.

Explicit Takings

The government, or entities exercising power delegated by the government, often engages in compulsory acquisitions of property, generally known in the United States as the power of condemnation or eminent domain. The most common uses of the power are for public infrastructure projects such as roads, sewers, power lines, and airport expansions. The power can also be used to acquire sites for government facilities such as courthouses, schools, or prisons. More controversially, the power has been used to reconfigure aging urban centers. Starting in the 1950s, eminent domain was used for massive urban renewal projects that bulldozed entire neighborhoods for redevelopment projects, a policy now widely discredited as destroying community ties and targeting minority groups. Most controversially, the power has sometimes been used to acquire sites for private business firms, as in the *Poletown* case,[31] which approved condemnation of a tract of land in Detroit for a General Motors assembly plant.

The U.S. Constitution and parallel provisions of state constitutions directly address explicit takings of property by the government. The Fifth Amendment provides: "nor shall private property be taken for public use without just compensation." This has been construed as imposing two limits on explicit takings. First, any such taking must be for a "public use." Second, such a taking requires the payment of "just compensation." Both of these requirements limit government interference with property rights, and hence promote forbearance.

---

31. Poletown Neighborhood Council v. City of Detroit, 304 N.W.2d 455 (Mich. 1981), overruled by County of Wayne v. Hathcock, 684 N.W.2d 765 (Mich. 2004).

Public Use

The public use limitation promotes the security of property rights by limiting the use of compulsory acquisitions to circumstances of public need. The government cannot force an exchange of property from *A* to *B* merely because *B* has more friends in the government, or because government officials harbor a dislike for *A*. The public use requirement also presumably means the government cannot set itself up as an all-purpose property acquisition service, forcing the transfer of property to any person willing to put up the money for the taking. By limiting the scope of compulsory acquisitions, the public use requirement promotes the stability of ownership, and allows people to make long-range plans for the development and use of their property.

Notwithstanding this important function, the U.S. Supreme Court has always given the public use requirement a weak interpretation. Although some state courts have flirted with the idea that public use means public ownership or a public right of access, the Supreme Court never explicitly adopted such a narrow definition, and beginning in the twentieth century, it has been increasingly explicit in its view that "public use" means public interest. Thus, government can take property as long as it can cite some public-regarding rationale for the taking, whether or not the property ends up in the hands of the government and whether or not the public can actually use it. Moreover, the Court has given great deference to legislative and administrative determinations of when property should be taken, suggesting that these decisions should be subject to only the requirement of minimum rationality as to the ends of the taking and whether the taking is an appropriate means to those ends.[32]

---

32. Hawaii Hous. Auth. v. Midkiff, 467 U.S. 229 (1984); Berman v. Parker, 348 U.S. 26 (1954).

The Court's highly deferential approach to public use was tested by *Kelo v. New London*,[33] a decision that sparked intense controversy about the use of eminent domain. At issue in *Kelo* was a project designed to revitalize the economy of New London, Connecticut, an economically depressed port city. Pfizer, the drug company, had purchased an abandoned factory on the waterfront, and was using the site to build a new research facility. The New London authorities decided to acquire a large tract of land next to the Pfizer facility. The plan was to level virtually all the buildings in the area, and retransfer the land to a private developer for a mixed-use project. The project would include some traditional public uses, such as a marina, a walkway, and a Coast Guard Museum. But most of it would be used for a hotel, commercial office buildings, and 80 new residences, which would be built and marketed by the developer.

Most property owners in the redevelopment area reached negotiated agreements to sell to the New London authorities. But ten owners of fifteen properties, many of which were owner-occupied residences, refused to sell, and the city instituted eminent domain proceedings against these owners. The dissident property owners argued in the state courts that the taking was not for a public use as required by the United States and Connecticut Constitutions, because the primary beneficiary would be an as-yet-to-be-determined real estate developer, and because there was uncertainty about whether the project would ever achieve its stated goal of revitalizing the New London economy. The city prevailed in the state supreme court, over a dissent.

The U.S. Supreme Court also held that the project was for a public use, although by a surprisingly close vote of five to four. Justice Stevens's opinion for the majority reaffirmed that the Takings Clause prohibits takings for a purely private purpose. The majority held there is no categorical constitutional rule against using

33. 545 U.S. 469 (2005).

eminent domain to promote economic development, even if the properties taken have not been found to be blighted.[34] Following prior decisions, the Court said that economic development is a legitimate government purpose, and that the decision whether to use eminent domain to achieve any legitimate government objective is largely left to the people's elected representatives. Justice Stevens concluded that the record showed the project was a bona fide effort to promote local economic development, and was not merely a pretext for private gain.[35]

The notion of pretext figured centrally in Justice Kennedy's concurrence.[36] According to Justice Kennedy, courts should strike down takings that are primarily meant to benefit a private party and have only incidental public benefits. He did not favor a remand, because he read the record in *Kelo* to include sufficient evidence for the conclusion that the exercise of eminent domain in New London was not pretextual. What exactly this potentially more robust standard of review would mean in practice is unclear, but courts may need to figure it out, because not unusually, Justice Kennedy supplied the crucial fifth vote for the result in *Kelo*.

Justice O'Connor, writing for four dissenting justices, viewed the decision with alarm. If economic development, without more, is a sufficient rationale for eminent domain takings, she wrote, then all properties are at risk of condemnation. All that is needed is a plausible argument that someone other than the current owner will put the property to a more valuable use.[37] She suggested limiting the use of eminent domain for economic development to circumstances where the precondemnation use of the property is

34. *Kelo*, 545 U.S. at 484.

35. *Id.* at 478.

36. *Id.* at 490 (Kennedy, J., concurring).

37. *Id.* at 503 (O'Connor, J., dissenting).

imposing affirmative harm on society, as where the property has been found to be blighted.[38]

In a separate dissent, Justice Thomas objected to the decision on two grounds.[39] He argued that a natural reading of the Takings Clause at the time it was adopted (1791) would have required that the property either be retained in government ownership or used by the public. Adverting to more recent history, Justice Thomas also pointed out that eminent domain has often been used against vulnerable groups such as African Americans, the poor, and the elderly, especially in the urban renewal era of the 1950s.

The lessons of early history alluded to by Justice Thomas are potentially instructive but in the final analysis ambiguous. The records of the Constitutional Convention and the ratification debates in the states provide very little guidance. The prohibitory word "without" appears before "just compensation," not before "public use." The words "public use" themselves may have been a paraphrase for "eminent domain," as if the Clause read, "nor shall private property be taken by eminent domain without just compensation." Would that mean that a government-sponsored private seizure (a taking from *A* to give to *B*) would not even require compensation? It has been almost universally assumed that taking from *A* merely to give to *B* is not permitted. Or would uncompensated *A*-to-*B* takings be prohibited by some other clause, such as the Due Process Clause? Even if the public use language meant only that takings by eminent domain require compensation, this still requires that we identify what it means to take by eminent domain (as opposed to take for some other purpose, such as to satisfy a tax liability). And eminent domain has always included some notion of publicness, so perhaps we circle back to the need to identify some public purpose, even if the Takings Clause is not read as directly prohibiting takings for private use.

---

38. *Id.* at 500.

39. *Id.* at 505 (Thomas, J., dissenting).

Early eminent domain practice is likewise ambiguous. Compensation was often not given for land taken for roads, but in early American history being close to a road was considered a benefit and undoubtedly increased the value of the land retained. Mill acts were also enacted that allowed private owners to build dams that flooded upstream lands, upon paying just compensation to the upstream owner. Grist mills were open to the public, and therefore satisfied the public access test. But other mills were private factories, and state laws granting them what amounted to a private right of eminent domain were also sustained, at least sometimes.[40] Some mill acts required the prospective mill builder to apply to an official and justify the taking, but others did not. Much of the litigation over mills also occurred in the nineteenth century and therefore sheds only indirect light on original understandings of the Takings Clause.

The analytical problem in determining the limits of eminent domain has always been that there are innumerable situations in which a forced exchange of rights can be useful in overcoming transaction-cost problems. Any project that requires the assembly of multiple contiguous parcels of land (think of a highway or an urban renewal project) will run into problems with holdouts, where some owners either behave strategically to exact a high price, or have an intense subjective attachment to their land, or just resent being forced to move. Even if only two parties are involved, as in the landlocked parcel problem mentioned in Chapter 8, this will be a bilateral monopoly and bargaining may break down. Moreover, any use of eminent domain to overcome transaction-cost problems has at least some public-interest justification—the assembly of land or the new access to land obtained through forced exchange presumably makes the community at least a little bit better off, and the additional wealth can be seen as a public good that redounds in some small degree to the benefit of everyone in the community,

40. *See, e.g.*, Head v. Amoskeag Mfg. Co., 113 U.S. 9 (1885).

if only in the form of more jobs and more tax revenues. So, practically any exercise in eminent domain can be described as satisfying a public-interest standard.

Yet few would advocate a universal right of eminent domain. This would undermine incentives to invest and would interfere with the market's ability to establish prices. The courts, however, have been singularly unsuccessful in drawing a line in the sand between permissible and impermissible uses of eminent domain. The U.S. Supreme Court, by holding public use to mean public interest, has effectively left the matter to the state courts and local political processes.

Given the Supreme Court's interpretation of public use as public interest and the reaffirmation of that interpretation in *Kelo*, one might think that the public use requirement would do little to promote forbearance. But this would be misleading, for two reasons.

First, although the Supreme Court has been very deferential about enforcing the public use requirement in the federal Constitution, state courts, where most condemnation cases are tried, have been more willing to hold that exercises of eminent domain do not satisfy the public use requirement in state constitutions. If we look only at reported appellate decisions, about one in six state appeals court decisions addressing a contested public use holds that the taking is not permitted.[41] These decisions suggest that state courts are not just rubber stamps approving any and all exercises in eminent domain. Cases in which property owners attach a high subjective value to property, or where eminent domain is being used to capture an assembly value for a private developer, appear to be particularly vulnerable to invalidation.

Second, the *Kelo* decision provoked a large backlash about the misuse of eminent domain. The result is that many states have amended their constitutions or statutes to tighten limits on the use

---

41. Thomas W. Merrill, *The Economics of Public Use*, 72 CORNELL L. REV. 61 (1986).

of eminent domain. One common reform is to limit takings of property for economic development to circumstances where the property being taken is blighted. Whether this makes sense from an urban planning perspective is debatable. But from the vantage of property owners, a blight limitation, at least in theory, enhances protection against government takings, as the property owner has it within his or her power to prevent an economic development taking simply by keeping the property sufficiently well maintained to avoid a finding of blight. To be sure, some definitions of blight are so capacious that it is doubtful that they provide much protection, and blight findings have historically been manipulated to the disadvantage of minority groups, as highlighted in Justice Thomas's dissent. In addition, there is some indication that state courts, chastened by the backlash against *Kelo*, will become more vigilant in policing proposed takings to make sure that there is a genuine public need and that all applicable legal requirements have been satisfied.[42] In short, compulsory acquisitions are likely to be more tightly rationed after *Kelo* than they were before.

Just Compensation

Federal and state constitutions also require that the owner be given "just compensation" for any compulsory acquisitions that take place. If just compensation meant complete indemnification—compensation so complete that the owner is indifferent between keeping the property and getting the compensation—then all concerns about explicit takings would presumably go away. Property owners would be just as happy with the compensation as with the

42. *See* Norwood v. Horney, 853 N.E.2d 1115 (Ohio 2006) (holding that taking of nonblighted property for economic development is not a public use under the Ohio Constitution); Centene Plaza Redev. Corp v. Mint Properties, 225 S.W.3d 431 (Mo. 2007) (en banc) (limiting definition of blight to preclude taking of functioning business property).

property and would have no objection. But the law has never required complete indemnification for takings. Instead, the general rule is that the owner receives the "fair market value" of the property taken—what the property would trade for in an arm's length transaction between a willing buyer and seller just before the taking by the government. The fair-market-value standard systematically undercompensates the owner, in two respects.

First, the market-value formula deprives the owner of the subjective premium the owner attaches to the property. There are many reasons why owners of discrete assets value them more highly than does the market. Psychological attachment is one. Owners of homes, in particular, often come to regard them as an extension of their selves. Personalized or idiosyncratic modifications are another. A home owner may have installed access ramps for a disabled child, or a factory owner may have configured the interior space to accommodate a unique production process, and the market will not value these modifications at cost. Loss of community ties or business good will is yet another reason. A restaurant or dry-cleaning shop may be uniquely dependent on its location for its customer base, such that being forced to move even a few blocks would put it out of business. Moving and relocation costs (including legal fees) are potentially a final reason. Eminent domain effectively expropriates the owner's subjective premium, whatever its source. This is a potent source of opposition to compulsory acquisitions.

Second, the market-value formula means that the condemning authority captures what may be called the assembly gain from the taking, and shares none of this with the owner. Eminent domain typically entails the assembly of many contiguous parcels of land, or the acquisition of a parcel that has some unique value to the condemning authority. Thus, the value of the assembled tract after the taking is greater than the sum of the parts before the taking, putting aside the value of any improvements. The assembled tract has scarcity value—it cannot be readily found in the market—for otherwise it would not be necessary to use eminent domain to put it together. Under the market-value formula, whereby the condemning authority pays the market value of what it takes, not what it gets, all of the assembly value is captured by the condemnor. This strikes many landowners as unfair, particularly in economic development takings, where the ultimate beneficiary of the assembly gain is often a private developer.

Why does condemnation law insist on undercompensating owners in these ways? The primary answer given by the Supreme Court is administrative costs.[43] Measuring the owner's subjective premium would be very difficult, might degenerate into a swearing contest, and would be prone to abuse. Measuring assembly gain would also be difficult, given the lack of a market for many assembled tracts (consider highway rights of way for example). And there is no obvious principle for how the gain should be divided between the condemnor and the condemnees.

Undercompensation may also be appropriate to discourage overreliance by owners. For example, we do not want to encourage owners to make elaborate improvements to their property when there is a high probability that it will soon be taken for some public project. Incomplete compensation for takings can be seen as a kind of co-payment requirement that creates an incentive for owners, as well as the government, to minimize the losses associated with takings. Too much government forbearance, as Chief Justice Taney recognized, can be a bad thing, not just too little forbearance.

Nevertheless, it is quite plausible that some reform of the fair-market-value formula in the direction of more complete compensation is warranted. The model here would be the federal Uniform Relocation Act, which mandates the payment of certain costs of takings that the fair-market-value formula ignores. The federal act, for example, pays moving costs, costs of temporary housing, and damage to personal property caused by a taking, subject to limits. Further modifications along these lines aimed at providing more

---

43. *See, e.g.*, United States v. 564.54 Acres, 441 U.S. 506, 510–12 (1979).

complete compensation would enhance the security of property rights, and would be consistent with a general objective of promoting government forbearance.[44]

Regulatory Takings

The Court has not limited the Takings Clause to explicit takings, but has held that it also applies to certain regulations of the use of property that have a particularly disruptive effect on owners. This has come to be known as the regulatory takings doctrine. The doctrine comes in two versions, weak and strong, with different implications for how much they promote government forbearance.

The weak version of the regulatory takings doctrine understands it as an antievasion rule. The Constitution requires that the government pay just compensation when it "takes" property. Consequently, the government should not be allowed to enact a regulation that achieves the same end as an explicit taking, and thereby evades the requirements of the Constitution. Under this weak version, the task of the courts is to ask whether the challenged regulation is "functionally comparable to government appropriation or invasion" and to force the government to pay compensation if the answer is yes.[45] The weak version provides modest support for forbearance, basically by preserving the integrity of the requirement that the government may engage in explicit takings only for public uses and only if it pays just compensation. The writings of Joseph Sax, who has argued that the regulatory takings doctrine should be limited to cases in which the government

44. A recent study suggests that because of relocation benefits some owners may not fare so poorly in terms of compensation once political realities are taken into account. Nicole Stelle Garnett, *The Neglected Political Economy of Eminent Domain*, 105 MICH. L. REV. 101 (2006).

45. Lingle v. Chevron U.S.A. Inc., 544 U.S. 528, 542 (2005).

is acting as an enterprise, as opposed to a regulator, are consistent with the narrow view.[46]

The strong version is considerably more ambitious. Under this version, the regulatory takings doctrine is designed to protect owners from any type of disproportionate loss in the value of their property caused by government regulation. As stated in one often-quoted case, the idea is to prevent "Government from forcing some people alone to bear public burdens which, in all fairness and justice, should be borne by the public as a whole."[47] The strong version has drawn intellectual sustenance from the pioneering work of Frank Michelman, who coined the term "demoralization costs" to refer to the disutility of an owner and the owner's sympathizers from an uncompensated taking as well as the loss of production stemming from the greater insecurity of property rights.[48] Michelman suggested that the government should always compensate if demoralization costs exceed settlement costs (which include compensation and administrative costs). He argued this was required on general utilitarian principles, and was also consistent with Rawlsian justice, insofar as the worst off in society would see this practice as part of an overall pattern that they would choose behind a veil of ignorance.

The contest between the Sax and Michelman perspectives, and more broadly between the narrow and broad visions of the regulatory takings doctrine, raises yet again far-reaching questions about the need for government forbearance. The broad version seems to suggest that the Takings Clause can be viewed as a form of mandatory insurance against losses in property values as a result of changes in government policy. The narrow version, in contrast,

---

46. *See* Joseph L. Sax, *Takings and the Police Power*, 74 YALE L.J. 36 (1964); Joseph L. Sax, *Takings, Private Property, and Public Rights*, 81 YALE L.J. 149 (1971).

47. Armstrong v. United States, 364 U.S. 40, 49 (1960).

48. Frank I. Michelman, *Property, Utility, and Fairness: Comments on the Ethical Foundations of "Just Compensation" Law*, 80 HARV. L. REV. 1165, 1214 (1967).

assumes that actors can anticipate that there will be change, and therefore mandatory government insurance is not called for; either self-insurance or private insurance would be better. Under the broad view, the government is both the insurer and the source of the risk—unlike private insurance companies that insure against earthquakes or lightning. The demand that the government insure against risks of its own creation brings us back to the question whether the main objective should be to require the government to internalize the costs of policy changes.[49]

Some find instructive evidence about the need for greater cost internalization in Oregon's recent experience with Measure 37, which very broadly requires local governments either to compensate landowners for decreases in land values caused by regulations, or to drop the regulation.[50] So far in every case, the government has chosen to drop the regulation rather than pay. This could be because the costs of the regulations were internalized by the governments and were found not to be worthwhile. Or it could be because the government has to pay for the costs imposed by its regulations but is not able to charge for the benefits those regulations provide. Or it could be because the legislature has refused to appropriate funds for compensation, leaving only the option of dropping the regulation. The explanation is unclear, and thus the competing intuitions underlying the narrow and broad versions of the regulatory takings doctrine still await a definitive empirical test.

Support for both the weak and strong versions can be found in the Supreme Court's decisions. The Court's first important

49. There is a similar problem of distinguishing between taxes and takings. Redistributive taxation would be impossible if compensation were required. Most commentators do not think that the Takings Clause prohibits progressive taxation. *But see* RICHARD A. EPSTEIN, TAKINGS: PRIVATE PROPERTY AND THE POWER OF EMINENT DOMAIN 295–303 (1985) (arguing that the Takings Clause, rightly construed, requires a flat tax and rules out progressivity).

50. OR. REV. STAT. § 197.352.

regulatory takings case, *Pennsylvania Coal Co. v. Mahon*,[51] involved a Pennsylvania statute protecting surface owners of land from subsidence caused by the mining of coal beneath their property. The Pennsylvania Coal Company, which owned the rights to mine the coal, challenged the statute as an uncompensated taking of the pillars of coal that would have to remain in place in order to prevent damage to the surface.

Elements of Justice Holmes's opinion for the Court read as if he was simply preventing the state from evading the requirement of paying compensation for an explicit taking. He stressed that the right of support is considered a separate "estate" under Pennsylvania law, and that the company had expressly reserved this right in the deed under which the Mahons claimed. The Pennsylvania statute, from this perspective, looked like an attempt to transfer a discrete property right from the coal company to the Mahons—something that ordinarily would require either a purchase of rights or an exercise of eminent domain.

Other elements in the Holmes opinion point toward a broader doctrine. He said that among the factors to be considered were the extent of diminution in value caused by the regulation, whether the statute seeks to regulate what would be regarded as a public nuisance, and whether the statute affords a rough reciprocity of advantage by restraining all property owners in a way that benefits each. The general rule, he concluded, is that "while property may be regulated to a certain extent, if regulation goes too far it will be recognized as a taking."[52] These elements of the opinion point toward an ad hoc balancing test in which courts decide whether particular regulations "go too far" and must result in a payment of compensation.

The ambiguity has persisted. In 1978, the Supreme Court restated the ad hoc regulatory takings doctrine in *Penn Central*

51. 260 U.S. 393 (1922).

52. *Id.* at 415.

Transportation Co. v. New York.[53] The case involved a takings challenge to a New York City landmark designation that prevented the owners of Grand Central Station from constructing a new office building in the air space above the station. The Court rejected the challenge, but in so doing offered up a different set of factors than the ones considered in *Pennsylvania Coal v. Mahon*. Writing for the majority, Justice Brennan agreed that the degree of diminution in value is relevant, but he identified the relevant "property" to be examined for these purposes as the "whole parcel" owned by the railroad, not just the air rights that were barred from development. Justice Brennan also said that courts should ask whether the regulation interfered with "distinct investment-backed expectations," thereby expressly linking the regulatory takings inquiry with forbearance values. Finally, he said courts should consider the nature of the government action, and in particular whether it has intruded directly onto the property or merely engaged in a regulation of its use.

The rhetoric of *Penn Central* points away from a minimalist concern with evasion toward a broader degree of protection of reasonable owner expectations. But the outcome of the case seemed to suggest that even highly intrusive regulations that disproportionately affect a small number of owners will not qualify as a regulatory taking. Over time, the latter signal appears to have dominated the former. After *Penn Central*, application of the ad hoc test has generally been fatal to regulatory takings claims.

Perhaps because of the uncertainty of the ad hoc approach of *Penn Central*, perhaps in response to the weak protection that case appears to afford to property owners, the Court in subsequent cases has developed exceptions to the *Penn Central* test in the form of certain "categorical" regulatory takings rules. In *Loretto v. Teleprompter Manhattan CATV Corp.*,[54] the Court held that any permanent physical occupation of property by the government or a

53. 438 U.S. 104 (1978).

54. 458 U.S. 419 (1982).

stranger acting with permission of the government is a taking, without regard to how the ad hoc *Penn Central* analysis would come out. Specifically, the Court held that a New York statute that allowed cable television companies to string cable transmission wires on rental buildings without the owner's consent was a taking, even though the addition of cable service was likely a net benefit to both the landlord and her tenants. And in *Lucas v. South Carolina Coastal Council*,[55] the Court ruled that unless it prohibits what would have been a nuisance at common law, a regulation that deprives an owner of all economically beneficial use of the property is a taking, again without regard to how the *Penn Central* balancing test would come out. The regulation at issue in *Lucas* prohibited construction of homes on two beachfront lots on a barrier island subject to periodic erosion, which the South Carolina courts had found rendered the lots "valueless."

Loretto and *Lucas* were greeted by property rights advocates as redressing an imbalance in favor of government regulation introduced by *Penn Central.* Paradoxically, however, their long-range effect may have been to push the Court back in the direction of the narrow, anti-evasion conception of the regulatory takings doctrine. The regulation in *Loretto* was "functionally comparable" to the condemnation of a utility easement. Ordinarily, if an electric or telephone company wants to string wires on someone's property, it must acquire an easement to do so, either by purchase or condemnation. The New York statute allowing cable companies to string wires on rental property without the owner's consent looks like a straightforward evasion of this settled understanding. Similarly, the regulation in *Lucas* was "functionally comparable" to the condemnation of a conservation easement. Again, conservation easements are ordinarily donated or purchased. The South Carolina statute looked like an attempt to acquire by regulation something that ordinarily would be purchased or condemned by eminent domain.

---

55. 505 U.S. 1003 (1992).

In any event, the history of the regulatory takings doctrine after *Lucas* has largely been one in which the Court has narrowly defined these categorical rules. For example, the Court declined to characterize a rent control statute that prohibited eviction of the tenant as a "physical occupation" under *Loretto*,[56] and it declined to characterize a temporary moratorium on development as a deprivation of all economically beneficial use under *Lucas*.[57] By confining the categorical rules to circumstances in which the government uses its regulatory power to acquire something that ordinarily would be purchased, the Court has effectively recast the regulatory takings doctrine as a narrow, antievasion principle.

Of course, the narrow version advances important forbearance values. It prevents the government from circumventing the protections the Takings Clause provides in cases of explicit takings. But, for the moment at least, the Court seems disinclined to expand the regulatory takings doctrine into a general source of insurance against government frustration of reasonable owner expectations. The regulatory takings doctrine is taking the shape that Chief Justice Taney would have given it, not the one advocated by Justice Story.

The problem of flexibility versus stability is characteristic of property in another sense. As we have seen in this book, some areas and elements of property law are fairly standardized and formalistic and achieve their goals indirectly. The basic exclusion strategy itself serves people's interests in use only indirectly. This simple basic structure is easy to use and manages a lot of complexity, and so stability is an emergent property of the system. It is when problems become great and urgent enough that more direct methods, from new governance rules on a micro scale to larger macro reforms, come onto the agenda. Debate over when and how

56. Yee v. Escondido, 503 U.S. 519 (1992).

57. Tahoe-Sierra Pres. Council, Inc. v. Tahoe Reg'l Planning Agency, 535 U.S. 302 (2002).

to make this shift will continue, but property's basic architecture has proven quite resilient.

Further Reading

Hanoch Dagan, *Takings and Distributive Justice*, 85 VA. L. REV. 741 (1999) (stressing the perspective of distributive justice in takings claims).

DAVID A. DANA & THOMAS W. MERRILL, PROPERTY: TAKINGS (2002) (providing a comprehensive survey of issues presented by the Takings Clause).

RICHARD A. EPSTEIN, TAKINGS: PRIVATE PROPERTY AND THE POWER OF EMINENT DOMAIN (1985) (arguing for expansion of takings liability to promote a minimalist state).

WILLIAM A. FISCHEL, REGULATORY TAKINGS: LAW, ECONOMICS, AND POLITICS (1998) (reviewing important historical disputes over takings from an economics perspective).

Louis Kaplow, *An Economic Analysis of Legal Transitions*, 99 HARV. L. REV. 509 (1986) (analyzing the economic significance of takings and related disputes).

Thomas W. Merrill, *The Landscape of Constitutional Property*, 86 VA. L. REV. 885 (2000) (providing a review of how the concept of property is used in due process and takings contexts).

Frank I. Michelman, *Property, Utility, and Fairness: Comments on the Ethical Foundations of "Just Compensation" Law*, 80 HARV. L. REV. 1165 (1967) (seminal article that explains and justifies takings liability from distributive justice and utilitarian perspectives).

Index

About the Editor

DENNIS PATTERSON holds the Chair in Legal Philosophy and Legal Theory at the European University Institute in Florence, Italy. He is also Board of Governors Professor of Law and Philosophy at Rutgers University School of Law, Camden, New Jersey and Chair in Jurisprudence and International Trade at Swansea University, UK. Patterson is the author of *Law and Truth* (OUP 1996) and *The New Global Trading Order* with Ari Afilalo (CUP 2008). He is General Editor of *The Blackwell Companion to the Philosophy of Law and Legal Theory*. He has published widely in commercial law, trade law and legal philosophy.